Affective intimacies

MANCHESTER
1824

Manchester University Press

Affective intimacies

Edited by
Marjo Kolehmainen, Annukka Lahti
and Kinneret Lahad

MANCHESTER UNIVERSITY PRESS

Published by Manchester University Press
Oxford Road, Manchester M13 9PL

www.manchesteruniversitypress.co.uk

British Library Cataloguing-in-Publication Data

A catalogue record for this book is available from the
British Library

ISBN 978 1 5261 5856 7 hardback

First published 2022

The publisher has no responsibility for the persistence or
accuracy of URLs for any external or third-party internet
websites referred to in this book, and does not guarantee
that any content on such websites is, or will remain, accurate
or appropriate.

Typeset
by Deanta Global Publishing Services, Chennai, India

Contents

Contributors

Tuula Juvonen works as a senior lecturer of Gender Studies at Tampere University, Finland. Her research interests focus on the sexualities and genders in flux, and the changing position of homosexuality in Finnish society. She leads the Academy of Finland-funded research project 'Affective activism: Sites of queer and trans world-making' (2021–2025) and led 'Affective inequalities in intimate relationships' (2015–2020). She recently co-edited a special issue of *SQS – Journal of the Society of Queer Studies in Finland* on Queer History Month, and as a chair of the Friends of Queer History association, she compiled an online *Dictionary of Queer History in Finland*.

Marjo Kolehmainen is a TIAS fellow at Turku Institute for Advanced Studies, University of Turku, Finland. Prior to joining TIAS, Kolehmainen worked on the project 'Intimacy in Data-Driven Culture', funded by the Strategic Research Council (SRC) at the Academy of Finland. Her work specifically concerns digital intimacies. At the time of writing, she is examining the diverse practices of teletherapy and telecounselling in the context of the COVID-19 pandemic. Kolehmainen has authored over twenty peer-reviewed publications. Recently, she has published articles in *Gender & Society*, *The Sociological Review*, *Body & Society*, *European Journal of Cultural Studies* and *Science, Technology, and Human Values*, to name a few. Moreover, she is a co-editor of the edited collection *Affective Inequalities in Intimate Relationships* (2018) and of a Special Issue on Affective Intimacies, published in *NORA – The Nordic Journal of Gender and Feminist Research* (2021).

Ilektra Kyriazidou is a social anthropologist affiliated with the Centre for Ethnographic Research at the University of Kent, UK. She holds a PhD in Social Anthropology from the School of Anthropology and Conservation, University of Kent, UK, an MA in Social Anthropology from the University of Bristol, UK, and a BA in Philosophy from the University of the West of England, UK. Her research interests include political anthropology, Greek ethnography, feminist and queer theory, intimacy, affect and emotions, gender, precarity, migration and urban social movements.

Kinneret Lahad is a senior lecturer at the NCJW Women and Gender Studies Program at Tel-Aviv University, Israel. Her research interests are interdisciplinary, spanning the fields of gender studies, sociology and cultural studies. Her open-access book, *A Table for One: A Critical Reading of Singlehood, Gender and Time*, was published by Manchester University Press in 2017. She is writing a monograph on friendships and time. Her publications have appeared in journals such as *Cultural Studies, European Journal of Women's Studies, Israeli Sociology, NORA – Nordic Journal of Feminist and Gender Research, Sociology, Sociological Forum, Sociological Review, Time and Society, Sociological Research Online, Theory and Criticism* and *Society and Women's Studies International Forum*. Her current projects include independent and collaborative studies on aunthood, friendships, time and temporality, emotions and affect, solo marriages and wellness culture. She has been a visiting scholar at Columbia University, a visiting scholar and lecturer at Venice International University, a visiting lecturer at the Master MIM Erasmus Mundus Graduate program at Ca' Foscari University in Venice, an honorary research fellow at Manchester University and an Erasmus visiting scholar at Aarhus University and Ludwig Maximilian University (Munich).

Annukka Lahti is a postdoctoral researcher at the University of Eastern Finland, in the Borders, Mobilities and Cultural Encounters Research Community. In her postdoctoral project, 'Where the rainbow ends: The becoming of LGBTIQ+ separations in two cultural locations', she explores the relationship break-ups of queer, lesbian, gay, bisexual, trans, intersex and asexual people in Finland and the UK through the theoretical lens of affect. She has studied the interrelations of intimacy, power, sexuality and affect for several years and has published studies on, for example, affective inequalities, bisexuality, heterosexual relationship contexts and LGBTIQ+ break-ups. She has authored more than fifteen peer-reviewed publications that have appeared in the *Journal of Sociology, NORA – The Nordic Journal of Gender and Feminist Research, Subjectivity* and *Feminism & Psychology*, among others. Moreover, she is a co-editor of the edited collection *Family and Personal Relationships under the Rainbow* (in Finnish, 2020) and of a Special Issue on Affective Intimacies, published in *NORA – The Nordic Journal of Gender and Feminist Research* (2021).

Andrea Lobb is completing a PhD in Gender, Sexuality and Diversity Studies in the Department of Politics and Philosophy at La Trobe University, Melbourne, Australia. Her research interests include psychoanalysis, feminist theories of empathy and affect and the critique of power in social and political thought. Her published work has appeared in the journals *Feminism & Psychology*, *Foucault Studies*, *Constellations: An International Journal of Democratic and Critical Theory* and *Feminist Philosophy Quarterly*.

Dresda E. Méndez de la Brena is a horizon postdoctoral researcher at the University of Concordia, Montreal in the Access in the Making Lab (AIM Lab). She holds a PhD in Women's Studies from the University of Granada, Spain, with a project focused on chronic pain, necropolitics, disability worlds and disability arts of living. She obtained an Erasmus Mundus Double Master's Degree in Women's and Gender Studies from Utrecht University, the Netherlands, and University of Granada, Spain. In 2010, she was awarded the prestigious Emerging Leaders International Fellowship of the Center of Philanthropy and Civil Society at The City University of New York. She was also awarded the XXI Carmen de Burgos National Essay Accessit Prize (2020), conferred by the Almería Provincial Council, Spain. Her current postdoctoral research focuses on disability, access, affordances, affective intimacies and human–non-human care.

Armi Mustosmäki is a postdoctoral researcher at the Department of Social Sciences and Philosophy, University of Jyväskylä, Finland. In her current project, 'Complaining mothers: Affect, moral and politics of medicalisation', she explores negative and forbidden feelings and experiences of mothers and the public responses to 'maternal complaint'. Her previous research focused on changing working life, as well as the specificities of the Nordic working life model, work-family policies and gender inequality in work life.

Nina Perger is an assistant at the Chair for Theoretical Sociology (Department of Sociology) and a researcher at the Centre for Social Psychology, Faculty of Social Sciences, University of Ljubljana, Slovenia. Her research interests include studies of everyday life with a focus on marginalised gender and sexual identities. Recently, she has been working on COVID-19-related social issues, focusing on often-overlooked social groups such as solo-living women and youth.

Tiina Sihto works as a postdoctoral researcher at the Centre of Excellence in Research on Ageing and Care (CoE AgeCare, Academy of Finland, 2018–2025) at the University of Jyväskylä, Finland. Her current work focuses particularly on the 'dark side' of care, experiences of care poverty and forbidden emotions of motherhood.

Yiran Wang was born and raised in China. In 2019 she obtained her PhD in anthropology from the University of Amsterdam, the Netherlands. Her research interests include female non-heteronormative intimacies, Chinese women's lived experiences, the 'queer Asia' that is embedded in a 'queer globe' and anthropological methodology and writing. Her articles have been published in *Journal of Gender Studies* and *Journal of Lesbian Studies*. At the time of writing, she is an independent researcher.

Acknowledgements

We warmly thank all the authors for their inspiring engagement with the topic of this book, and who further have made thought-provoking contributions. The impressive work of the authors has spurred our thinking on affective intimacies, and we wish that the readers will find their work as valuable as we do. Thank you for your excellent contributions. Our deepest thanks go to our editor Thomas Dark – we are grateful for his encouragement and invaluable guidance – as well as to Lucy Burns, whom we praise for her excellent support during the production process, and to all the good people at Manchester University Press. It was a true pleasure working with you. We are also very grateful to the Knowledge Unlatched project for making our book available to readers and scholars free of charge. It is close to our heart to support the aim of making publications open access and we really appreciate your work, in regard to this volume and beyond. We would also like to express our gratitude to the anonymous peer-reviewer of this collection for their unquestionable support and insightful feedback.

This edited collection has its origins in an international workshop entitled 'Affective Intimacies: A Workshop with Sasha Roseneil and Kinneret Lahad' which was held at Tampere University on 18–19 November 2019. It consisted of two public keynotes by Professor Sasha Roseneil (University College London, UK) and Dr Kinneret Lahad (Tel-Aviv University, Israel) followed by commentaries from Dr Tuula Juvonen (Tampere University, Finland) and Professor Susanna Paasonen (University of Turku, Finland). Marjo Kolehmainen and Annukka Lahti were members of the organising team. During the preparations, we became interested in editorial collaboration, which has already resulted in a special issue that was published in NORA – *The Nordic Journal of Gender and Feminist Research* (2021). Many thanks to our fellow organisers of the 'Affective Intimacies' event, as well as to all participants, keynote speakers and commentators.

Marjo Kolehmainen's work was supported by Intimacy in Data-Driven Culture (IDA), a research consortium funded by the Strategic Research Council at the Academy of Finland. Marjo would like to thank Professor

Susanna Paasonen and Professor Anu Koivunen for their own inspiring work on affect and intimacy and for the support they have provided, as well as her other colleagues from IDA. Further, during her employment in IDA, she also visited the IAS at University College London, UK. She would like to thank Professor Sasha Roseneil for sponsoring that fruitful and in many ways unforgettable visit. She would like to thank Professor Johanna Kantola and the vibrant gender studies community at Tampere University. Further, she would like to thank Marja Vehviläinen and the naturecultures reading group on feminist post-humanism for several inspiring discussions and engagements. Warm thanks to Annukka Lahti and Kinneret Lahad for their co-editorship. Finally, her heartfelt thanks go to her everyday human and cat companions: Jaakko, Einari, Aukusti, Otsu and Mitsu.

Annukka Lahti's work was supported by the Kone Foundation and the University of Eastern Finland. In UEF she has the privilege to work under the mentorship of Professor Laura Assmuth, Professor Eeva Jokinen and Professor Jaana Vuori, whom she would like to thank for inspiration, encouragement and support. Her warmest thanks go to Marjo Kolehmainen and Kinneret Lahad for inspiring collaboration in co-editing this book. Many thanks also to the naturecultures reading group at Tampere University for offering a platform to discuss and learn about feminist post-humanisms. Further, her heartfelt thanks go to fellow feminists, colleagues and friends Heidi Elmgren, Laura Mankki, Armi Mustosmäki, Tiina Sihto and Jenny Säilävaara for sharing everyday ups and downs of (academic) life, as well as to her friends, partner and family.

Kinneret Lahad wishes to thank Marjo Kolehmainen and Annukka Lahti for inviting her to take part in this fascinating intellectual research project. She offers them her deepest thanks. She also thanks her wonderful colleagues at Tel-Aviv University as well as her close friends and family. Special thanks to her nephew and nieces, Neta Lahad, Nitzan Lahad, Noam Shaanan, Niri Lahad and Yuval Shaanan; she is grateful for all the laughter and love she shares with them.

Tampere and Jyväskylä, Finland, and Tel-Aviv, Israel
24 November 2021
Marjo Kolehmainen, Annukka Lahti and Kinneret Lahad

Introduction: Affective intimacies

Marjo Kolehmainen, Annukka Lahti and Kinneret Lahad

This edited collection, *Affective intimacies*, provides a novel terrain for rethinking intimacies through the lens of affect theories. It departs from the assumptions that, on one hand, there are a priori affective domains, such as care relationships or sexuality, that form a primary locus for intimacy, and on the other hand, that intimacy is about what is private and special (Kolehmainen, Lahad and Lahti, 2021).[1] It argues that the social sciences and humanities have not yet recognised and utilised the potential to imagine intimacy and affect in alternative ways, without starting from the already familiar terrains, theories and conceptualisations. Rather than assuming that we could parse affect and intimacy in a pre-defined way, this book asks how the study of affect would enable us to rethink intimacies – what the affect theories can do to the prevailing notions of intimacy and how they might renew and enrich contemporary theories of intimacy. This book has three sections that address the importance of re-imagining affective intimacies, the politics of affect, and the queering of intimacies. The chapters within those sections examine contemporary topics and push forward the current state of the art.

While pioneering in scholarship on both intimacy and affect, feminist scholars in particular have recognised intimacy as an important issue and advanced the field of affect studies. They have stressed how intimacy makes a contested field of power (Wilson, 2016; Illouz, 2007) and entails inequalities that operate through affective registers (Juvonen and Kolehmainen, 2018). Yet intimacy has often been discussed mainly in the context of certain issues, such as care responsibilities, heterosexual relationships or domestic work. These pre-defined domains, however, foster the idea of intimacy as something already known and defined (Kolehmainen and Juvonen, 2018). The bracketing of intimacy to certain domains, such as sexuality, private life or interpersonal relations, has historically made it difficult for intimacy to be a subject of importance writ large (Latimer and Gómez, 2019). It has also led to associations of intimacy with 'positive' closeness, such as in (assumedly) close relationships and encounters (Wilson, 2016; Gabb and

Fink, 2015). Yet this is highly problematic and results in very narrow definitions and operationalisations of the concept. Intimacy also takes normative and even violent forms (Zengin, 2016). Proximity and closeness are not neutral practices but are imbued with power; that is, besides protection or pleasure, they might provide exposure or pain (Kinnunen and Kolehmainen, 2019). The open-ended use of intimacy supports an alternative that is useful in understanding intimacy in critical terms (Wilson, 2016). Thus, there is a lacuna in scholarship that asks how the study of affect would enable us to rethink intimacies in unforeseen ways.

While there are alternative definitions of affect, this book builds on Gilles Deleuze's understanding of affect – who for his part was inspired by the Spinozist notion of affectus – as bodies' capacities to affect and become affected (Deleuze and Guattari, 2004; Coleman and Ringrose, 2013; Fox and Alldred, 2013; Ringrose and Renold, 2014; Seyfert, 2012). Here bodies are not limited to human bodies, but entail all kinds of bodies – non-human, material, discursive, collective, inorganic (Bennet, 2010; Seyfert 2012). Thus, affect should be seen neither as human-only nor as private and personal. In other words, affect can entail emotions, but it is not synonymous with individual human emotion – even if one persistent way of defining affect is to discuss its relation with emotion. In relational affect studies, affects – understood as intensities, energies and flows, for instance – are conceptualised as emerging out of the dynamic encounters between bodies and things (Gregg and Seigworth, 2010; Kolehmainen and Juvonen, 2018; Seyfert 2012). These multiple encounters, intimate in themselves, challenge the prevailing notions of intimacy as a human relation. Moreover, a lens provided by affect theory enables situated analysis of intimacies, as affect emerges and entangles in asymmetrical networks of power. This further highlights the political potential of affect in studying intimacies.

This book taps directly into this challenge, making an effort to enrich the prevailing scholarship and imagination concerning affective intimacies. As a point of departure, we seek to reject such assumptions that human relations are the main nexus for intimacy and that the most intimate of encounters happen in human–human relations, and that non-humans (from animals to technology) can at best merely facilitate human-only intimacies. Thus, one of the aims of this book is to refuse the human-only notions of affective intimacies and rather post-humanise both affect and the notion of intimacy. Post-humanising both affect and intimacy is crucial (Lykke, 2018) as intimacies surface and wither in networks of human and non-human actors (Paasonen, 2018a). We thus perceive this edited collection as an invitation to radically and openly attune to affective intimacies as they unfold in the happenings of everyday lives and in their more-than-human entanglements.

From 'intimate relationships' to affective intimacies

In social sciences and the humanities, the shifting forms of intimate lives have provided a major object of study. Paradigms such as individualisation and relationality have been important starting points when studying transformations concerning expectations, commitments and practices in intimate relationships in Western countries during the past few decades (Gabb and Silva, 2011; Roseneil, 2006). The shifts and pluralisation of intimate lives are connected to the decline of traditional institutions and social structures and to the impact of individualisation upon intimate lives (e.g. Beck and Beck-Gernsheim, 1995; Giddens, 1992). The critics of the individualisation thesis have pointed to the continuing connectedness, interdependencies and relationalities of intimate lives and to genderedness and classedness of intimate practices (Jamieson, 1998; Roseneil, 2007; Gabb and Silva, 2011). For example, it has been noted that in mixed-sex relationships men withdraw from emotional intimacy with women, making intimacy rather a source of control than a shared experience (O'Neill, 2018; Jurva and Lahti, 2019), and that same-sex intimacies have gained increased social acceptance and legal recognition in several Western countries, but this has largely happened at the expense of incorporating LGBTIQ+ relationships into already existing models of intimacy, such as marriage and the nuclear family (Warner, 2000; Duggan, 2002).

In previous research, there have been attempts to shift the focus from certain privileged forms of intimacy to pluralised forms of families and intimate practices. New concepts have been created to capture the everyday 'makings and mouldings' of intimacies: for example, family practices (Morgan 1996), relatedness (Carsten, 2000), personal life and living 'connected lives' (Smart, 2007) and practices of intimacy (Jamieson, 2011). By moving the paradigm from 'being' to 'doing' intimacies, these attempts are designed to better grasp the diverse forms of relationships, rather than to draw on limited understandings of intimacy (Gabb and Silva, 2011). Thus, various forms of relationships beyond the conjugal couple with children have been made visible (Budgeon, 2008; Holmes, 2015; Roseneil, 2007). Yet, despite the foregrounding of practices, which cumulatively and in combination enable, create and sustain a sense of closeness and the special quality of a relationship (Jamieson, 2011), the focus still dwells upon the interpersonal bonds.

As long as only human–human relationships are seen as the nexus of intimate relations, the relevance of more-than-human intimacies remains underdeveloped. For instance, scholars drawing upon queer theory have challenged the idea that only certain intimate relationships are of importance, starting from making visible the hierarchical valuation of intimate practices, from marriage to distinct sex acts (Rubin, 1993). Whereas the earlier work within queer theory provided such pivotal ideas as the concept of chosen families (Weston, 1991) – which illustrated how intimate lives in gay and lesbian communities were not arranged so centrally around couple relationships and biological ties, but friendship and community played a central role – or the concept of couplenormativity (Roseneil *et al.*, 2020) – which highlights how monogamous couple relationships are persistently valued more than other ways of arranging intimate lives – the most recent insights now ask what queer intimacies might look like when we think beyond human–human relations and consider intimacies with other species. For instance, attempts have been made to widen the idea of chosen families; that is, besides not being based on genetic kinship and the nuclear family, non-human-centred forms of kinship are to be included (Irni, 2020).

In recent years, scholars from different disciplinary backgrounds have suggested a shift away from human–human intimate relationships to more-than-human intimacies. For instance, the category of kinship has been broadened to include more-than-human intimacies. Yet while many concepts mobilised in the research on intimacies are bound to humans only, alternative concepts that both queer and post-humanise intimacy are also emerging. For instance, Nina Lykke (2018) uses the notion of compassionate companionship to resist normative terms, such as relative, to pay attention to corpo-affective dimensions and to the bodily becomings that extend into the more-than-human worlds. Companionship is a deeply affective relation of being for and with one other, and companionships extend to more-than-human bodies (Lykke, 2019). Kuura Irni (2020) asks what queer intimacies might look like when we think beyond human–human relations and consider intimacies with other species. Rethinking affective intimacies, therefore, is not only about rethinking the new forms and shapes of human relationships within and outside of institutional, legal and conventional frames; it is about rethinking, for instance, human–animal, human–plant and human–matter relations (see also Lykke, 2019; Puig de la Bellacasa, 2017). Within this book, we wish to provide such 'food for thought' that helps to recognise and understand more-than-human intimacies.

Infrastructures and structures of intimacy

One way to re-imagine intimacies is to look beyond the Western ontologies, both metaphorically and in concrete ways. In other words, we propose that re-imagining intimacies also requires a collective un-imagining of settler colonialism, nationalism, consumer capitalism, familism and patriarchy. Contemporary ideas of the early twenty-first century that are related to intimacy, such as chastity and respectability, are linked to capitalist ideas of ownership, monopoly and the accumulation of goods (Duggan, 2002; Halberstam, 2005; Hennessy, 2000). Researchers examining post-colonialism, indigenous studies scholars, as well as academics, politicians and activists from the 'Global South', have also pointed out that the normative categories governing intimacies, such as monogamy, are often Western phenomena (Monro, 2015; TallBear, 2018). Yet these normativities extend beyond couple relationships, for instance, to widely accepted yet restricted notions of love and attachment that influence, for example, the practices of adoption (Myong and Bissenbakker, 2021). As Irni (2020) argues, calling into question colonialist politics and thinking not only requires a rethinking of Western modes of relating but also the human-centredness of intimacies. For example, Mel Y. Chen's (2012) concept of animacies raises concerns that the relentless drawing of a distinction between human and inhuman, animate and inanimate is produced through racialised and sexualised means and political consequences. In this book, we especially foreground affect studies as a way to rethink and question this kind of human centrism.

In addition to un-imagining the prevailing notions of intimacy, novel imaginations, mappings and explorations are needed in order to widen the scope of studies on intimacy. Feminist scholar Laurent Berlant (2000) addresses intimacy as the connections that impact people and on which they depend for living. The most evident form of this kind of intimacy in contemporary societies is networked connectivity that has grown into a matter of infrastructure reminiscent of electricity, gas, water or heating – they are, in many ways, what living depends on (Paasonen, 2018a). In connection to digital infrastructures, many also consider the growing importance of data intimacies, such as the intimate role of algorithms, AI or datafication as a key development in our everyday lives. Yet in a similar vein we can discuss, for instance, chemical or toxic intimacies – referring to multiple entanglements, from drug use that aims to increase emotional closeness between partners or lower inhibitions during sex acts (e.g. Anderson *et al.*, 2018; Hakim, 2019) to the cumulative exposure to endocrine disruptors, neurotoxins, asthmagens, carcinogens and mutagens that is an inseparable and unavoidable part of everyday lives (Cielemecka and Åsberg, 2019; Chen, 2012). In other words, our lives are entangled with a multiplicity of intimacies, many of which, perhaps, occur without us even noticing.

Finally, intimacy does not require physical proximity nor is it limited to the material presence of (at least) bodies, objects or things. Whereas even the novel conceptualisations – from data intimacies to chemical intimacies – foreground proximity, companionship and entanglement, intimacies extend beyond this kind of closeness. Thus, intimacy should not be understood solely through physical proximity and, in addition to material intimacies, immaterial intimacies provide one way to re-imagine affective intimacies. To give a few examples, bodies and minds have capacities to communicate – to affect and become affected – largely in immaterial ways (Dernikos, 2018); meaning that material and other-than-human elements participate in producing post-mortem forms of affective intimacies (Alasuutari, 2021). Intimacies hence also take novel shapes; from dreams to fantasies, and from cravings to memories that haunt us. These can take both individualised and collective forms. Through thinking of the embodied experience of history, it becomes possible to explore how the experience of oppression and exploitation is embodied and transmitted across communities and generations and can, thus, continue to haunt us (Walkerdine, 2015; also, Rajan-Rankin, 2021). Affective intimacies thus exist on the limits of the phenomenal (also Lury, 2015), meaning that their explorations require methodological sensitivity and imagination.

Affective intimacies: Signposts for alternative research designs

From the perspective of this book, then, the relevant questions start by asking how to approach affective intimacies. For instance, what is recognised as 'affective' or 'intimate' is a key question, yet the relation between affect and intimacy certainly forms another. We accept that methodology should enrich, not flatten the research process and thus think one should be aware of the limitations of working with stabilising concepts (Kolehmainen, 2019) – rather, mapping both fixity and movement is an essential part of a research process (Renold and Ringrose, 2008). Notably, this collection is not about affect and intimacy, but affective intimacies. Instead of foregrounding certain pre-defined categories of affects or intimacies, we wish to shift the focus to the processes, entanglements and encounters between humans – as well as between human and non-human bodies – that provide key signposts for comprehending affective intimacies. While recent years have seen advances in the theoretical and methodological scholarship on affect, thus far affect studies have not been fully utilised in rethinking intimacies. We advocate that thinking about intimacies through more-than-human entanglements offers a novel perspective to attune to the affective intimacies that emerge through relational networks and encounters, which include multiple elements and which are alive and vibrant, intimate in themselves (Bennet, 2010; Fox and Alldred, 2015, 2017; Kolehmainen, 2018). Taking this kind of co-constitution into account requires methodological elaboration.

Further, affect, we claim, offers new perspectives on the intimate as it is sensed and lived, networked across human and non-human bodies. One of the challenges in the examination of intimacy is to look at the socio-material constitution of intimacy and its more-than-human constituencies (Latimer and Gómez, 2019). Complex, non-reductive understandings of materiality are key here (Wilson, 2016). This translates to a quest for methodologies that foreground processes (Knudsen and Stage, 2020). Further, for working with non-reductive understandings of affective intimacies it is important to pay attention to how they emerge in varying and unfolding conditions of the world (Tiainen *et al.*, 2020). Reclaiming the heterogeneous materiality of the intimate – with intimacy being made of and with multiple entangled materialities – counters the invisibilisation of affect (Latimer and Gómez, 2019). Yet, as indicated earlier, what is conventionally seen as immaterial also contributes to these un/makings of intimacy. Thus, we highlight the importance of explorations of and experiments with immaterial intimacies, even if this also means new methodological challenges.

Instead of static events or certain relational forms, affective intimacies often emerge as barely perceptible events in the process of 'becoming' across social, material, discursive, human and more-than-human worlds (e.g. Tiainen *et al.*, 2020; MacLure, 2013). Entering the middle – an approach stemming from Deleuzian tradition (Coleman and Ringrose, 2013) – is especially fruitful in examining affective intimacies. It can be used to examine the entanglement of affect and intimacy, thus foregrounding the process or the relations instead of two distinct categories. Another beneficial avenue is provided by assemblage theory, which also offers methodological tools for the exploration of affective intimacies. Affective intimacies can be conceived of as assemblages wherein multiple and complex elements entangle. They are therefore temporal groupings of relations that are both unfinished and open-ended. Such intimate assemblages connect bodies with other bodies, matter, affect, ideas and societal processes in many different directions. An alternative approach is provided by the concept of meshwork, which stresses how individuals and forms of knowledge are entanglements: they emerge through encounters with others – they are not pre-existent, self-contained and separate entities, but a meshwork of interwoven lines of growth and movement (Ingold, 2007). In a research process, attunement to affective intimacies thus translates as a quest to become skilful in recognising the entanglements and loose ends (Ingold, 2011). In any case, such engagements that do not assume the separateness of affect and intimacy are crucial.

Rethinking affect and intimacy

The first section of this book delves into the importance of re-imagining affective intimacies. Aligning with the notion that the concept of affect helps us to reconsider intimacy as something of which its existence does not require our conscious attention or recognition (see Blackman, 2012), this book makes a serious intervention in its attempt to rethink the entanglements of affects and intimacies. We further propose that affective intimacies are about the happenings of the social (Lury and Wakeford, 2012) where the social is not restricted to humans (Tsing quoted in Mitman, 2019). Yet still, several concepts from meanings to discourses and from narratives to identities prioritise human-only agencies, without fully allowing an acknowledgement of the more-than-human and the entangled agencies. We thus align with such bodies of work that have emphasised either the employment of non-human centred concepts – meaning that, for instance, affect is not equated with human emotion (Colebrook, 2002) or intimacy with human sexuality (Fox and Alldred, 2013; Lahti and Kolehmainen, 2020) – or who have stressed the importance of reconsidering the uses of such familiar conceptualisations as 'the social' or 'the political' (e.g. Bennett, 2010; Tsing quoted in Mitman, 2019).

While many affect theories highlight the importance of the human body, as Jane Bennett (2010) reminds us, affect is not specific to humans, organisms or even to bodies: we should consider the affect of technologies, winds, vegetables, minerals – or, as we do within the first section of this book, we reach towards the affects of smoke, digital intimate publics and technological infrastructures. Further, when affect refers to registers best described as trans-subjective, non-conscious, inter-corporeal and immaterial (Blackman and Venn, 2010; Blackman, 2012), it cannot be reduced to individual physical responses even when registered or felt personally (Kolehmainen and Juvonen, 2018). Rather, it inherently entails the notion of relationality, providing important insights into the ways that bodies – human, non-human, animate, inanimate, virtual, material – are conditioned and condition themselves to one another in a set of unequal and uneven relations of power (also, Ahmed, 2000; Zengin, 2016). Hence, in the context of this book, the catchphrase characterisation of affect as 'capacities to affect and become affected' should not be understood as entailing a symmetry or a balance between 'affecting' and 'becoming affected' (Schuller, 2018) but rather as a concept that points to the multiple entanglements of affect and intimacy.

It is widely acknowledged that affect as a concept resists such binaries as body/mind, self/other and subject/object, yet there is more to that: since affect also helps to question such dichotomies as individual/collective, human/animal or animate/inanimate, we believe that the lens provided by affect theories presents fruitful insights into the rethinking of more-than-human intimacies. Affect also allows ambivalence, uncertainty and multiplicity to be addressed, thus having the potential to enliven and renew the scholarship on intimacies. The three chapters in this section do not privilege human-only intimacies, but rather consider intimacies as they surface and unfold in multiple matterings. These more-than-human intimacies remind us that the becomings of bodies, as well as their intimate entanglements, extend into more-than-human worlds. That is, bodies enter and exit trans-corporeal (Alaimo, 2008) relationships with the more-than-human world (Neimanis, 2017; see also Lykke, 2019). Further, bodily in/capacities to affect and become affected pinpoint different co-dependencies (e.g. Puig de la Bellacasa, 2017; Tsing, 2015) as essential for all forms of living. These co-dependencies are formed historically and culturally and across species, technologies, bodies and matterings. Their examination provides an important entry point to the study of affective intimacies.

The politics of affect: Spatial and societal entanglements

The second section of the book examines the politics of affect in particular, by looking at the spatial and societal entanglements that are intertwined with affective intimacies. With the help of affect theories, it is possible to shift the focus onto the intimacies that emerge in the process of the 'happening' of everyday life (Stewart, 2007) that reach beyond pre-defined and top-down operations of power, such as capitalism, colonialism, sexism and heteronormativity. Yet still, economic, social and cultural forces hide in the happening of everyday life and might intensify in a person, an event or a scene (Stewart, 2007; Fannin *et al.*, 2010). It is in these encounters and events that these forces and forms of power come to matter (Fannin *et al.*, 2010). In particular, ordinary life has a peculiar materiality, where bodies of all kinds – people, atmospheres, spaces, expectations and institutions – are momentarily thrown together and then they fall apart again (Stewart, 2007). Attuning to this kind of materiality of everyday life opens up new ways of thinking about affective intimacies, as the three chapters in this section illustrate. They especially tap into the ways in which spatial and societal relations condition and co-produce such affective intimacies that are difficult to grasp empirically.

We also take a cue from Ann Cvetkovich's (2012) suggestion that affects provide important entry points to diagnose political problems as well as an immanent force for societal change. We further claim that the study of affective intimacies enriches our understanding of politics by contributing to the exploration of mundane experiences of exclusion and injustice, where differences are also affectively, spatially and materially made and unmade (see also Kolehmainen, 2019; Lahti, 2018). By attending to affective intimacies, the chapters yield insights into how austerity, white privilege and sexuality emerge, entangle and become registered and felt through multiple encounters across human and non-human bodies. Hence, the focus on affective intimacies opens up novel perspectives on the politics of power, but also refuses to centre solely on human-only notions of affective intimacies. Thus, the political potential of affect lies in the ways in which thinking with affect helps to address co-constitutions and interdependencies as a condition of life – also in its more-than-human forms.

A lens provided by relational affect theories enables us to resist such depoliticising, neoliberalist stances that rely upon individualising rhetoric and choice-driven logics, and that foster the idea of bounded, sovereign and human-only subjects (e.g. Blackman, 2012). An approach that foregrounds affect provides tools for the simultaneous consideration of multiple entanglements that co-constitute each other. From this perspective, vulnerability becomes the condition of life (Chouliaraki, 2020; Koivunen *et al.*, 2018). Affect theory provides a productive framework for the conceptualisation of vulnerability as an affective relation which entails both the entanglements with political conditions that hinder one's life, and the affective becoming of bodies that allow transformation and movement beyond a fixed and stable subject position (Rozmarin, 2021). This also has consequences for our understanding of the political: these vary from resisting such notions of intimacy where it is seen as opposed to the political (Kolehmainen and Juvonen, 2018) to the limiting of politics to humans only (Bennett, 2010; Tsing, 2015). This displaces the individual human or a human collective from the core of political analysis (Bennett, 2010), making space for affective, psychic, material and spatial considerations – as the three chapters in this section eloquently do.

Queering intimacies: Affective un/becomings

The third section explores those forms of intimacy that (at least at times) escape the cultural recognition and intelligibility that would allow them to be acknowledged. Traditionally, mainly queer intimacies have been seen in this kind of culturally not-apprehensible form, even if, for instance, invisibility has perhaps also secured the survival of same-sex intimacies. Queer theoretical concepts of heteronormativity and homonormativity have been groundbreaking in highlighting how heterosexuality is naturalised and privileged in everyday life in various ways, and how LGBTIQ+ intimacies have gained social acceptance and legal recognition by affirming the heteronormative model of long-term monogamous relationships that produce children (Duggan, 2002). However, we wish to highlight how sexuality-related norms function depending on how they are assembled with other elements, from intersecting (power) relations to multiple intimacies. When discussing 'normativities', there are elements that are more fluid and elements that are less open to fluidity (Lahti and Kolehmainen, 2020; Osella, 2019). For instance, desire – often seen as fluid – also works through affective flows, surges and intensities. Thus, the relationship between norms and affect is not at all straightforward, and this relationship cannot be frozen and stabilised as it would be if norms were affectively attached to it, or if it were determined by pre-existing norms.

The internationally dominant systems for categorising sex, sexuality and gender, and the social inequalities they are likely to produce, at least partly stem from the Western colonial past (Monro, 2015). These categorisations were developed in synchrony with the racialised, sexualised and gendered social inequalities on which many societies are based (Haritaworn, 2015; Monro, 2015). However, the legacies of colonialism have proven very hard to decolonise (Singh, 2016) even if decolonisation would offer the potential to map intimacies in alternative and novel ways. In this section, though it focuses on queer intimacies, we advance a view that affective intimacies as a framework enables the destabilisation of the Western dichotomies, including the hetero/homo-binary. Affect theory, in particular, allows new questions to be raised that simultaneously tap into the continuing dominance of heterosexuality and refuse old, worn-out explanations and concerns. As Caroline Osella (2019) reminds us, our questions cannot be binary. Binary questions and concepts necessarily come up with binary answers, such as labelling objects as normative or non-normative. Alternative conceptualisations – many of which are sensitive to affect, such as feeling entities (Steinbock, 2014) or play (Paasonen, 2018b) – help us to see sexuality in a more vivid way than just normativity or lack thereof.

Again, a lens provided by affect theory shifts the focus to entanglements and encounters between human and non-human bodies. It also invites us to see gender and sexuality as unstable categories that are on the move (re) assembling and connecting in new ways and taking new forms through intimate world-making practices (Fox and Alldred, 2013; Kolehmainen, 2018; Lahti, 2018). Furthermore, while post-humanist conceptualisations of sexuality point to the processes, entanglements and encounters of multiple bodies (Fox and Alldred, 2013; Lahti, 2018, 2020a, 2020b; Weiss, 2020), gender can also be conceptualised as a multiplicity that emerges as an effect of entanglements of multiple elements (Kolehmainen, 2020; Schuller, 2020). Gender and sexuality can be seen as the products of bodies' relations with other bodies; in other words, they are about 'becoming rather than being' (e.g. Coleman, 2009; Kolehmainen, 2018; Lahti, 2018, 2020a, 2020b), which allows for a consideration of queer intimacies and queering intimacies without reducing gender and sexuality to stable, individualised identity categories. In this book, we propose a shift away from human-centred and identity-based notions of gender and sexuality. The chapters in this section

propose that the relevance of gender or sexuality is dependent on the particular assemblages that it forms with other bodies (Malins, 2004; Renold
and Mellor, 2013). By focusing on encounters, relationalities and entanglements that connect us queerly to others (Weiss, 2020) we take up the task
of queering the whole notion of sexuality. The three chapters in this section
re-imagine sexuality and gender as collective, embodied and affective processes. The chapters illustrate that it is relevant to ask how unpredictable
and unruly affect might participate in queering intimacy.

Mapping affective intimacies

The edited collection, *Affective intimacies*, provides a novel platform for
re-evaluating the notion of open-ended intimacies through the lens of affect
theories. In particular, it addresses the embodied, affective and psychic
aspects of intimate entanglements across various contemporary phenomena.
It advances the value of interdisciplinary perspectives in thinking in terms
of affective intimacies. The diverse chapters introduce topical themes and
contribute to current topics in social sciences, representing multiple disciplines from gender studies, sociology and cultural studies to anthropology
and queer studies. In addition, the authors come from different academic
backgrounds. This kind of diversity is also present in the methodological
approaches, which both present and push forward different onto-episte-
mological points of departure. Theoretically, the chapters make significant
advances: rethinking well-known concepts of care, lesbianism, the re-exam-
ination of debates on topics such as austerity or motherhood and the re-
imagining of notions of empathy or gender. The attunement to experiences
that are not usually afforded recognition, that remain ordinary or unspoken
and invisible is characteristic to all chapters; thus, they enrich the study
of the workings of power by addressing the under-the-radar operations of
power. In this way, by addressing racism, capitalism, sexism and heteronormativity they also make the political aspects of affective intimacies visible,
yet they avoid any shorthand explanations of power (Latour, 2005; Stewart,
2007). In their nuanced, vivid and rich elaborations of interdependencies
and vulnerabilities across different sites from intergenerational to transnational they all contribute to the study of affective intimacies.

Affective matterings

The collection starts with a section on 'Rethinking affect and intimacy'. The
brilliant chapter '"Caring matter": A love story of queer intimacies between

(her) body and object (her cigarette)' by Dresda E. Méndez de la Brena opens this section and the whole book. Méndez de la Brena starts by asking what 'care' means when we go about thinking and living interdependently with beings other than humans in disabled worlds. In queering the concept of care in relation to matter, the chapter foregrounds the affective entanglements between persons and objects. Méndez de la Brena eloquently pinpoints the limits of human care while introducing two queer love stories, one about the process of becoming-in-love between her and her partner, and the second love story between her narcoleptic partner and smoking. Here cigarettes are acknowledged to be providing crucial care since they help the narcoleptic partner to cope with her illness – even if this is not the author's desired situation. Different ways to write academically are not only looked for but successfully created when Méndez de la Brena discusses love and care in their manifold forms. Using an approach provided by 'auto-phenomenography', the chapter thus rethinks how we can create and imagine new possibilities. From these points of departure, the chapter beautifully contributes to the study of affective intimacies, in particular by introducing the novel concept of 'caring matter'. The chapter concludes that caring matter can show us how non-human care 'works' when human-provided care is absent or insufficient. Finally, it asks for the rejection of normative and ableist notions of smoking, reminding us that for many people smoking offers possibilities for performance, survival and endurance. It invites us to rethink many ideas that are often taken for granted concerning intimacies and provides thought-provoking, eloquent work on affective matterings between people and objects.

Armi Mustosmäki's and Tiina Sihto's chapter, 'The figure of a regretful mother on an online discussion board', analyses a discussion thread in response to a post on regretting motherhood on an anonymous Finnish online discussion board. The chapter analyses the affective responses to the figure of a regretting mother, highlighting how negative maternal feelings are (not) allowed to enter a digital intimate public. The analysis shows that in the context of motherhood, the affective registers of regret are discredited and are instead subsumed by various motivations and pathological explanations. For example, expressions of regret are interpreted as symptoms of individualised perfectionism and 'overdoing' of motherhood, or as the mother's inability to resist the societal pressure put on mothers. There are also responses that blame regretting mothers for parental incompetence or lacking the will to enjoy motherhood. The chapter insightfully suggests that the affective registers of regret are associated with weak or damaged agency and mothers' inability to take charge of their lives. Mustosmäki and Sihto's analysis makes an important contribution to affective intimacies by demonstrating how a mother's negative feelings are pathologised and devalued.

Affect plays a prominent role within the formations of neoliberalism, where therapeutic ethos becomes visible in the ways in which women are expected to be resilient and self-sufficient. The chapter innovatively sheds light on normative intimacies, exploring how maternal affects are mediated in the digital intimate public.

Marjo Kolehmainen's chapter, 'Intimate technology? Teletherapies in the era of COVID-19', examines affective intimacies in teletherapy settings. Empirically, the study explores therapy and counselling professionals' experiences of the role of technology in their work, particularly in relation to the 'digital leap' brought about by the COVID-19 pandemic. Rather than pre-defining teletherapies as similar or different to traditional therapies, the chapter takes the position that technological infrastructures condition and shape the affective processes of support-seeking and support-giving. In particular, the analysis taps into the question of how intimacy comes to matter in teletherapy practices, tracing the ways in which intimacy is being made and unmade, of and with multiple entangled materialities. Kolehmainen argues that therapy and counselling could best be understood through the Baradian lens of intra-action, wherein agency is distributed across various human and non-human actors: from professionals and clients to therapy venues, from psychic conditions to legislation, from technological equipment and software apps to economic factors. With this approach, Kolehmainen makes visible the socio-material constitution of intimacies in teletherapy practices, thus enriching our understanding of affective intimacies. The chapter thus develops tools to rethink intimacy as co-constituted by several dynamic processes that have capacities to affect and become affected. The chapter concludes by arguing that the distancing capacities are not distinct from those capacities that generate the feelings of intimacy. Rather they both exemplify the distributed agencies of entangled materialities.

Spatial and material politics of affect

The following three chapters are a part of the section 'The politics of affect: Spatial and societal entanglements'. 'The empathiser's new shoes: The discomforts of empathy as white feminist affect', Andrea Lobb's theoretical chapter, asks how and why the capacity for empathy – long celebrated in Anglo-American feminism – no longer appears to be such a straightforward ethical virtue when read through the double lens provided by affect and critical race studies. Engaging with philosophical theories, Lobb views the empathy of the white feminist as an acutely ambivalent affect – one tied up in complex ways with the asymmetric power relations of race. In her contribution, she argues that the efforts of feminists from white settler societies are embedded in moral ambivalence as, on one hand, they wish to maintain their empathetic identifications but, on the other hand, they must divest themselves of willful ignorance regarding their racial privilege. Lobb thus suggests that white feminist politics needs to be prepared to relinquish the attachment to feeling virtuous and good, and work instead with the affective dissonance of ambivalent empathy. By so doing, she offers a fascinating critique of the affective building of the intimate-political assemblages of feminist solidarity and argues that paying attention to the imbrications of racial domination and the intimacies of affect dislodges the taken-for-granted normative 'goodness' so often ascribed to empathy within feminist theory. As Lobb eloquently shows, there is an urgent need to rethink the affective politics of empathy within white feminist politics.

In Ilektra Kyriazidou's chapter, 'Neighbouring in times of austerity: Intimacy and the "noikokyrio"', we are presented with an incisive analysis of female residents' experiences of austerity in a low-income neighbourhood in Thessaloniki, Greece. Her contribution to affective intimacies unfolds the ways in which politics of austerity are lived and felt – in her words experienced as a 'blow to the body', as bodies are overwhelmed by daily obstacles and commitments. By drawing upon an ethnographic study, the chapter provides novel insights into the ways that intimacy between neighbours is constructed in everyday relations developed from sharing the difficulties and the exhaustion they face in their efforts to help their families during austerity. Yet, as Kyriazidou underscores, the affective patterns within these intimate relations also take different and exclusionary forms as they are driven by the wider political climate of austerity and a particular affective economy of antagonism. This is further oriented by the conservative ethos of the 'noikokyrio', the local model of the family household. Kyriazidou attunes to models of support but also to criticism and judgements as they unfold in the everyday relations between neighbours, painting a vivid picture of these intimate affective dynamics. More generally, her chapter also illuminates how evaluations of one's neighbours are well-matched with the ideological reinforcements of austerity and neoliberalism. Thus, the affective intimacies of the neighbourly relations, as discussed in the chapter, are conditioned by diverse political and economic circumstances and effects of austerity.

Tuula Juvonen's chapter, 'Becoming a lesbian at lesbian and gay dance parties: Lesboratories as affective spaces', introduces the groundbreaking idea of 'lesboratories', opening up a completely new research strand in the study of affective intimacies and in lesbian studies. Looking at past gay and lesbian communities, the chapter taps into the question of venues that were also actively participating in the production of what was then an emerging idea of a lesbian. Lesboratories acknowledge the role of matter in the making of lesbians – as Juvonen eloquently illustrates, a lesboratory as a novel conceptualisation argues for understanding lesbianism as a collective, embodied and affective formation. Here Juvonen departs from such scholarship that has mostly theorised LGBTIQ+ identities as being based on language, discourse and norms; or focused solely on the social relations between people. Instead of following these paths, Juvonen applies the thinking of Karen Barad to her study, arguing that bodies and spaces cannot be separated, as both arise together in an intra-action in which they are entangled. Empirically, the chapter draws upon accounts from oral history interviews regarding lesbian and gay party venues run by the local lesbian and gay organisation in Tampere, Finland in the 1980s. It argues that lesboratories influenced both the ways in which women were able to become lesbians and how they were able to create communities of their own. Lesboratories underline the intimate, collective bonds through which the affected bodies became with the materiality of the spaces of lesbian and gay dance parties. The chapter vividly enlivens political imaginaries of the past, and leads us to the next section, which highlights how approaching sexuality and gender as collective, affective processes offers fresh perspectives on the embodied entanglements that connect us queerly to others.

Collective formations of gender and sexuality

Yiran Wang's chapter, '"Lack" of languages: Affective experiences of female same-sex intimacies in contemporary China', opens the section titled 'Queering intimacies: Affective un/becomings'. It examines the collective, trans-subjective processes of becoming a women-loving woman in China. Drawing upon an ethnographic study, her analysis taps into the complicated relationship between affect and language. There is often a lack of 'proper' language for expressing female same-sex love and describing sexual practices, since the dominant discourses do not acknowledge them. Wang examines ineffable feelings, 'misused' words and affective and bodily practices, and illustrates insightfully how it is not despite this 'lack' but through it that it becomes possible to understand the inter-corporeal processes of becoming intimate and becoming a women-loving woman. By applying concepts and ideas that are sensitive to affect and embodiment she investigates assembled, relational subjectivities, particularly utilising the ideas of 'nomadic subjectivity' theorised by Rosi Braidotti and intra-action by Karen Barad. By theorising '(first) love without articulation' and re-appropriating the notion of 'penetration', she shows how the women's affective memories reach beyond available discourses. Through her analysis that is sensitive to embodiment, she is able to grasp the inter-corporeal entanglements and affective forces that shape affective intimacies. In other words, by attending to the trans-corporeal aspects of becoming a women-loving woman in con-temporary China, Wang makes a unique contribution to the exploration of affective intimacies of these collective processes.

The experiences of gender non-binary individuals in Slovenia are the focus of Nina Perger's chapter. In 'Affective obligations and obliged affections: Non-binary youth and affective (re)orientations to family', the young people illuminate the affects of being silenced or rejected by their fami-lies in response to their gender non-binary identities. By bringing together Sara Ahmed's (2014) conceptualisation of affective orientations and Pierre Bourdieu's (2000, 2001) conceptual pairing of affective obligations and obliged affections, Perger offers a complex analysis into the ways in which affective orientations towards family as a happy object and a 'straightening' device are maintained. Taking up this line of inquiry her research demon-strates that the promise of familial happiness is bound up with the securing of social hierarchy, as the analysis of interview data vividly illustrates. By acknowledging the embodiment of affective obligations, family life emerges as a space where affects are entangled with bodily sensations and thoughts that move agents towards and away from certain objects. The chapter dem-onstrates how this movement can be stuck in an ambivalent experiential mess of belonging and alienation, which in turn can entail guilt and shame alongside memories of care and pleasure among gender non-binary indi-viduals. The chapter thus makes a valuable contribution to the study of affective intimacies from the perspective of non-binary gendered people and their familial ties, as it departs from viewing these affective processes as individual but rather highlights their collective entanglements.

Annukka Lahti's chapter, 'Affective intimacies of gender assemblages: Closeness and distance in LGBTQ+ women's relationships', explores the sig-nificance of gender in LGBTQ+ women's relationships. The chapter begins with an observation of the closeness and easiness of certain LGBTQ+ wom-en's relationships, while others struggle with unequal approaches to shar-ing childcare and domestic responsibilities in ways that strikingly resemble the gendered conventions of heterosexual relationships. Arguing that the framework of gendered conventions is limited, Lahti analyses gender as becoming in and through affective assemblages. The chapter thus shifts the focus from the human-centred paradigm that would approach gender as an identity that 'belongs to a person', to seeing them as collective formations. A more nuanced approach, where multiple elements and affective intimacies of a gender assemblage can be identified. For the purposes of the chapter, she analyses two data sets: interviews with LGBTQ+ women who have expe-rienced a recent relationship break-up, and a longitudinal set of interviews with bisexual women and their variously gendered (ex)partners. Her analy-sis shows how the accumulating affective intimacies of a gender assemblage, which are a co-constitution of many elements – e.g. sexual desire, cultural norms and ideas about gender, (shared) interests, events and material spaces – have an ability to bring certain gendered bodies closer to one another, while pushing others away from one another. The chapter also shows how equalities and inequalities emerge in temporally shifting ways in LGBTQ+ women's gender assemblages and how this is entangled with closeness and distance in their relationships.

Note

1 Marjo Kolehmainen's work was supported by 'Intimacy in Data-Driven Culture', a research consortium funded by the Strategic Research Council at the Academy of Finland (327391).

References

Ahmed, S. (2000), *Strange Encounters: Embodied Others in Post-Coloniality* (London: Routledge).

Ahmed, S. (2014), *Cultural Politics of Emotion* (Edinburgh: Edinburgh University Press).

Alaimo, S. (2008), 'Trans-Corporeal Feminisms and the Ethical Space of Nature', in *Material Feminisms*, S. Alaimo and S. Hekman (eds) (Bloomington, IN: Indiana University Press), 237–64.

Alasuutari, V., 'Tied Together by Death – Post-Mortem Forms of Affective Intimacy in LGBTQ People's Stories of Partner Loss', *NORA – Nordic Journal of Feminist and Gender Research* (online, 21 April 2021). doi: https://doi.org/10.1080/08038740.2021.1903554

Anderson, K., Reavey, P., and Boden, Z. (2018), 'An Affective (re) Balancing Act? The Liminal Possibilities for Heterosexual Partners on MDMA', in *Affective Inequalities in Intimate Relationships*, T. Juvonen and M. Kolehmainen (eds) (London: Routledge), 19–33.

Beck, U., and Beck-Gernsheim, E. (1995), *The Normal Chaos of Love* (Cambridge: Polity Press).

Bennett, J. (2010), *Vibrant Matter: A Political Ecology of Things* (Durham, NC: Duke University Press).

Berlant, L. (2000), 'Intimacy: A Special Issue', in *Intimacy*, L. Berlant (ed.) (Chicago, IL: University of Chicago Press), 1–8.

Blackman, L. (2012), *Immaterial Bodies: Affect, Embodiment, Mediation* (London: SAGE Publications).

Blackman, L., and Venn, C. (2010), 'Affect', *Body & Society*, 16:1, 7–28. doi: https://doi.org/10.1177/1357034X09354769

Bourdieu, P. (2000), *Pascalian Meditations* (Palo Alto, CA: Stanford University Press).

Bourdieu, P. (2001), *Masculine Domination* (Cambridge: Polity Press).

Budgeon, S. (2008), 'Couple Culture and the Production of Singleness', *Sexualities*, 11:3, 301–25.

Carsten, J. (ed.) (2000), *Cultures of Relatedness: New Approaches to the Study of Kinship* (Cambridge: Cambridge University Press).

Chen, M. Y. (2012). *Animacies. Biopolitics, Racial Mattering, and Queer Affect* (Durham, NC, and London: Duke University Press).

Chouliaraki, L. (2020), 'Victimhood: The Affective Politics of Vulnerability', *European Journal of Cultural Studies*, 24:1, 10–27. doi: https://doi.org/10.1177 /1367549420979316

Cielemęcka, O., and Åsberg, C. (2019), 'Introduction: Toxic Embodiment and Feminist Environmental Humanities', *Environmental Humanities*, 11:1, 101–7.

Colebrook, C. (2002), *Gilles Deleuze* (London: Routledge).

Coleman, R. (2009), *The Becoming of Bodies: Girls, Images, Experience* (Manchester: Manchester University Press).

Coleman, R., and Ringrose, J. (eds) (2013), *Deleuze and Research Methodologies* (Edinburgh: Edinburgh University Press), 164–83.

Cvetkovich, A. (2012), *Depression: A Public Feeling* (Durham, NC: Duke University Press).

Deleuze, G., and Guattari, F. (2004), *A Thousand Plateaus: Capitalism and Schizophrenia* (London: Continuum).

Dernikos, B. (2018), 'Reviving Ghostly Bodies: Student-Teacher Intimacies as Affective Hauntings', in *Affective Inequalities in Intimate Relationships*, T. Juvonen and M. Kolehmainen (eds) (London: Routledge), 218–30.

Duggan, L. (2002), 'The New Homonormativity: The Sexual Politics of Neoliberalism', in *Materialising Democracy: Towards a Revitalized Cultural Politics*, R. Castronovo and D. D. Nelson (eds) (Durham, NC: Duke University Press), 175–94.

Fannin, M., Jackson, M., Crang, P., Katz, C., Larsen, S., Tolia-Kelly, D., and Stewart, K. (2010), 'Author Meets Critics: A Set of Reviews and a Response', *Social and Cultural Geography*, 11:8, 921–31.

Fox, N. J., and Alldred, P. (2013), 'The Sexuality-Assemblage: Desire, Affect, Anti-Humanism', *Sociological Review*, 61:4, 769–89.

Fox, N. J., and Alldred, P. (2015), 'New Materialist Social Inquiry: Designs, Methods and the Research-Assemblage', *International Journal of Social Research Methodology*, 18:4, 399–414.

Fox, N., and Alldred, P. (2017), *Sociology and the New Materialism* (London: SAGE Publications). https://dx.doi.org/10.4135/9781526401915

Gabb, J., and Fink, J. (2015), *Couple Relationships in the 21st Century* (Basingstoke: Palgrave Macmillan).

Gabb, J., and Silva, E. B. (2011), 'Introduction to Critical Concepts: Families, Intimacies and Personal Relationships', *Sociological Research Online*, 16:4, 104–8.

Giddens, A. (1992), *The Transformation of Intimacy: Sexuality, Love and Eroticism in Modern Societies* (Cambridge: Polity Press).

Gregg, M., and Seigworth, G. J. (eds) (2010), *The Affect Theory Reader* (Durham, NC: Duke University Press).

Hakim, J. (2019), 'The Rise of Chemsex: Queering Collective Intimacy in Neoliberal London', *Cultural Studies*, 33:2, 249–75. doi: https://doi.org/10.1080/09502386 .2018.1435702

Halberstam, J. (2005), *In a Queer Time and Place: Transgender Bodies, Subcultural Lives* (New York, NY: New York University Press).

Haritaworn, J. (2015), *Queer Lovers and Hateful Others: Regenerating Violent Times and Places* (London: Pluto Press).

Hennessy, R. (2000), *Profit and Pleasure: Sexual Identities in Late Capitalism* (New York, NY, and London: Routledge).

Holmes, M. (2015), 'Couples Living Apart Together', in *The Blackwell Encyclopedia of Sociology*, G. Ritzer (ed.) (online). doi: https://doi.org/10.1002 /9781405165518.wbeosc141.pub2

Illouz, E. (2007), *Cold Intimacies: The Making of Emotional Capitalism* (Cambridge, MA: Polity Press).

Ingold, T. (2007), *Lines: A Brief History* (London: Routledge).

Ingold, T. (2011), *Being Alive: Essays on Movement, Knowledge and Description* (London: Routledge).

Irni, K. (2020), 'Queer-visioita lajirajat ylittävistä perheistä ja läheissuhteista', in *Perhe- ja läheissuhteet sateenkaaren alla*, A. Lahti, K. Aarnio, A. Moring, and J. Kerppola (eds) (Helsinki, Finland: Gaudeamus), 214–30.

Jamieson, L. (1998), *Intimacy: Personal Relationships in Modern Societies* (Jackson, MS: University Press).

Jamieson, L. (2011), 'Intimacy as a Concept: Explaining Social Change in the Context of Globalisation or Another Form of Ethnocentrism?', *Sociological Research Online*, 16:4, 151–63.

Jurva, R., and Lahti, A. (2019), 'Challenging Unequal Gendered Conventions in Heterosexual Relationship Contexts Through Affective Dissonance', *NORA – Nordic Journal of Feminist and Gender Research*, 27:4, 218–30.

Juvonen, T., and Kolehmainen, M. (eds) (2018), *Affective Inequalities in Intimate Relationships* (London: Routledge).

Kinnunen, T., and Kolehmainen, M. (2019), 'Touch and Affect: Analysing the Archive of Touch Biographies', *Body & Society*, 25:1, 29–56.

Koivunen, A., Kyrölä, K., and Rydberg, I. (eds) (2018), *The Power of Vulnerability* (Manchester: Manchester University Press).

Kolehmainen, M. (2018), 'Mapping Affective Capacities: Gender and Sexuality in Relationship and Sex Counselling Practices', in *Affective Inequalities in Intimate Relationships*, T. Juvonen and M. Kolehmainen (eds) (London: Routledge), 63–78.

Kolehmainen, M. (2019), 'Rethinking Heteronormativity in Relationship Counseling Practices: Toward the Recognition of Nonlinearity, Uncertainty, and Rupture', in *The Everyday Makings of Heteronormativity: Cross-Cultural Explorations of Sex, Gender, and Sexuality*, S. Sehlikoglu and F. G. Karioris (eds) (Lanham, MD: Lexington Books), 65–79.

Kolehmainen, M. (2020), 'Re-Imagining Gender and Sexuality: Feminist New Materialisms, Affect Theory and the Feminist Futures', presentation at Gender

Studies Conference Reclaiming futures 2020, 15 November 2020 (Tampere University, Finland).

Kolehmainen, M., and Juvonen, T. (2018), 'Introduction: Thinking With and Through Affective Inequalities', in *Affective Inequalities in Intimate Relationships*, T. Juvonen and M. Kolehmainen (eds) (London: Routledge), 1–16.

Kolehmainen, M., Lahad, K., and Lahti, A. (2021), 'Introduction: Editorial for Special Issue on Affective Intimacies', *NORA – Nordic Journal of Gender and Feminist Research*, 29:3, 147–51.

Knudsen, B., and Stage, C. (eds) (2015), *Affective Methodologies: Developing Cultural Research Strategies for the Study of Affect* (Basingstoke and New York, NY: Palgrave Macmillan).

Lahti, A. (2018), 'Listening to Old Tapes: Affective Intensities and Gendered Power in Bisexual Women's and Ex-Partners' Relationship Assemblages', in *Affective Inequalities in Intimate Relationships*, T. Juvonen and M. Kolehmainen (eds) (London: Routledge), 49–62.

Lahti, A. (2020a), 'The Becoming of Family Relationships and Friendship Circles After a Bisexual Break-Up', in *Bisexuality in Europe*, R. Baumgartner and E. Maliepaard (eds) (London: Routledge), 85–99.

Lahti, A. (2020b), 'Research Perspectives on Bisexuality', in *The SAGE Handbook of Global Sexualities, vol. 1*, Z. Davy, A. C. Santos, C. Bertone, R. Thoreson, and S. E. Wieringa (eds) (London: SAGE Publications), 119–40.

Lahti, A., and Kolehmainen, M. (2020), 'LGBTIQ+ Break-Up Assemblages: At the End of the Rainbow', *Journal of Sociology*, 56:4, 608–28.

Latimer, J., and López Gómez, D. (2019), 'Intimate Entanglements: Affects, More-Than-Human Intimacies and the Politics of Relations in Science and Technology', *The Sociological Review*, 67:2, 247–63.

Latour, B. (2005), *Reassembling the Social: An Introduction to Actor-Network-Theory* (Oxford: Oxford University Press).

Lury, C. (2015), 'Postscript: Beside(s) the Empirical', in *Affective Methodologies*, B. T. Knudsen and C. Stage (eds) (London: Palgrave Macmillan), 237–46.

Lury, C., and Wakeford, N. (eds) (2012), *Inventive Methods: The Happening of the Social* (London: Routledge).

Lykke, N. (2018), 'When Death Cuts Apart: On Affective Difference, Compassionate Companionship and Lesbian Widowhood', in *Affective Inequalities in Intimate Relationships*, T. Juvonen and M. Kolehmainen (eds) (London: Routledge), 109–25.

Lykke, N. (2019), 'Co-Becoming with Diatoms: Between Posthuman Mourning and Wonder in Algae Research', *Catalyst: Feminism, Theory, Technoscience*, 5:2, 1–25.

MacLure, M. (2013), 'Classification or Wonder? Coding as an Analytic Practice in Qualitative Research', in *Deleuze and Research Methodologies*, R. Coleman and J. Ringrose (eds) (Edinburgh: Edinburgh University Press), 164–83.

Malins, P. (2004), 'Machinic Assemblages: Deleuze, Guattari and an Ethico-Aesthetics of Drug Use', *Janus Head*, 7, 84–104.

Mitman, G. (2019), *Reflections on the Plantationocene: A Conversation with Donna Haraway and Anna Tsing* [podcast and transcript]. Retrieved from https://edgeeffects.net/haraway-tsing-plantationocene/ (Accessed: 16 April 2021).

Monro, S. (2015), *Bisexuality: Identities, Politics, and Theories* (Basingstoke: Palgrave Macmillan).

Morgan, D. H. J. (1996), *Family Connections: An Introduction to Family Studies* (Cambridge: Polity Press).

Myong, L., and Bissenbakker, M. (2021), 'Attachment as Affective Assimilation: Discourses on Love and Kinship in the Context of Transnational Adoption in Denmark', *NORA – Nordic Journal of Feminist and Gender Research* (online, 2021). doi: https://doi.org/10.1080/08038740.2021.1891133

O'Neill, R. (2018), *Seduction: Men, Masculinity and Mediated Intimacy* (Cambridge: Polity Press).

Neimanis, A. (2017), *Bodies of Water. Posthuman Feminist Phenomenology* (London: Bloomsbury Publishing).

Osella, C. (2019), '"Tell Me, What Made You Think You Were Normal?": How Practice Will Always Outrun Theory and Why We All Need to Get Out More', in *The Everyday Makings of Heteronormativity: Cross-Cultural Explorations of Sex, Gender, and Sexuality*, S. Sehlikoglu and F. G. Karioris (eds) (Lanham: Lexington Books), 13–26.

Paasonen, S. (2018a), 'Infrastructures of Intimacy', in *Mediated Intimacies: Connectivities, Relationalities and Proximities*, R. Andreassen *et al.* (eds) (London: Routledge), 103–16.

Paasonen, S. (2018b), *Many Splendored Things: Thinking Sex and Play* (London: Goldsmiths University Press).

Puig de la Bellacasa, M. (2017), *The Matters of Care* (Minneapolis, MN: University of Minnesota Press).

Rajan-Rankin, S. (2021), 'Material Intimacies and Black Hair Practice: Touch, Texture, Resistance', *NORA – Nordic Journal of Feminist and Gender Research* (online, 2021). doi: https://doi.org/10.1080/08038740.2021.1912172

Renold, E., and Mellor, D. (2013), 'Deleuze and Guattari in the Nursery: Towards an Ethnographic Multi-Sensory Mapping of Gendered Bodies', in *Deleuze and Research Methodologies*, R. Coleman and J. Ringrose (eds) (Edinburgh: Edinburgh University Press), 23–41.

Renold, E., and Ringrose, J. (2008), 'Regulation and Rupture: Mapping Tween and Teenage Girls' Resistance to the Heterosexual Matrix', *Feminist Theory*, 9:3, 313–38. doi: https://doi.org/10.1177/1464700108095854

Ringrose, E., and Renold, J. (2014), '"F**k Rape!" Exploring Affective Intensities in a Feminist Research Assemblage', *Qualitative Inquiry*, 20:6, 772–80.

Roseneil, S. (2006), 'The Ambivalences of Angel's "Arrangement": A Psychosocial Lens on the Contemporary Condition of Personal Life', *Sociological Review*, 54:4, 847–69.

Roseneil, S. (2007), 'Queer Individualization: The Transformation of Personal Life in the Early 21st Century', *NORA – Nordic Journal of Feminist and Gender Research*, 15:2, 84–99.

Roseneil, S., Crowhurst, I., Hellesund, T., Santos, A. C., and Stoilova, M. (2020), *The Tenacity of the Couple-Norm: Intimate Citizenship Regimes in a Changing Europe* (London: UCL Press). Open Access available at: www.uclpress.co.uk/products/166273# (Accessed: 24 June 2021).

Rozmarin, M. (2021), 'Navigating the Intimate Unknown: Vulnerability as an Affective Relation', *NORA – Nordic Journal of Feminist and Gender Research*, 29:3, 190–202. doi.org/10.1080/08038740.2021.1899284

Rubin, G. S. (1993), 'Thinking Sex: Notes for a Radical Theory of the Politics of Sexuality', in *The Lesbian and Gay Studies Reader*, H. Abelove, M. A. Barale, and D. M. Halperin (eds) (New York, NY: Routledge), 3–44.

Schuller, K. (2018), *The Biopolitics of Feeling: Race, Sex, and Science in the Nineteenth Century* (Durham, NC, and London: Duke University Press).

Schuller, K. (2020), 'The Future of Gender: Rethinking the Sex/Gender Distinction', keynote speech at Gender Studies Conference 2020, 13 November 2020 (Tampere University, Finland).

Seyfert, R. (2012), 'Beyond Personal Feelings and Collective Emotions: Toward a Theory of Social Affect', *Theory, Culture & Society*, 29:6, 27–46. doi: https://doi.org/10.1177/0263276412438591

Singh, P. (2016), 'Between Legal Recognition and Moral Policing: Mapping the Queer Subject in India', *Journal of Homosexuality*, 63:3, 416–25.

Smart, C. (2007), *Personal Life: New Directions in Sociological Thinking* (Cambridge: Polity Press).

Steinbock, E. (2014), 'On the Affective Force of "Nasty Love"', *Journal of Homosexuality*, 61:5, 749–65. doi: https://doi.org/10.1080/00918369.2014.870446

Stewart, K. (2007), *Ordinary Affects* (Durham, NC: Duke University Press).

TallBear, K. (2018), 'Making Love and Relations Beyond Settler Sex and Family', in *Making Kin Not Population*, A. E. Clarke and D. Haraway (eds) (Chicago, IL: Prickly Paradigm Press), 145–64.

Tiainen, M., Kontturi, K.-K., Leppänen, T., and Mehrabi, T. (2020), 'Making Middles Matter: Intersecting Intersectionality with New Materialisms', *NORA – Nordic Journal of Feminist and Gender Research*, 28:3, 211–23.

Tsing, A. L. (2015), *The Mushroom at the End of the World: On the Possibility of Life in Capitalist Ruins* (Princeton, NJ: Princeton University Press).

Walkerdine, V. (2015), 'Transmitting Class Across Generations', *Theory & Psychology*, 25:2, 167–83.

Warner, M. (2000), *The Trouble with Normal: Sex, Politics, and the Ethics of Queer Life* (Cambridge, MA: Harvard University Press).

Weiss, M. (2020), 'Intimate Encounters: Queer Entanglements in Ethnographic Fieldwork', *Anthropological Quarterly*, 93:1, 1355–86.

Weston, K. (1991), *Families We Choose: Lesbians, Gay Men and Kinship* (New York, NY: Columbia University Press).

Wilson, A. (2016), 'The Infrastructures of Intimacy', *Signs*, 41:2, 247–80. doi: https://doi.org/10.1086/682919

Zengin, A. (2016), 'Violent Intimacies: Tactile State Power, Sex/Gender Transgression, and the Politics of Touch in Contemporary Turkey', *Journal of Middle East Women's Studies*, 12:2, 225–45. Available at *Project MUSE* muse.jhu.edu/article/625055.

Part I

Rethinking affect and intimacy

1

'Caring matter': A love story of queer intimacies between (her) body and object (her cigarette)

Dresda E. Méndez de la Brena

'What does "care" mean when we go about thinking and living interdependently with beings other than human' in disabled worlds (Puig de la Bellacasa, 2017)? In what way do 'things matter' to the life of chronically ill and disabled individuals? What kind of 'care arrangements' do they enter into and make with the material world so that they can live as well as possible? These are the questions addressed in this chapter. My empirical focus is a specific case. I unfold my reflections on 'caring matter' and 'affective intimacies' in the context of the love story of caring for my partner, who is narcoleptic and a heavy smoker. Against this background, I am committed to a discussion of the 'intimate act of love' between disabled individuals and objects, where love is neither pure nor liberatory but 'caring' nonetheless. Overall, I discuss what I call 'caring matter' – that is, as an intimate entanglement created between disabled bodies and objects in affective moments where human care cannot fit into their world to provide it.

The focus is on the concept of 'caring matter'. I coined this concept as a queer re-elaboration of disability scholar Arseli Dokumaci's (2020) concept of 'care intimacy' and feminist science and technology studies scholar María Puig de la Bellacasa's (2017) notion of 'matter of care'. Care is a widely contested, multifaceted and unstable term with varying connotations including burden, necessity, as well as (inter)dependence and emotional and affective fulfilment. All these engagements with care reveal how 'care' implicates different relationalities, issues and practices in different settings. In particular, scholars who cover issues of care investigate these fundamental issues – including dependency, informal and formal care, caretaking work and the 'ethics of care' – in the context of human care relationships. However, care, in this context, is normally positioned as something only humans do. In queering the concept of care in relation to matter, I align my analysis with this volume's broad and inclusive definition of affective intimacies, bringing to the foreground the affective entanglements between persons and objects, the human and non-human as constituents of various forms of care production.

The analysis presented here is part of a more comprehensive research project on chronic pain, care, intimacy and affective methodologies undertaken during my PhD studies. The method used in this chapter is an auto-phenomenographic (auto-ethnography with a phenomenological approach) exploration of autobiographical writing on everyday intimate moments between me and my partner. The material that I explore consists of personal excerpts from poetic narratives, speculative storytelling and photography as visual/narrative imaginaries, motivated by my attempts to create a different way to write academically. As Deborah Bird Rose (2012) argues, 'writing is an act of witness; it is an effort not only to testify to the lives of others but to do so in ways that bring into our ken the entanglements that hold the lives of all of us within the skein of life' (139). Auto-phenomenography invites us to re-evaluate knowledge-seeking outside the rigidity of academic writing, using any available 'semiotic technologies' – that is, practices and arts (i.e. art, poetry or any other sensual method of telling) of creating meaning with signs, metaphors, figurations, words, ideas, descriptions and theories to invigorate an ethical sensibility and response-ability for the Other (Allen-Collinson, 2010; Haraway, 1988; Puig de la Bellacasa, 2012).

Consequently, I decided to start this chapter with a love story. A story of unexpected (queer) love between my partner and myself as we enter into a process of being-in-love.[1] The story leads to excerpts of conversations associated with my partner's smoking habits on a day that was as good as any other. Secondly, I introduce the concept of 'caring matter', through which I theorise queer intimacies between persons and objects and the ways in which this affective relationality is performed against the background of my unsuccessful attempts to provide her with the care required. Thirdly, with 'caring matter' as a theoretical frame, I analyse the excerpts of our conversations with a focus on the 'intimate act of love' framed in the smoking-and-breathing encounter. Love, here, is not equivalent to romantic, innocent love or a love that leads to a healthier life, but a kind of love that offers a multi-layered, non-pure approach to the meanings and complexities of caring in disability worlds (Weaver, 2013). In the conclusion, I summarise my reflections on 'caring matter', and the ways matter can show us how non-human care 'works' when human-provided care is absent or insufficient. Ultimately, I call for critical thinking on smoking from the perspective of feminist intersectionality and disability studies.

A (queer) love story

I met her on Tinder. I was in Vienna for an academic conference and since my academic companions were younger than me, their party night interests were quite different from my own. I wanted to meet someone to show me the city. We matched on Saturday and we started to talk on Sunday. We set a date, Monday at 7:00. She chose the bar. Before saying good night, she asked me if I was familiar with narcolepsy. I wittily replied, 'Are you telling me this in case you fall asleep abruptly so I do not think I am boring you?' 'Yes, exactly that', she replied.

I remember her entering the room wearing a long grey coat and rounded vintage glasses. The beautiful mane of her curly hair distracted me from her formal introduction. She sat in front of me. I was nervous and she could tell. She was nervous but I did not realise. I no longer remember what we talked about, but I remember with clear lucidity the moment that made us unfold ourselves into each other. While I was sharing my long-standing interest in and practice of photography and my desire to engage in ways to represent illness, I remember her looking at me forcefully, as if she wanted to see beyond me, through me. At first, I thought I was making her feel uncomfortable. Thousands of worried thoughts rushed through my head. Was I telling her something politically incorrect? Was I assuming in my understanding and speaking about disability? Was I boring her? My egocentric concerns vanished when she suddenly held my hand while losing her bodily composure. Without further notice, she was having a sleeping attack in front of me. I first became terribly stressed; then, I was thwarted by my inability to help her appropriately. A few minutes later, when she regained all her vitality, she jokily said to me: 'you cannot say I did not warn you'. We both started to laugh. That was the moment in which our love story unfolded: she fading away while holding my hand and I falling in love while touching hers.

Since that unforgettable evening I was pulled into her wonderful world. A world of a truly warm-hearted loving person who had built a positive environment around her in order to navigate through the difficulties of living with narcolepsy. A number of difficult situations come along each day for the both of us: the tiredness that limits her in daily activities such as cleaning or organising; the difficulty of waking her up – due to cataplexy (i.e. a person experiencing total cataplexy stays awake and is cognisant of the surroundings but is completely unable to move) – knowing that by doing it, I am provoking in her the most excruciating pain. But without a doubt, the most striking moment of our day is when she is having a sleeping attack. I can now identify these moments by looking at her eyes. Her beautiful brown-caramel eyes start to become surrounded by the most visible dark circles. This can happen at any time of the day. However, she has developed certain habits in order to control her sleeping attacks such as not eating before an important event or writing with her left hand – although she is right-handed – to focus her mind and physically challenge her body to stay awake. But by far, the most effective of these habits is smoking. And, oh my, does she smoke considerably. I am not a frequent smoker but I have succumbed to it particularly while going through moments of stress, sadness or depression. However, I had never co-habited or been-in-love with a genuinely committed smoker, and consequently, I never realised how much I had incorporated the negative idea of the smoker into my own attitudes towards what I consider 'too much smoking'. My limited perspective narrowed my view of why individuals whose 'health' is considered in decline engage in acts that are presumably 'harmful' to or 'endanger' their own health. My narrow perspective on an individual's smoking history and the specificities of their bodily experience while smoking led me to judge my partner's smoking habits more frequently than I dare to recognise.

> Could you please open the window? The living room smells like a canteen. You have just finished smoking one cigarette. Is it really so necessary to light up another one so soon? – I ask half kindly, half mad.
>
> I am sorry, I will move next to the window. I will try to remember to open the window the next time. – She kindly replies. I know I should reduce my smoking. I will try but it is not as easy as you think, at least for me. I have been smoking since I was 14 years old, and my relationship with my cigarette is more complicated than you dare to imagine. This [referring to the cigarette] is the only thing I know that *helps me* to be here talking to you without losing my concentration or falling asleep.

My partner's habits are not dissimilar to the statistics on the prevalence of smoking in adults with chronic pain (Orhurhu *et al.*, 2015). In particular, narcoleptic smokers' statistics report relief from symptoms by smoking tobacco cigarettes (Ebben and Krieger, 2012). It is widely studied how narcoleptic patients perceive nicotine as helping them to decrease excessive daytime sleepiness and cataplexy, but also how smoking can lead to injuries when narcoleptics fall asleep (Barateau *et al.*, 2016; Krahn *et al.*, 2009). She and I read these studies identifying how while driving, she rolls up a cigarette to help herself stay focused on the road, or how most of her clothes are damaged by falling asleep holding a cigarette butt. However, there is something else at stake other than mere statistics. In her excessive daytime sleepiness, sucking on a cigarette is a self-referential moment that not only settles the craving for falling asleep but also provides her with a more intimate relation to more-than-human others.

There is a 'relationship', a sort of affective exchange performed or enacted between my partner and her cigarette. A form of care that surpasses traditional imaginaries of the intimate. A (queer) love story that unfolds between her mouth and the touch of smoke. A sense of help emerges as an affective dimension in daily practices of use and encounters with objects, essential to different kinds of world-making and world-surviving. In this encounter, my partner finds something she can count on. My partner's body has developed a particular relationality with cigarettes that brings together different situated intimate experiences and theoretical engagements with matter. In this 'caring moment', relief, help, comfort, intimacy, love and life support are provided by matter when it is not possible for care to be performed by human contact. Sometimes, 'caring matter' is an indispensable living-ground constituent for the everyday sustainability of the lives of disabled people. 'Caring matter', therefore, asks us to consider the elusive phenomenological realm of illness/disability and care, and how it pushes us to speculate on intimate entanglements, queer love stories and queer socialities that matter.

'Caring matter'

As a theoretical framework for the analysis, the concept of 'caring matter' brings together affective intimacies as other-than-human intimacies. First, allow me to reveal the personal motivations and theoretical engagements behind the formulation of this concept. As a trans feminist scholar, I am familiar with the different theoretical debates that address the complex emotional and material concerns that caring entails (Engster, 2005; Noddings, 2013; Ruddick, 1995; Tronto, 1998). As an activist, I recognise the variety of caring processes that are crucial for the articulation and the organisation of everyday life, and how care comes to matter as a political and material performance. As a daughter, I face and struggle with the feminisation of care (in its two main connotations: 'caring about' – the feeling part of caring; and 'caring for' – the practical work of tending to others) (Glenn, 1992; Lutz, 2018) when parental care is assumed to be my responsibility and not that of my two brothers. As a partner, my concern for care intersects with disability contexts due to the emotional relationship I have with my narcoleptic partner (Watson *et al.*, 2004). Care, in this context, comes with ableist self-identifications, particularly when reflecting upon the complexities of growing old together with a smoker and/or when thinking about the difficulties and fatigue of physical care that being with my partner entails.

In the recollection of my personal biography, care is and has been lived through struggle, contradiction and flux. However, despite – or rather because of – its complexities, care has also become a bridge between the rational knowing of what epistemologically I think I know and the affective and bodily dimensions of care that make it essential to different kinds of 'knowledge-making' and 'world-making' for me, for my partner and for other disabled people. As a person dwelling in another's experience of disability, I have become particularly interested in how to build worlds where companionship can make possible certain kinds of affordances (Dokumaci, 2017, 2019, 2020) or where my body can work as a 'prosthetic extension' (Lykke, 2018) to ameliorate my partner's life in moments of sleepiness or pain. 'Thinking with care' (Puig de la Bellacasa, 2012) through the lens of disability has helped me to explore new ways to think and write about what care does when performed, and what kind of actors are entangled or neglected in the process of caring. Thinking with care also requires thinking with relational processes and interdependent worlds. Care, in this context, necessitates not only a profound vision of caring (Puig de la Bellacasa, 2010, 2012, 2017) but a speculative exploration of forms of care, unfolded through the prism of what is possible rather than what is probable (Haraway, 2008, 2016, 2019; Wilkie *et al.*, 2017). The concept of 'caring matter' is therefore articulated in the midst of a series of theoretical threads that weave disability and technoscience thinking and speculative writing practices, offering a more specific and intimate understanding of care and caring as 'matters of care' (Puig de la Bellacasa, 2010).

To untie the first theoretical knot of 'caring matter', I draw attention to the work of Turkish/Canadian disability scholar Arseli Dokumaci. Given her background in performative studies and informed by her own chronic illness, Dokumaci is interested in how disability and performance can offer a 'new way to think through how disabled individuals might transform the very materiality of the environment through the most mundane and micro of their performances' (Dokumaci, 2017: 395). To articulate this idea, Dokumaci relies on James Gibson's (1986) theory of affordances which describes the possibilities of action ensuing from the inextricability of the perception of the self and the environment and the reciprocity of organism–environment relations. According to Dokumaci, in disease (and/or disability) the affordances received by the environment cannot be compared to the affordances made for disease-free, able-bodied persons. In disease the world shrinks, reducing its complementarities and no longer affording a living with ease. In order to avert and accommodate pain (although recognising that not all disabled people have pain or disease), disabled individuals will have to perform and actualise their relations with the environment in order to hold on to the everyday.

In Dokumaci's commitment to exploring disabled subjects' lives, she explores the intimate worlds that come to the foreground when the environment shrinks due to disability. Dokumaci finds that since disability is always in relation to someone (or something), people who accompanied another's experience of disability can also provide, enable or become an affordance for one another, especially where no other affordances exist. 'People-as-affordance' involves other people's properties which can provide new ways of care and understanding (Dokumaci, 2020). Within this framework, 'being-for and being-with each other' (Lykke, 2018) become affordances that entwine the experience of living with pain and the companion's experience of living with someone in pain. In this intimate scenario, 'care intimacy' describes 'how the need for care can be articulated, responded to, and engaged with through intimate and unspoken means as people provide or become affordances in and of themselves' (Dokumaci, 2020: S203). Care intimacy is meeting the other's needs and desires, and being ready to support and help the other, willingly.

However, as the author recognises, in living disability worlds (s = in plurality, in difference, in mutuality) sometimes care intimacy from others fails to materialise. There are circumstances 'where there are no readily available affordances or convenient tools, objects, and infrastructures to respond to their pain, ill health, and bodily particularities' (Dokumaci, 2020: S105). There are moments in disabled worlds where 'care intimacy' cannot be provided and people cannot become affordances for one another, 'not because an otherwise unimaginable action possibility is co-created but because an already established and socialised action possibility is not undertaken' (Dokumaci, 2020: S105). There are forms of care that emerge by not pursuing the caring engagement with the other at all, but by letting the possibility of caring go.

To illustrate this, I share another fragment of the shared world my partner and I inhabit:

> We are sitting on the couch talking about our next Christmas vacation. We really want to go to the beach, rent a small apartment, make a fire and enjoy the nice weather. We are both really enthusiastic about spending our first holiday season together, so our conversation is really pleasant and charged with a lot of positive energy. I think I get distracted for a second. A WhatsApp message comes in. It is not an important matter to attend to so I reply with a smiley emoticon. I turn my eyes to her in an attempt to keep on with the conversation. I can see how her eyes are abandoning me. By now, I know I am not supposed to touch her since my touch provokes her pain. So, I call her by her name. I see her struggling to be awake, to stay with me. When her muscles are finally alert again, her immediate action is to look for her cigarette case and roll one up. There she is, in front of me, the person I care about the most, and my touch, my words or even more my sole presence hurts her. I try to offer her some relief but my proximity is not enough at this moment. I cannot be of any assistance; I am relegated to being a mere witness of her pain and tiredness. I am just there, in front of the person I care about the most, without being able to provide her with my care.

There are moments where 'not touching her' is the only act of care I can perform to alleviate her pain. At this moment, following Dokumaci, 'not touching' is an affordance because it is the unrealised potential of care that matters. 'Care intimacy' can happen, therefore, when the proximity of care is not performed. While my partner's environment shrinks due to the force of her sleeping attack and her corporeality vanishes as she fades out, the only way I can help her is by 'being alongside' (Latimer, 2013) during her worst moments of pain. However, in the space that opens up between her body and my touch, other forms of care emerge that offer her the possibility to go on, which do not involve human action. There are moments when care comes from unexpected places, bringing into being new 'caring' kinship imaginaries (Dokumaci, 2020). Caring kinships make it possible to build disability worlds of care even when human care is not possible or not feasible. Here, I speculate on the different 'caring' kinship imaginaries that open up between a disabled body and the non-human touch that allows other forms of care, not involving human presence. Forms of care build up by not performing the act of care, but by the most intimate act of love with non-human companions, disrupting our understanding of both love and care as exceptionally only-human affairs. I introduce the concept of 'caring matter' to refer to this form of care – that is, a momentary entanglement with matter, where the body is always-already touched by other beings which give a form of care that humans cannot provide (Méndez de la Brena and Schoenmann, 2021). As such, my use of 'caring matter' incorporates a post-human analysis of care that I will highlight and will be further expanded in what follows.

'Intimate act of love'

Thinking of 'caring kinship imaginaries' is only possible by speculating on multiple affective possibilities. It requires imaginative 'propositions' for thinking together with, and for, the creation of connections between things that don't yet exist but may become possible. In other words, a proposition is a speculative sensibility in our engagements with the world, or better said, a speculative sensibility of world-making. Speculating, therefore, is a 'process of imagination of a very specific kind', one that does not operate in a vacuum but can 'move beyond the field from which [it] originate[s]' (Shaviro, 2014: 55). This means that speculation has a point of departure; it has a context and it is grounded. It does not respond to the unknown but instead it is settled within acts of thoughts. In other words, speculation is situated; it cannot be applied out of a context.

It is widely known that the speculative can be traced back to a long list of feminist scholars and writers of colour working with and through speculative thinking (Isabelle Stengers, Donna Haraway, Octavia Butler, Sun Ra, Nalo Hopkinson and Karen Lord, to name a few, and Chicana

Figure 1.1 *Smoking*, Dresda E. Méndez de la Brena, 2019, Colour, Paper, 38.74 × 47.63 cm. Courtesy of the artist.

writers Rosaura Sánchez and Beatriz Pita). My use of speculative storytelling is particularly informed by Haraway's feminist speculative fabulation and her crafty formation of knowledge-making and world-making that calls on the factual, fictional and fabulated. This refers to the creation of hypothetical worlds wherein 'it matters what stories tell stories; it matters whose stories tell stories' (Haraway, 2019). In what follows, I use speculative storytelling accompanied by photography as visual imaginary to entice the reader with what I call 'caring matter'. I invite the reader to let themselves feel touched by the smoke that comes out from the frame of the photograph and by my words, since both provide alternative ways of thinking and imagining caring propositions and an affective speculative outcome.

> She immediately rolls up a cigarette; she starts smoking and her sleepiness and pain start to subside. In that moment I realise that, in the worst sleeping attacks, it is a cigarette, not me, that can offer her the best comfort and act of care. It is in her worst state that an intimate connection with a cigarette happens. I can see her pain and tiredness going away with every inhalation she takes. I am there; in front of the person I treasure the most, while she is having

the most intimate and sensual act of love with a body that is not mine. I am a witness of the more intimate act of love, care and relief between my lover and a cigarette, an intimate act of love I cannot provide.

I wrote this paragraph after witnessing my romantic (queer) lover being loved by her cigarette. As I was watching the smoke coming out of her nose, entwining itself through her clothes, embracing her body, caressing her face, touching her lips, I was witnessing an intimate act of love between my girlfriend and a body that is not mine. I was there, observing how a cigarette offers her the vitality to keep going, as smoking is a 'vital affordance' that allows the 'multiplication of the conditions of living, exactly when and where those existing conditions least afford living' (Dokumaci, 2017: 408). After the cigarette was totally consumed and my partner's sleeping attack was over, I started a speculative exploration of the significance of 'care intimacy' when care is provided by things other than humans. When human touch is not allowed, there are other forms of care that happen in the more-than-human web of life, which brings maintenance and vibrancy to specific relations, particularly when the environment shrinks and no other person can fit in there to provide it. What happened between my girlfriend and her cigarette was an act of care; a loving connection that revealed to me how, in that particular moment, care was co-enacted by non-humans. In this moment, human care did not disappear but the agency of who provided it was distributed (Bellacasa, 2017).

In 'thinking with care' and non-human actants, a conversation with scholar María Puig de la Bellacasa is mandatory. In her book *Matters of Care*, Puig de la Bellacasa offers a speculative notion of care by asking 'what does "caring" mean when we go about thinking and living interdependently with beings other than human, in "more than human" worlds?' (Puig de la Bellacasa, 2017: 13). Puig de la Bellacasa's speculative project is to approach care as something open-ended where 'more than human' beings are both subjects and objects of care in a complex web of interdependencies. The author argues, 'care is a human trouble, but this does not make of care a human-only matter' (Puig de la Bellacasa, 2017: 2). By extending care to account for non-human worlds, the author situates care as any act of maintenance of life that places 'interdependency as the ontological state in which humans and countless other beings unavoidably live' (4). The author summons 'matter of care' to the idea of care in the materiality of more-than-human others and its manifestations in the everyday practices promoted by human and non-human worlds. Interestingly, Puig de la Bellacasa articulates a new re-evaluation of the sense of touch, to rethink the reciprocity or reversibility of care in the living web of care. Thus, care is sustained, distributed and reciprocated by 'touch' of some sort. A human/ non-human differentiated touch, that is 'the touch of entangled beings (be) coming together-apart' in ways that enable response-ability (Barad, 2012: 208) and is aware of the multiple ways to engage with the needs and desires of what/whom it reaches for.

Here, Mel Y. Chen's (2012) loving episode with their couch comes to mind. Chen works on de-differentiated intimacies provoked by metal poisoning, which led them[2] to differentiate an intimacy act of their couch due to the comfort it provided them. In the author's argument, there are queer socialities or living animacies that disrupt the difference between a body and object. Chen's body moves beyond its ostensible bounds, generating a space for queer affectivity between non-human and human agents. My partner's pain moves beyond its ostensible bounds into the midst of (human and non-human) bodies that momentarily care for each other. The use of speculative storytelling and photography as a visual imaginary tell a queer love story that speculates on momentary and contingent entanglements between cigarettes, lungs, hands and air. A love affair with the non-human world, where my partner is always-already touched by other beings which return to her the care that my 'humanity' cannot provide. As Barad (2012) poetically states:

> In an important sense, in a breathtakingly intimate sense, touching, sensing, is what matter does, or rather, what matter is: matter is condensations of response-ability. Touching is a matter of response. Each of 'us' is constituted in response-ability. Each of 'us' is constituted as responsible for the other, as the other. (Barad, 2012: 215)

Perhaps a better understanding of the touch of the cigarette can be traced if we once again look at the photography and let ourselves be captivated by my girlfriend's act of smoking and by the smoke itself. Here, I argue two possible approaches to understand the act of love between my girlfriend and her cigarette: the phenomenological and the new materialistic. The first approach corresponds to the idea that smoking is a corporeal extension of the smoking person in the world. Following the Merleau-Pontyan phenomenological tradition of the body, which goes against the notions of bodily containment, Katz (1999) noted how smoking illustrates how the body is always intertwined with the world. In every exhalation, smoking makes visible the respiratory process, exposing how the body exceeds itself. Consequently, the body is not a contained entity but it extends itself into the things of the world. In smoking, the 'I will exceed the I' (Dennis, 2011: 26) and becomes a 'we', since by breaking the proper integrity of the body, we breathe one another, we ingest one another. As

Chen (2012) writes, 'I am ingesting their exhaled air, their sloughed skin, and the skin of the tables, chairs, and carpets of our shared rooms' (209). The I is the world and its content. A world where we are intrinsically always touched by others; always affected and being affected by others. In a phenomenological tradition, the visibility of smoke reveals my partner's bodily pain being extended to the air, touched by and taking care of it, until it travels from her body to mine. With every smoky breath she takes, her painful body is my own. In every breath I take I ingest her pain. A pain that is 'as part of me, as not part of me, as a part of the world' (Winance, 2019: 429).

In a less speculative account of my girlfriend's smoking, one could argue that the pleasure, relief and love that my partner feels are derived from the feeling of chemicals rushing through her body. That my partner's relief is the result of the possession of the cigarette and the relations it allows her. However, this approach centres my partner's body as the sole actant that 'brings together all of these aspects of human and non-human objects to draw in the pleasures of smoking' (Dennis, 2018: 72). I step away from this idea by incorporating a new materialist approach to smoking in which 'smoking pleasure has more to do with certain kinds of confluence, rather than any fixed property within or subjectivity of the agent herself' (Dennis, 2018: 71). In her new materialist approach to smoking, Simone Dennis (2018) argues that smokers become 'enwinded'[3] in the intra-activity with the air and with the relief this encounter provides. This is only possible if we avoid the option (a) 'to differentiate between a broadly constituted "environment" or "atmosphere" and humans, and so [refuse] essentialism in favour of relationality, and [(b) acknowledge] the capacity of non-human things – even atmospheres like the air – to impact and influence'. Following this idea, as the air comes out of her lungs, her pain and tiredness are displaced and move beyond her body. The air is embracing my girlfriend's tiredness in a simultaneous material, affective and aesthetic choreography of queer love and care.

I do not pretend to romanticise love and care. As Puig de la Bellacasa (2010) warns us, caring is 'non-innocent', it comes with tension and must therefore be handled with care. Caring is an act that most often involves asymmetry (56) that can lead to acts of love and care of a 'different kind' (Weaver, 2013). In the last part of this chapter, I want to explore the caring/love tensions in the smoking-breathing encounter and how this friction intersects with normative and ableist understandings of the smoker's body in articulations of a healthy future, arguing for a feminist intersectional approach to smoking in relation to disability studies. To this end, I analyse a poem I wrote as part of my personal understanding of my partner's heavy smoking habits and the perils of a relationship with a dead end.

'Love is a dead end'

Dead End
(Poem, Dresda Méndez, 2020)

Only for tonight,
you breathed me in
you blew me out.
Can't tell when it was done,
'Til I faded off this touch.

Only for the night,
the cigarette remained alight.
Without so much as a second thought,
you penetrated the snow fog around us,
Filled with each inhale
Fallen with each exhale.

Only in the night,
I watch your chest rise.
As you made it harder to breathe,
I fall with the pressure of your lips.
Was it too much?
Cannot leave your lungs for long.
Who's never smoked for love?

Tonight,
There's something burning inside you.
Strong. Overwhelming. Suffocating.
Enwinded to relieve the pain
Whilst you reach to find nothing but air.
Dancing in the night,
With each inhale, there is life.

I guess, there is a charm.
Why can't we say each exhale brings you life?
In endless creativity and stuttering breaths,
in every exhale that brings no end,
a love with dead end.

Smoking and breathing share a complex relationality as well as a hierarchical positionality. Humans (although not only humans) become alive by breathing. Consequently, implicit in the fact of living, breathing is the primal condition of bodily existence (Sloterdijk, 2009). As such, breathing is the quintessential force of life that engages us with and put us in relation to the world (Gorska, 2016). However, breathing is far from being defined as merely an ongoing metabolic bodily action. The vast relationalities that breathing enacts upon the world unfold diverse and heterogenous respiratory interventions that have been of much interest within different interdisciplinary fields of study in the twenty-first century. The relationship between 'air-and-breathing-bodies' (Allen, 2020) has been taken by phenomenological studies of environmental exposures, intersectional feminism, interdisciplinary social and environmental justice politics.

When we talk about breathing and respiration as a lived phenomenon in relation to smoking, smoking is usually treated as a menace that reduces the capacity of breathing and, therefore, the possibility of human survival and endurance. In common conversations, smoking is related to phrases such as shortness of breath, breathless, catching one's breath, out of breath, taking a breath of fresh air. As Górska (2016) points out, 'while breathing is a force of life, it is also a matter of dying' (28), and smoking is considered a deliberate act with the capacity to invade the body, via inbound breath, to literally take the breath away. As we are familiar with public health discourses on the dangers of smoking (inhaling nicotine and other toxic chemicals may cause illnesses like heart disease, strokes and lung cancer), breathing also 'contains a set of ideas, morals, values, and hierarchies [over the act of smoking] that can be drawn into and absorbed by bodies just as readily as oxygen' (Dennis, 2006: 9). As such, if we pinpoint breathing as the vital source of life, we largely ignore or misconceive how for some bodies which are deemed 'sick', to compromise breathing by self-induced air-and-breathing poisoning, more than a menace, becomes the ultimate 'chemical sublime' intoxication (Shapiro, 2015). In this sense, if we take Górska's invitation for adopting an intersectional perspective of breathing as never homogenous and consequently always differently enacted in relation to differently lived circumstances, understandings, capacities, specificities and privileges of who is breathing, we should also extend this comprehensive approach to those bodies that against human normative (in)securities about breathing, challenge the 'proper' or the 'healthy' aesthetics about it. Ultimately, if breathing is not a homogeneous phenomenon, then nor is smoking. For those for whom the world is a difficult place, smoking is the possibility of performance, survival and endurance. For some, smoking is a survival strategy only possible or meaningful under certain social, cultural, economic and historical conditions. An intersectional feminist approach to smoking has to work towards an anti-ableist vision of survival.

However, this is not easy. The poem I wrote refers to the perils of the smoking-and-breathing encounter. Even when I rethink and re-ontologise the particular vulnerability to the detrimental impact of smoking on her health, the questions that follow are 'if smoking is ruining [her] health, why do[es] [she] persist in [her] habit? Why do[es] [she] not make a rational, informed decision to quit?' (Macnaughton *et al.*, 2012: 458). My partner is well aware of the risks and dangers of smoking, but she also knows about the potential of smoking to reduce her sleepiness and her pain in her immediate present. Engaging in smoking and its potentially future damages is for my partner a way to be with me in the present. For me, her engagement in smoking is a rupture of my (linear) temporality, that is, my (normative and ableist) future-oriented stance of being together. In my normative account, our love story has a dead end.

As the reader can assume by now, this chapter was not about our love story, but my lover's love story with her cigarette. And, in this love story, what is important is to ask what kind of love is, especially given the many ways in which love is neither innocent nor liberatory. Here, I want to bring back Chen's (2012) analysis of toxicity as more than a simple (social) metaphor but as an agent that does something in the body. For Chen, toxins are queer agents that mediate the ambiguous boundaries between life, death and disability. If (cigarette) toxins violate the very proper intimacies between death and vitality, toxins are a part of queer socialities that are built upon the simultaneity of pleasure and pain. What Chen proposes is a different kind of intimacy, a different kind of love; or using Weaver's (2013) concept, a love in the form of 'becoming in kind'. Love that is neither good nor bad; love that can come from the darkest places; love that is sometimes oppressive, dangerous and noxious, but love nonetheless. In loving her cigarette, my partner is not abandoning or neglecting its possible consequences, but she has acknowledged and embraced them instead of living in opposition to it. My partner has learned to make friends with her (present) medical condition, and the (future) conditions of her illness.

Through the development of 'caring matter', I have tried to show the importance of speculating on different understandings of care, wherein it matters 'the ways sick and disabled people attempt to get the care and support [they] need, on [their] own terms, with autonomy and dignity' (Lakshmi Piepzna-Samarasinha, 2018: 41). 'Caring matter' brings with it the possibility to respond affectively to certain caring corporeal-experiences that might be perceived in, for example, the deterioration of health, but that, implicitly, indicate a need for further analysis of the affective intimate relations between objects and people that create the specificity of 'caring' in a particular moment. In this way, 'caring matter' is a relevant concept for the study of intimate affections between disabled individuals and other-than-humans. It also makes an important contribution to the fields of feminist intersectionality and disability studies, since it stresses 'caring' as a multi-layered, multi-shaped and multi-modal arrangement with the material world, even if that implies for those who are standing close to them a different path of care that is defined by not touching, not holding, not caressing, but just caring alongside.

Notes

1 In working towards new ethics of describing intimate relations, new forms of authorship-companionship emerge. Through the speculation on my life partner's disability, we are working together towards new ethics of being there for each other, and materialising new forms of support and help for the other, when possible. I most profoundly appreciate my partner's loving feedback and allowing me to share our friendship, love and intimate companionship's experiences. In my words, I find your voice. In your voice, I find myself. Always.

2 They/them are Chen's pronouns.

3 The word 'enwinded' is first used by Tim Ingold (2007, 2011) to refer to the agential properties of air itself – that is, it is not that air has agency; air is agency itself. Air has a power in its own right which refuses to be arranged and enclosed by bodies. As such, air is not contingent to the bodies' embodiment; rather the air itself enwinds us. Ingold (2007) states: 'It is as though every breath was one's first, drawn at the very moment when the world is about to disclose itself for what it is. In this, it is not so much the wind that is embodied as the body, in breathing, that is *enwinded*' (S32, Ingold's italics).

References

Allen, I. K. (2020), 'Thinking with a Feminist Political Ecology of Air-and-Breathing-Bodies', *Body & Society*, 26:2, 79–105. doi.org/10.1177/1357034X19900526

Allen-Collinson, J. (2010), 'Running Embodiment, Power and Vulnerability: Notes toward a Feminist Phenomenology of Female Running', in *Women and Exercise: The Body, Health and Consumerism*, E. Kennedy and P. Markula (eds) (London: Routledge), 280–98.

Barad, K. (2012), 'On Touching – The Inhuman That Therefore I Am', *Differences*, 23:3, 206–23. doi.org/10.1215/10407391-1892943

Barateau, L., *et al.* (2016), 'Smoking, Alcohol, Drug Use, Abuse and Dependence in Narcolepsy and Idiopathic Hypersomnia: A Case-Control Study', *Sleep*, 39:3, 573–80.

Chen, M. Y. (2012), *Animacies: Biopolitics, Racial Mattering, and Queer Affect* (Durham, NC: Duke University Press).

Dennis, S. (2006), 'Four Milligrams of Phenomenology: An Anthrophenomenological Analysis of Smoking Cigarettes', *Popular Culture* Review, 17:1, 41–57.

Dennis, S. (2011), 'Smoking Causes Creative Responses: On State Antismoking Policy and Resilient Habits', *Critical Public Health*, 21:1, 25–35.

Dennis, S. (2018), 'Becoming Enwinded: A New Materialist Take on Smoking Pleasure', *The International Journal on Drug Policy*, 51, 69–74.

Dokumaci, A. (2017), 'Vital Affordances, Occupying Niches: An Ecological Approach to Disability and Performance', *Research in Drama Education: The Journal of Applied Theatre and Performance*, 22:3, 393–412. doi.org/10.1080/13569783.2017.1326808

Dokumaci, A. (2019), 'Micro-Activist Affordances', *Somatosphere*, 18, March. Available at: http://somatosphere.net/2019/micro-activist-affordances.html/ (Accessed: 12 April 2020).

Dokumaci, A. (2020), 'People as Affordances: Building Disability Worlds Through Care Intimacy', *Current Anthropology*, 61:S21, S97–S108.

Ebben, M. R., and Krieger, A. C. (2012), 'Narcolepsy with Cataplexy Masked by the Use of Nicotine', *Journal of Clinical Sleep Medicine: JCSM: Official Publication of the American Academy of Sleep Medicine*, 8:2, 195–6.

Engster, D. (2005), 'Rethinking Care Theory: The Practice of Caring and the Obligation to Care', *Hypatia*, 20:3, 50–74.

Gibson, J. (1986), *The Ecological Approach to Visual Perception* (New York, NY: Taylor & Francis).

Glenn, E. N. (1992), 'From Servitude to Service Work: Historical Continuities in the Racial Division of Paid Reproductive Labor', *Signs*, 18, 1–43.

Górska, M. (2016), *Breathing Matters: Feminist Intersectional Politics of Vulnerability* (Linköping, Sweden: Linköping University).

Haraway, D. (1988), 'Situated Knowledges: The Science Question in Feminism and the Privilege of Partial Perspective', *Feminist Studies*, 14:3, 575–99. doi.org/10.2307/3178066

Haraway, D. (2008), *When Species Meet*. Minnesota, MN: Minnesota University Press.

Haraway, D. (2016), *Staying with the Trouble*. Durham, NC: Duke University Press.

Haraway, D. (2019), 'It Matters What Stories Tell Stories; It Matters Whose Stories Tell Stories', *a/b: Auto/Biography Studies*, 34:3, 565–75. doi.org/10.1080/08989575.2019.1664163

Ingold, T. (2007), 'Earth, Sky, Wind, and Weather', *The Journal of the Royal Anthropological Institute*, 13, S19–S38.

Ingold, T. (2011), *Being Alive: Essays on Movement, Knowledge and Description* (New York, NY: Routledge).

Katz, J. (1999), *How Emotions Work* (Chicago, IL: University of Chicago Press).

Krahn, L. E., Martin, K. A., and Silber, M. H. (2009), 'Narcoleptic Patients' Perceptions of Nicotine', *Journal of Clinical Sleep Medicine: JCSM: Official Publication of the American Academy of Sleep Medicine*, 5:4, 390. doi.org/10.5664/jcsm.27554

Lakshmi Piepzna-Samarasinha, L. (2018), *Care Work: Dreaming Disability Justice* (Vancouver, BC: Arsenal Pulp Press).

Latimer, J. (2013), 'Being Alongside: Rethinking Relations Amongst Different Kinds', *Theory, Culture & Society*, 30:7–8, 77–104. doi.org/10.1177/0263276413500078

Lutz, H. (2018), 'Care Migration: The Connectivity between Care Chains, Care Circulation and Transnational Social Inequality', *Current Sociology*, 66:4, 577–89. doi.org/10.1177/0011392118765213

Lykke, N. (2018), 'When Death Cuts Apart: On Affective Difference, Compassionate Companionship and Lesbian Widowhood', in *Affective Inequalities in Intimate Relationships*, T. Juvonen and M. Kolehmainen (eds) (London: Routledge), 109–24.

Macnaughton, J., Carro-Ripalda, S., and Russell, A. (2012), '"Risking Enchantment": How Are We to View the Smoking Person?', *Critical Public Health*, 22:4, 455–69.

Méndez de la Brena, D. E., and Schoenmann, C. (2021), 'Lucid Dreaming as a Method for Living Otherwise', *Sociology and Technoscience*, 11:1, 125–51. doi. org/10.24197/st.1.2021

Noddings, N. (2013), *Caring: A Relational Approach to Ethics and Moral Education* (Berkeley, CA: University of California Press).

Orhurhu, V. J., Pittelkow, T. P., and Hooten, W. M. (2015), 'Prevalence of Smoking in Adults with Chronic Pain', *Tobacco Induced Diseases*, 13:1, 17.

Puig de la Bellacasa, M. (2010), 'Matters of Care in Technoscience: Assembling Neglected Things', *Social Studies of Science*, 41:1, 85–106. doi.org/10.1177/0306312710380301

Puig de la Bellacasa, M. (2012), '"Nothing Comes Without Its World": Thinking With Care', *The Sociological Review*, 60:2, 197–216. doi.org/10.1111/j.1467-954X.2012.02070.x

Puig de la Bellacasa, M. (2017), *Matters of Care: Speculative Ethics in More Than Human Worlds* (Minneapolis, MN: University of Minnesota Press).

Rose, D. B. (2012), 'Multispecies Knots of Ethical Time', *Environmental Philosophy*, 9:1, 127–40.

Ruddick, S. (1995), *Maternal Thinking: Toward a Politics of Peace* (Boston, MA: Beacon Press).

Shapiro, N. (2015), 'Attuning to the Chemosphere: Domestic Formaldehyde, Bodily Reasoning, and the Chemical Sublime', *Cultural Anthropology*, 30:3, 368–93. doi.org/10.14506/ca30.3.02

Shaviro, S. (2014), *The Universe of Things: On Speculative Realism* (Minneapolis, MN: University of Minnesota Press).

Sloterdijk, P. (2009), 'Airquakes', *Environment and Planning D: Society and Space*, 27:1, 41–57.

Tronto, J. C. (1998), 'An Ethic of Care', *Generations: Journal of the American Society on Aging*, 22:3, 15–20.

Watson, N., McKie, L., Hughes, B., Hopkins, D., and Gregory, S. (2004), '(Inter) Dependence, Needs and Care: The Potential for Disability and Feminist Theorists to Develop an Emancipatory Model', *Sociology*, 38:2, 331–50. https://doi.org/10.1177/0038038504040867

Weaver, H. (2013), '"Becoming in Kind": Race, Class, Gender, and Nation in Cultures of Dog Rescue and Dogfighting', *American Quarterly*, 65:3, 689–709. doi.org/10.1353/aq.2013.0034

Wilkie, A., Savransky, M., and Rosengarten, M. (2017), *Speculative Research: The Lure of Possible Futures* (London: Routledge).

Winance, M. (2019), '"Don't Touch/Push Me!" From Disruption to Intimacy in Relation with One's Wheelchair: An Analysis of Relational Modalities between Persons and Objects', *The Sociological Review Monograph*, 67:2, 428–43. doi. org/10.1177/0038026119830916

2

The figure of a regretful mother on an online discussion board

Armi Mustosmäki and Tiina Sihto

Introduction

In recent years, the digital intimate public, such as that on social media and online discussion forums, has become an important site where intimate lives are shared, played out, recorded, commodified and constituted (Berlant, 2008; Dobson *et al.*, 2018). Berlant (2008) argued that the proliferation of therapeutic discourses has increasingly impelled us to express or confess our intimate thoughts on public platforms. For instance, mothers can complain about children going through the terrible twos, lament the lack of time for themselves, vent about the unequal sharing of childcare and household chores and gauge the appropriateness and legitimacy of frustrations and 'negative' maternal emotions, such as exhaustion, anger, irritation and dissatisfaction (Ehrstein *et al.*, 2019; Mustosmäki and Sihto, 2021; Pedersen and Lupton, 2018). Intimacy is created by individuals sharing details of their private lives, private experiences and feelings, often with expectations of validation, relief, connection and a sense of belonging (e.g. Kanai, 2017). However, these interactions might redirect expressions of cultural and intimate discontent in ways that uphold normativity. Post-feminist sensibilities that are affectively mediated in the (digital) intimate public invite women to govern themselves and their intimate relationships, including how they navigate the pressures and burdens of motherhood despite disappointments and relentlessly invest in the happiness of their families (e.g. Gill and Orgad, 2018; Jensen, 2018; Wilson and Chivers Yochim, 2017).

This chapter contributes to discussions on digital and affective intimacies by analysing a discussion thread on regretting motherhood on an anonymous Finnish online discussion board. First, our analysis focuses on the darker side of intimacy. In the discussion thread, protected by the anonymity of the online platform, mothers confessed their struggles with parenthood and experiences of 'the most forbidden' emotion of motherhood – that they regret motherhood. Although the mother–child relationship is often culturally considered the most intimate and even symbiotic relational bond, intimate relations are not only about closeness and warmth but are experienced and lived in varying, often messy, ways. Consequently, intimacy is also 'always relational to detachment' (Paasonen, 2018: 110). A child is born into intimacy with their mother, as the newborn does not perceive themselves as a singular subject separate from their mother (e.g. Mjöberg, 2009). This intimacy, which can be seen as life-sustaining and rewarding for the mother, also has a darker side: for the mother, the intimacy and dependency of child/ren might equate with fears or actual experiences of losing one's autonomy, draining oneself and being 'swallowed' by motherhood (e.g. Donath, 2015a, 2015b, 2017; Mustosmäki and Sihto, 2019).

Second, we seek to contribute to discussions on how normative intimacies and 'pedagogies of intimate lives' are affectively mediated and also resisted (Dobson *et al.*, 2018). Confessions of exhaustion, loss of autonomy and regret spurred some vivid discussions dense with affect; others targeted these mothers with contempt, dismay and moral judgement; whilst others evinced attempts to understand, provide advice and support, and even relate to the experiences described by mothers who expressed regret. Inspired by Sara Ahmed's notions of affect (2004) and work on affective figures (2000, 2010), we trace how the affect and meanings that participants directed towards and attached to these confessing and complaining mothers constitute the figure of a regretful mother. However, our analysis is not restricted to the negative affect and moral judgement attached to these confessing mothers (see also Ahmed, 2000; Tyler, 2008). With our open affective-discursive approach that maps a broad range of affective reactions, tenors and orientations towards mothers who expressed unhappiness related to their maternal role, we demonstrate that intimacies are about gradations of proximity and distance (Paasonen, 2018), affectively constituted in the digital intimate public. Thus, in our analysis, the figure of a regretful mother is not constituted as a static, othered abject figure; rather, the qualities of the figure are negotiated and the result of affective formations which are dynamic (inter)connected and becoming in various forms and ways. We aim to bring new perspectives to studies on how normative intimacies are challenged and possibly disrupted in the digital intimate public (e.g. Ehrstein *et al.*, 2019).

Il/legible maternal emotions and regretting motherhood

Despite the vast body of feminist research that has shed light on how motherhood might be a double-edged sword for women, bringing forth emotions that many would consider negative, such as anger, exhaustion, anxiety and mourning for the loss of one's freedom (Lupton, 2000; Miller, 2005; Sevón 2009; Rich, 1977), some emotions are considered largely outside the spectrum of acceptable or even possible maternal emotions. One of them is regret. According to Israeli sociologist Orna Donath's (2015a, 2015b, 2017) groundbreaking research on maternal regret, there are many feeling rules and cultural narratives that govern the spectrum of possible and acceptable maternal emotions. While it seems culturally acceptable for mothers to temporarily experience 'negative' emotions related to the maternal role, motherhood is ultimately always constructed as worthwhile. Consequently, maternal regret has remained largely invisible because it does not fit the cultural master narrative of motherhood which states that one might regret not having children, but nobody (at least no woman) regrets having children.

Once Donath's book (2017) on regretting motherhood were translated into various languages and spurred wider societal controversy. Heffernan and Stone (2021a, 2021b) showed how in this debate in Germany, Spain and Anglophone countries, maternal regret was seen as unimaginable and regretful mothers were deemed self-centred, shameless and cold-hearted. Yet confessions of regret also raised considerable discussion that was supportive and sympathetic, evincing that mothers were overburdened and exhausted, in part, due to cultural ideals and demands of good motherhood and the lack of political and social support for (working) mothers (see also Sihto and Mustosmäki, 2021). However, redirecting the discussion to cultural ideals and family policy arguably dilutes the more radical emotion of regret, as regret can be seen as 'treatable' with increasing support to mothers. Consequently, research on regretting motherhood has shed light on a phenomenon that has remained hidden but also illuminates 'the systems of power that compel women to see motherhood in positive terms and as the only available script for femininity' (Heffernan and Stone, 2021: 337). We seek to contribute to these discussions by showing the workings of this system of power in the digital intimate public and how difficult it is to legitimate struggles in motherhood.

Affect and figures in the digital intimate public

To analyse the discussion at hand and especially the affective reactions to maternal regret, we draw on figurative methodology developed by Ahmed (2000, 2004, 2010) and Tyler (2008). In her analysis of the figure of the stranger, Ahmed (2000) proposed that negative feelings and meanings become associated with certain groups of people or figures. This negative affect is not something that resides within an individual but is generated through the association between objects and signs (Ahmed, 2004). The word *figure* may be used to describe the way that specific bodies become overdetermined and are publicly imagined and represented (and are figured) in excessive, distorted and/or caricatured ways (Tyler, 2008). In her work, Ahmed (2010) constructed the figures of a melancholic migrant, unhappy queer and happy housewife and unpicked the cultural and political work these figures do.

These affective formations of figures resonate with our data as well as 'imagining' and 'figuring', as on the anonymous discussion board, the public's knowledge of the situations and lives of the mothers confessing regret was limited to the information about their most intimate feelings and relations revealed in the comments made on the forum. However, the audience mobilised affect and meanings attached to the figure of a mother who regrets having children; they imagined regretful mothers' personal qualities (as well as the lack of them), choices and failings as well as resources and circumstances in which they lived.

In Ahmed's (2010) research on genealogy and objects of happiness, she also discussed unhappiness in intimate relations and identified the figure of the (un)happy housewife. Her analysis drew on Betty Friedan's work in *The Feminine Mystique*, which identified a problem that has no name, exposing the unhappiness and frustrations of American housewives. For Ahmed (2010), 'the happy housewife is a fantasy figure that erases the signs of labor under the sign of happiness' (50). The function of this 'happiness' is to justify gender norms, such as unequal distribution of labour. Furthermore, 'bad feelings' are attributed to other bodies and objects, such as feminism, instead of to the happy object itself. As Ahmed pointed out, 'feminists are read as being unhappy, such that situations of conflict, violence, and power are read as about the unhappiness of feminists, rather than being what feminists are unhappy about'. For instance, Friedan described how housewives' unhappiness is often attributed, for instance, to an unskilled plumber instead of the role of stay-at-home mother. Inspired by Ahmed (2010), we analyse what the mothers' 'negative' feelings, regret and struggles are attributed to.

Figurative methodology has been widely applied and developed especially by feminist and media scholars to study cultural re/production and mediation of un/desirable 'maternal femininity' (McRobbie, 2013). Scholars have analysed the mobilisation of negative affect, discourse and meanings and drawn out the figures of 'chav mums' (Tyler, 2008), 'benefit broods' and 'welfare mothers' (Jensen and Tyler, 2015) and highlighted how intensely these affective figures have been mobilised in the media, policy and public discourses as symbols of welfare dependency, moral breakdown and anxieties around contemporary motherhood (e.g. Jensen, 2018).

Conversely, there are figures such as the thrifty, happy housewife, who experiences the 'domestic' as a site of contentment and the related romance of retreat, or the figure of the do-it-all working mum, emphasising the meaning of hard work and commitment to family and striving for work–life balance (Allen *et al.*, 2015; Orgad, 2019). These figures call into being subjects who are rational and self-motivated, who govern themselves and make sense of their lives through discourses of freedom, responsibility and choice. Such governance also operates at the level of emotions and feelings, inviting women to adjust their feeling states to maintain happiness (e.g. Ehrstein *et al.*, 2019). Such maternal subject positions shape normative ideals about 'good' and 'bad' motherhood, what mothers are allowed to feel and be and how to manage their intimate relations, and they invite women and mothers to judge themselves and others against these post-feminist models of successful (and abject) femininity and maternity.

However, in our analysis of mothers who experience regret, we avoid simplifying and distinguishing only monolithic 'good' or 'bad' maternal figures. While this may pit mothers who regret against normative notions of intimacies and post-feminist ideals, our affective-discursive analysis shows that post-feminist ideals are not simply accepted and circulated. We suggest that analysing affect and meaning-making processes, as they potentially open a wider range of subject positions made available to women and mothers, will reveal some fractures in wider power relations.

Data and methods

We obtained our data from a thread on the anonymous online discussion board Vauva.fi. Vauva.fi is one of Finland's most popular websites, attracting around 400,000 visitors and 5.7 million page views per week in 2021 (a relatively high number, as Finland's population is 5.5 million). The majority of its discussions focus on pregnancy, children and family life (*vauva* is the Finnish word for *baby*). The topic of the analysed discussion thread can be loosely translated as 'Those of you who regret having children: does the feeling ease as the children get older?' The thread, consisting of 754 comments, appeared online in February 2017. Although the first commenter explicitly addressed those who have experienced regretting having children, affective intensities intermeshed and clustered in complex ways as the discussion progressed (cf. Paasonen, 2015). After the first comment, the thread soon filled with other kinds of comments than those describing personal experiences of regret, such as comments trying to make sense of maternal regret, giving advice to those expressing regret or to mothers in general, responding to previous comments, reflecting on one's own experiences of being or becoming a mother or being a child of a regretful mother/parent.

Analysing affective reactions in the discussion necessitates taking into account the digital architecture of the discussion board from which we collected our data. Discussions can become heated quickly, but even for the most popular topics, the interest is often short-lived. In the case at hand, the popularity of the discussion thread was intense but relatively short-lived: the comments were written within the span of seven days, with most of the comments (483 in total) written within the first three days of the thread's appearance online.

The way we read online threads often follows a particular pattern: individual comments are often skimmed through quickly or skipped entirely (see Paasonen, 2015). Consequently, reading and replying can be considered an affective practice, as some comments are 'sticky' and garner attention, whereas others do not. On Vauva.fi, this skipping is supported to some extent by the architecture of the discussion board, which regulates the format and order in which comments appear. In discussion threads, users see the comments in chronological order, with the twenty oldest comments appearing on the first page of the thread and the newest comments appearing on the last page of the thread.

The thread analysed in this chapter consisted of thirty-nine pages of comments; consequently, commenters most often engaged with the comments appearing on the first page of the thread (i.e. the twenty oldest comments). This can also be seen in the distributions of upvotes and downvotes that particular comments received: the comments on the first page typically attracted the most votes, and as the thread continued, individual comments generally received fewer votes. To examine the affective intensities and 'stickiness' of particular views and comments in the discussion thread, in our analysis, we also pay attention to the numbers of upvotes and downvotes comments received whilst also taking into account that these numbers not only reflect the (un)popularity of particular views but are also shaped by the website's architecture.

In addition to the infrastructure of the board, its anonymity plays a major part in how affect comes into being and circulates in discussions, as anonymous forums have their own, specific affective circuits. Anonymity can invite highly polarised and emotional discussion and commenting styles as participants search for affective intensity (Jensen, 2013; Paasonen, 2015). The dynamics and interaction in threads can appear non-linear, hectic, chaotic and filled with moments of affective intensity. What is often characteristic of online discussions is fast intensification and circulation, the sharpening of affect and the possible flattening of people into 'types' (Paasonen, 2015).

For the purposes of this study, to define affect, we rely on Ahmed's (2004) and Wetherell's (2012) understanding of the interwovenness of meaning-making, discourse and affect. This framework is useful for our analysis of affect circulating in the digital intimate public because it allows us to perceive affect as a social process shaped by a social order but also by digital technologies and architectures of websites, involving bodies, feeling states and discourses aimed at making sense of the world. In line with Ahmed (2000, 2004, 2010) and Wetherell (2012), we perceive affect and emotions as related and as connected to the meaning-making process. Thus, the public's affective reactions are results of complex becomings of cultural narratives and norms, moods and sensibilities, their personal histories and the architecture of the site. Ahmed (2010) has also defined affect as 'sticky' and as 'what sustains or preserves the connection between ideas, values and objects' (230). This notion is useful for our analysis because regret appears sticky, drawing the public towards itself, as well as fascinating and simultaneously appalling and worrying. This conceptualisation of affect contrasts with theories of affect that perceive it as sensations, moods and atmospheres that escape the discursive and are ultimately detached from meaning, representation or consciousness (Wetherell, 2012).

Affective re/orientations towards the figure of a regretful mother

We first present the affective orientations that mobilised negative affect towards mothers expressing regret. The figure of a regretful mother was constituted as a maternal figure lacking *will, mothering skills* and *competence*. These affective orientations attributed the source of regret to mothers' personal qualities, individualising both the source and solutions to difficulties faced in the maternal role. There were also affective orientations constituting the figure of a regretful mother as a *perfectionist* – somebody who takes the pressures and ideals of motherhood too seriously and ends up 'overdoing' motherhood or who is *unable* to make her own choices regarding motherhood. These orientations recognised external pressures stemming from society yet ultimately saw that individual mothers should 'deal' with these pressures.

However, at times, the source of regret was not directly highlighted as within or outside the mother, and the affective tenor was cooler. Instead of regretful, the mothers were understood as suffering from *mental disorders* or *post-natal depression* and were advised to seek professional help. In these comments, the affective orientations were caring and advising, and regret was seen as a difficult, temporary phase. At times, notions of mental disorders were dense with negative and judgemental affect including resentment, anger and moral worry, and regret was pathologised and deemed unnatural. Although we present the affective orientations and meanings attached to regret as somewhat distinct, the features often overlapped, were sometimes in conflict with one another and also evinced resistance to certain affect and meanings.

Regret as a matter of attitude?

Earlier studies on maternal regret shed light on the various ways mothers describe their struggles with parenting. Typical descriptions include loss of autonomy and freedom, exhaustion and missing one's life before children (Donath, 2015a, 2015b, 2017). Similarly, in our earlier analysis of women who expressed regretting motherhood (Mustosmäki and Sihto, 2019), mothers confessed that they missed having time for themselves and that, as mothers, they could not live their lives in the way they wanted. Often, these mothers recognised the promise of happiness embedded in the 'happy object' of the nuclear family (see Ahmed, 2010) and experienced disappointment and affective dissonance because they did not 'feel the right way' when in proximity to this happy object (Mustosmäki and Sihto, 2019; Sihto and Mustosmäki, 2021).

In this study, many commenters in the discussion thread directed negative affect towards mothers expressing regret. These comments were often filled with judgement that invited the public to trace the reason for troubles to the mothers themselves, constituting these mothers as weak, incompetent and unable to manage their lives and emotions. According to some comments, what is characteristic of the figure of a regretful mother is *lacking the will* to enjoy her life as it is and to enjoy motherhood. One commenter framed regretful mothers as follows: 'This is a perfect example of an attitude problem. You can be happy now, it is only a matter of attitude' (three upvotes, seventeen downvotes). The existence of regret as such was not denied or reframed. However, regret was seen as originating in mothers wanting 'the wrong things' and their incapability to be happy. Thus, the mother is at fault. This was highlighted in statements such as 'the killjoy and barrier to happiness is looking back at you in the mirror' (ten upvotes, twenty-four downvotes).

The above comment resonates with the notion of 'feminist killjoys' (Ahmed, 2010) who vocalise unhappiness lying beneath happy objects, thus killing the joy of others and causing discomfort in others by revealing their experiences. Such comments also resonate with research on affective and psychic life of neoliberalism and how women are invited to take individual responsibility for their lives and shape their dispositions, behaviour and emotional states to respond with a positive mental attitude to any challenge they face (e.g. Ehrstein *et al.*, 2019).

Comments were also dense with advice on how to 'cure' regret. Regretful mothers were seen as stuck in or paralysed by their feelings and were advised to control their emotions and frustrations (e.g. Jensen, 2018). Such comments suggest that regretful mothers can be 'rehabilitated' by changing their attitude, either towards mothering or towards the feeling of regret. It is not individual actions but emotions that are quintessential, and one's emotions should be dealt with, as evinced a comment emphasising that 'feelings are just feelings to which one shouldn't give too much space' (one upvote, five downvotes).

Regretful mothers were not only seen as lacking the will to do the things that a mother should do but also as lacking the *will* to enjoy doing those things. Commenters expressed certainty that children can sense that the mother does not have the right affective state attached to motherhood – that she does not enjoy mothering and does not want to do things with her children – and therefore, the children act out to get the attention they desperately need: 'The poor child must be screaming for attention, as you just want to be left alone and not spend time with your child' (119 upvotes, 302 downvotes). These commenters empathised with children as innocent and vulnerable. Making children visible in this way is also a strong affective orientation that invites the intimate public to focus on the alleged damaged morality of mothers expressing regret. These commenters feared that the children would be damaged as well. Such comments mark the problem as originating within the individual and, thus, imply strong but damaged agency: the mothers could enjoy motherhood and their children if they wanted to, but they do not.

In addition to mothers' attitudes and emotion management, another affective orientation invited the public to perceive the figure of a regretful mother as somebody who *lacks the ability to parent*, encouraging the public to see regretful mothers as *incompetent* and lacking knowledge, which results in difficulties and challenges in their everyday lives, leading to maternal regret. This view is reflected in statements such as 'you're not having fun because for some reason your children were not raised to behave well. [...] Raising [children] is a skill, like playing the piano, nothing mystical' (eight upvotes, eighteen downvotes). Thus, the problem was seen as originating in the mothers themselves and their lack of expertise. Mothering was constructed as a skill which every mother should have and which is possible to acquire. These evaluations are explicit in comments stating that children might also be misbehaving because they are going through 'a phase' in their development: 'children have several phases in their development, and parents should be equipped with sufficient information and knowledge of how to cope with these situations. However, the majority of parents do not seem to have any understanding of raising a child' (seven upvotes, nine downvotes). Here, the affective tone invites the public to orient and respond to mothers with (perhaps unsolicited) advice.

These comments highlight that mothers must possess expert knowledge, and this will help them understand how children should be raised. Thus, problems that cause regret, such as difficulties with one's children, can be solved by seeking knowhow – acquiring more skills in raising children and developing a more thorough understanding of what children are like. This was expected to make the lives of both mothers and children easier and smoother. Commenters sometimes justified their statements with references to research and expert knowledge on (early) childhood, but often, the source of commenters' expertise or knowledge was not considered. In these comments, the use of passive voice asserted a position of power and a connotation that this is shared knowledge. However, these individualising and judgemental comments received more downvotes than upvotes, indicating that these views were also rejected by many participants in the discussion thread. We analyse resistance to these comments offering advice more in the following section.

Tired mother, perfectionist mother?

Many commenters in the discussion forum recognised the ideals of good, intensive motherhood (Hays, 1996) as stemming from society and suggested that mothers' feelings of exhaustion and regret come from 'overdoing' motherhood. Thus, they understood the mothers' perfectionism as the problem and the source of regret. The tendency towards perfectionism was projected onto and from other mothers who have set (unnecessarily) high standards in their everyday lives. These other regretful, exhausted mothers have internalised the (impossible) demands and pressures that society imposes on them:

> Nobody benefits from a martyred mother who submerges her own needs in favour of others and who is grumpy all the time. [...] The mother does not have to wake up at 6 a.m., even if others would. [...] Nobody has to stay awake when the kids eat their sandwiches whilst sitting on the sofa watching cartoons. [...] Going to restaurants is part of normal upbringing. The age gap between children is nobody's business. Every parent has a right to adjust their routines to cope. Children will just sense that their mom can cope and is not in danger of exploding. I do know some 'supermoms', but I do not believe their children are any happier in reality than the kids of my type of parent, who are a bit less fanatical about 'the job'. (Fourteen upvotes, one downvote)

The above comment shows that regretful mothers were seen as lacking the ability to control their 'need for perfection' and their everyday lives to make things manageable. The discussion thread included detailed instructions, such as in the comment above, on how mothers can cope and find time for themselves in between and during their daily routines. Commenters emphasised that children will not be damaged if a mother strives to be 'less perfect'. These comments reflect ideas about deterministic parenting (see e.g. Lee *et al.*, 2014), where 'bad, careless parenting' is a risk to the child's emotional development. However, resistance to such deterministic ideas and the affective allure of intensive mothering prevailed in (unsolicited) advice to recognise and resist the cultural demand that a mother should be constantly present for her children. It is notable, however, that mothers were advised to be self-sufficient and not to expect more from society or to seek help. Thus, while recognising the ideals as socially constructed, the advice circulated individualistic solutions and neoliberal sensibilities about individual responsibility, self-sufficiency, the importance of managing one's feelings and possibilities of 'having it all with the right mindset' (Gill and Orgad, 2019). However, these comments dispensing advice were often also met with resistance. The comment below ironises the advice and the striving for 'optimising' motherhood present in the previous comment:

> Do you think that your children do not understand that when you prepare breakfast for them in the evening, it's because you do not want to wake up to eat with them? Do you think that your children have not understood that you took them to restaurants early on so that they could get used to it and that it would be easier? Do you think that your children have not understood why they have such a big age gap? Because YOU cannot stand their whining. Your children do sense what kind of mother you are and were. (Ten upvotes, twenty downvotes)

The commenter above opted for 'humorous trolling' (Sanfilippo *et al.*, 2018) in reference to an earlier comment which gave detailed advice on how to cope with the everyday challenges of motherhood and suggested that children can 'sense' the mother's emotional states. There were also responses from mothers who rejected these meanings and effects associated with their issues, resisting the idea that difficulties in motherhood can be dealt with by 'not minding the opinions of others':

> Others do cause enormous stress for me and without children, those others would not be in my life. If I don't pay attention to them, it won't make them go away. On the contrary, that would cause even more harm and stress. So, the options are bad and worse.
>
> I feel that the freedom to do things on my terms has been completely taken away from me. Now, I do things on my child's terms or on the terms of people who have something to do with my child. (Thirty-six upvotes, six downvotes)

Comments such as the one above challenged the idea(l) of happiness embedded in the maternal role and brought forth narratives of loss. Very similarly, regretful mothers rejected suggestions that their feelings and emotions could be dealt with by 'taking time for yourself':

> Exhausted parents are always advised to take time for themselves and organise childcare, etc. ... But it does not really resolve our issues, at least not for

us who genuinely miss the time before we had our children. These emotions are not just being tired. It is also about the fact that having children has permanently and fundamentally changed our lives and there is no turning back.

The everyday realities of motherhood and the loss of personal autonomy might contrast starkly with the expectations of happiness (Ahmed, 2010) these mothers had prior to having children (Mustosmäki and Sihto, 2019). The affective orientations here created connections and proximities between struggling mothers who expressed regret and sought to explain why they regret and what they miss. Yet the regretful mothers simultaneously created distance by rejecting empathy from those offering the perhaps well-intentioned but unsolicited advice.

Struggling mother, mentally ill mother?

Some commenters questioned whether it is possible to genuinely regret motherhood or whether it is, in fact, merely a symptom of depression or other mental health issues. Some of these comments expressed tones of moral condemnation, contempt or even hatred. Regretting motherhood was understood as 'not healthy' (seventeen upvotes, 141 downvotes), the result of a bad relationship with one's own mother or a symptom of psychological problems or 'defects on the emotional side' (five upvotes, twenty-nine downvotes). Interestingly, the downvotes show some resistance to the script, suggesting that regret cannot be reduced to mental health issues. Some comments even suggested that regret about having children is so far from the cultural narrative of (good) mothering that it is seen as a sign of severe mental disorders or monstrous characteristics. In these comments, regretful mothers were called *sociopaths, madwomen, child haters* or *potential child murderers*. Such judgemental comments did not open a window for temporarily tired or depressed mothers to grow into good mothers (see also Donath, 2017).

However, many commenters approached the complaints of struggling mothers with sympathy, understanding and support, suggesting that these mothers on the forum were suffering from (post-natal) depression. One commenter stated, 'I don't think anyone genuinely regrets their children, the moms here just sound depressed and exhausted to me' (eighty-one upvotes, 252 downvotes). These expressions are somewhat hesitant, but depression is a more plausible explanation for difficulties experienced with motherhood than the idea that someone might not want to be a mother. The affective tone in these comments could also be rather cool and matter-of-fact and without blame or shame directed towards struggling mothers. It is interesting that users expressed disagreement with and resistance to the idea of depression explaining the struggles with downvotes.

At times, affective proximity and support were constructed through statements based on personal experience that regret, exhaustion and feeling overwhelmed by motherhood represented a temporary phase and were connected to a phase of life when the commenter was diagnosed with post-natal depression:

> I fell into post-natal depression, and when my illness was at its worst, I cried and regretted that I had ever decided to have a child, I was so tired and low. Now that I have received the necessary treatment and help, and some six months have passed, I am doing great with my child and my husband.

These caring, affective orientations were also created in comments perceiving regret as tiredness or depression and freeing the subject of responsibility for the difficult situation and from moral condemnation. Caring orientations were often accompanied by advice on how to move forward in such difficult situations, as regretting mothers were advised to seek professional help and go to therapy. Such messages convey a firm belief that seeking medical help and therapy will help the regretful mothers, which highlights the insinuation of therapeutic culture into intimate relations and parenting (see e.g. Becker, 2005; Furedi, 2003). Therapeutic culture does not deny the existence of negative emotions, as it is emphasised that there is no perfect happiness and relationships are not trouble-free. Rather, it highlights the importance of discussing one's emotions openly and dealing with them, as well as the 'therapeutic capacity' of individuals to analyse themselves and their relationships in cooperation with therapists and medical experts (Illouz, 2008; Nehring and Kerrigan, 2019).

Yet again, these affective orientations attached to the figure of a regretful mother aligned regret with exhaustion and depression and the solutions provided by therapeutic and medical help were downplayed or even rejected:

> I've too been disturbed by these ideas that nowadays mothers are only allowed to be tired or depressed, and in that case, they talk at the maternal care centre, are prescribed some medication, take some time for themselves – and abracadabra – mythical maternal figure is ready to continue.

Thus, being tired or depressed have become culturally acceptable and intelligible emotions and feeling states that might be part of the maternal experience (e.g. Jokinen, 1996). These comments also reflect therapeutic ideas about intimate relations, how these ideas have influenced the ways we perceive mother–child relations: although motherhood is demanding and complex, it is essential to recognise difficult feelings and emotions, reflect on them and deal with them. While some mothers testified from their own experience that, for them, regret was part of temporary depression, and they found therapeutic and medical treatments helpful, not all mothers were willing to align themselves with this figure and these meanings (see also Donath, 2015a, 2015b, 2017). Instead, they wanted to carve out space for a figure that just does not necessarily grow into motherhood.

Conclusion

In this chapter, we have brought new perspectives to studies on affective intimacies by analysing a discussion on regretting motherhood on an anonymous Finnish online discussion board. First, our analysis focused on the darker side of intimacy. In the discussion thread, protected by the anonymity of the online platform, mothers confessed their struggles with parenthood and experiences of 'the most forbidden' emotion of motherhood – that they regret motherhood. Second, our analysis of affect and meanings attached to mothers expressing regret demonstrated that while neoliberal sensibilities and therapeutic ideals were circulated, they were also resisted and ridiculed.

The figure of a regretful mother was constituted as a maternal figure lacking the *will* to mother as well as mothering *skills* and *competence*. There were also affective orientations that constituted the figure of a regretful mother as a *perfectionist* – as somebody who takes the pressures and ideals of motherhood too seriously and ends up 'overdoing' motherhood or who is *unable* to make her own choices regarding motherhood. These orientations recognised external pressures stemming from society yet ultimately saw that individual mothers should 'deal' with these pressures. These affective orientations attributed mothers' personal qualities as the source of their regret, individualising both the sources and solutions to difficulties faced in the maternal role. These orientations circulated and reinforced neoliberal and therapeutic understandings of how individualism has affected our perception of the self not only as a solution but also as the source of problems (Becker, 2005). However, in these comments, addressing regret as regret often seemed difficult. Regret was given various meanings and explanations that affectively circulated around regret but often failed to address it in its own right. Consequently, many of the problems women face were seen as medical rather than societal and personal rather than political (see also Furedi, 2003).

The ideal of personal development, which is characterised by specific social norms and beliefs that act as moral resources from which the public draws, both consciously and unconsciously, were often present in the discussion (Nehring and Kerrigan, 2019). The commenters often highlighted their own willpower, their control over their own lives and the abilities and competence they possessed – all qualities and dispositions they deemed the mothers who expressed regret were lacking. These comments highlight the ideal of the individualistic neoliberal subject who is self-sufficient, resilient and positive, whatever the outer circumstances are (see also Gill and Orgad, 2018). This ideal subject is self-reliant: she expects a lot from herself but little, if any, help or support from others or the surrounding society.

In some comments, the figure of a regretful mother was affectively constituted as somebody who is not 'truly' regretful but suffers from a *mental disorder* or *post-natal depression* and was advised to seek professional help. In some of these comments, the affective orientations were caring and advising, as regret was not seen as regret but as a difficult, temporary phase from which mothers can eventually 'recover'. Again, neoliberal sensibilities and notions of therapeutic culture were apparent in comments to regretful mothers that promoted the idea that one can overcome such problems either by taking control of one's life or by talking about the problems and seeking medical help. These notions do certain cultural work on intimate relations as well as on the nature of the mother–child relationship. According to Maksimainen (2010), the biggest promise of therapeutic culture is that relationships between people can always be fixed through negotiation and by dealing with one's emotions. In its most extreme form, therapeutic culture denies the possibility of tragedy (see also Illouz, 2008).

However, the contribution of this analysis to discussions on the digital intimate public is that the notions of neoliberal, therapeutic and medicalised meanings and affect were not just recognised and reinforced, they were also debated and rejected. Thus, revealing one's most intimate thoughts and emotions in the digital intimate public, even anonymously, may offer possibilities for new becomings and affective formations to exist. Our analysis of regret and ambivalence and contradictions has shed light on how intimacy, even in the mother–child relationship, is always relational to detachment and gradations of proximity and distance. Mothers miss their own lives, identities, time for themselves and might seek validation for their hopes, desires and frustrations. Yet the vulnerability of children limits the possibilities to resist the intimacy between mothers and children. This vulnerability created distances between women confessing regret, exhaustion and negative feelings as well as commenters in the digital intimate public. The worries over children create complex affective relations, meanings and moralities, limiting mothers' possibilities to voice out their regret. Thus, motherhood is a fragile terrain on which to combat power relations and act politically outside the intimate public.

References

Ahmed, S. (2000), *Strange Encounters: Embodied Others in Postcoloniality* (Abingdon: Routledge).

Ahmed, S. (2004), 'Affective Economies', *Social Text*, 22:2, 117–39.

Ahmed, S. (2010), *The Promise of Happiness* (Durham, NC, and London: Duke University Press).

Allen, K., Mendick, H., Harvey, L., and Ahmad, A. (2015), 'Welfare Queens, Thrifty Housewives, and Do-It-All Mums', *Feminist Media Studies*, 15:6, 907–25.

Becker, D. (2005), *The Myth of Empowerment: Women and the Therapeutic Culture in America* (New York, NY: New York University Press).

Berlant, L. (2008), *The Female Complaint: The Unfinished Business of Sentimentality in American Culture* (Durham, NC: Duke University Press).

Dobson, A. S., Robarts, B., and Carah, N. (2018), 'Digital Intimate Publics and Social Media: Towards Theorising Public Lives on Private Platforms', in *Digital Intimate Publics and Social Media*, A. S. Dobson, B. Robarts, and N. Carah (eds) (Cham, Switzerland: Palgrave Macmillan), 3–27.

Donath, O. (2015a), 'Choosing Motherhood? Agency and Regret within Reproduction and Mothering Retrospective Accounts', *Women's Studies International Forum*, 53, 200–9.

Donath, O. (2015b), 'Regretting Motherhood: A Sociopolitical Analysis', *Signs: Journal of Women in Culture and Society*, 40:2, 343–67.

Donath, O. (2017), *Regretting Motherhood: A Study* (Berkeley, CA: North Atlantic Books).

Ehrstein, Y., Gill, R., and Littler, J. (2019). 'The Affective Life of Neoliberalism: Constructing (un)Reasonableness on Mumsnet', in *Neoliberalism in Context*, S. Dawes and M. Lenormand (eds) (Basingstoke: Palgrave), 195–213.

Furedi, F. (2003), *Therapy Culture: Cultivating Vulnerability in an Uncertain Age* (London: Routledge).

Gill, R., and Orgad, S. (2018), 'The Amazing Bounce-Backable Woman: Resilience and the Psychological Turn in Neoliberalism', *Sociological Research Online*, 23:2, 477–95.

Hays, S. (1996), *The Cultural Contradictions of Motherhood* (New Haven, CT: Yale University Press).

Heffernan, V., and Stone, K. (2021a), '#regrettingmotherhood in Germany: Feminism, Motherhood, and Culture', *Signs: Journal of Women in Culture and Society*, 46:2, 337–60.

Heffernan, V., and Stone, K. (2021b), 'International Responses to Regretting Motherhood', in *Women's Lived Experiences of the Gender Gap*, A. Fitzgerald (ed.), Sustainable Development Goals Series (Singapore: Springer). https://doi.org/10.1007/978-981-16-1174-2_11

Illouz, E. (2008). *Saving the Modern Soul: Therapy, Emotions, and the Culture of Self-Help* (Berkeley and Los Angeles, CA: University of California Press).

Jensen, T. (2013), '"Mumsnetiquette": Online Affect within Parenting Culture', in *Privilege, Agency and Affect*, C. Maxwell and P. Aggleton (eds) (Basingstoke: Palgrave Macmillan), 127–45.

Jensen, T. (2018), *Parenting the Crisis: The Cultural Politics of Parent-Blame* (Bristol: Policy Press).

Jensen, T., and Tyler, I. (2015), '"Benefits Broods": The Cultural and Political Crafting of Anti-Welfare Commonsense', *Critical Social Policy*, 35:4, 470–91.

Jokinen, Eeva (1996), *Väsynyt äiti. Ätiyden omaelämänkerrallisia esityksiä* (Helsinki, Finland: Gaudeamus).

Kanai, A. (2017), 'Girlfriendship and Sameness: Affective Belonging in a Digital Intimate Public', *Journal of Gender Studies*, 26:3, 293–306. https://doi.org/10.1080/09589236.2017.1281108

Lee, E., Bristow, J., Faircloth, C., and Macvarish, J. (2014), *Parenting Culture Studies* (London: Palgrave Macmillan).

Lupton, D. (2000), '"A Love/Hate Relationship": The Ideals and Experiences of First-Time Mothers', *Journal of Sociology*, 36:1, 50–63.

MacRobbie, A. (2013), 'Feminism, the Family and the New "Mediated" Maternalism', *New Formations*, 80:81, 119–37.

Maksimainen, J. (2010), *Parisuhde ja ero: Sosiologinen analyysi terapeuttisesta ymmärryksestä.* (Doctoral dissertation/Studies in Social sciences 3:2010. Helsinki, Finland: Helsinki University Press).

Miller, T. (2005), *Making Sense of Motherhood: A Narrative Approach* (Cambridge: Cambridge University Press).

Mjöberg, J. (2009), 'Challenging the Idea of Intimacy as Intimate Relationships', in *Intimate Explorations Readings across Disciplines*, A. Cervantes-Carson and B. Oria (eds) (Oxford: Interdisciplinary Press).

Mustosmäki, A., and Sihto, T. (2019), 'Äitiyden katuminen intensiivisen äitiyden kulttuurissa', *Sosiologia*, 56:2, 157–73.

Mustosmäki, A., and Sihto, T. (2021), '"F*** This Shit" – Negotiating the Boundaries of Public Expression of Mother's Negative Feelings', *NORA – Nordic Journal of Feminist and Gender Research*, 29:3, 216–28.

Nehring, D., and Kerrigan, D. (2019), *Therapeutic Worlds: Popular Psychology and the Sociocultural Organisation of Intimate Life* (New York, NY: Routledge).

Orgad, S. (2019), *Heading Home: Motherhood, Work and the Failed Promise of Equality* (New York, NY: Columbia University Press).

Paasonen, S. (2015), 'A Midsummer's Bonfire: Affective Intensities of Online Debate', in *Networked Affect*, K. Hillis, S. Paasonen, and M. Petit (eds) (Cambridge, MA: MIT Press), 27–42.

Paasonen, S. (2018), 'Infrastructures of Intimacy', in *Mediated Intimacies: Connectivities, Relationalities and Proximities*, R. Andreassen, M. N. Petersen, K. Harrison, and T. Raun (eds) (London: Routledge), 103–16.

Pedersen, S., and Lupton, D. (2018), '"What Are You Feeling Right Now?" Communities of Maternal Feeling on Mumsnet', *Emotion, Space and Society*, 26, 57–63.

Rich, A. (1977), *Of Woman Born. Motherhood as Experience and Institution* (London: Virago).

Sanfilippo, M. R., Fichman, P., and Yang, S. (2018), 'Multidimensionality of Online Trolling Behaviors', *The Information Society*, 34:1, 27–39.

Sevón, E. (2009), *Maternal Responsibility and Changing Relationality at the Beginning of Motherhood* (Jyväskylä Studies in Education, Psychology, and Social Research 365) (Jyväskylä, Finland: University of Jyväskylä).

Sihto, T., and Mustosmäki, A. (2021), 'The Most Invisible Maternal Experience? Analysing How Maternal Regret Is Discussed in Finland', in *Women's Lived Experiences of the Gender Gap: Gender Inequalities from a Global Perspective*, A. Fitzgerald (ed.) (Singapore: Springer), 109–120.

Tyler, I. (2008), '"Chav Mum Chav Scum": Class Disgust in Contemporary Britain', *Feminist Media Studies*, 8:1, 17–34.

Wetherell, M. (2012), *Affect and Emotion: A New Social Science Understanding* (London: Sage).

Wilson, J. A., and Yochim, E. C. (2017), *Mothering through Precarity: Women's Work and Digital Media* (Durham, NC: Duke University Press).

3

Intimate technology? Teletherapies in the era of COVID-19

Marjo Kolehmainen

Some personas are like, they like remote consultations. And they can speak in a more intimate manner when remote. It's intriguing, and them some cannot talk [of] anything intimate in this way, this is so alien this connection. (Psychotherapist)

Introduction

This chapter investigates teletherapies, aiming to produce novel insights into how human well-being is co-constituted with technological infrastructures.[1] Drawing upon a study on the diverse practices of remote therapy and counselling in the context of the COVID-19 pandemic, it explores the ways in which Finnish psychotherapists and other counselling professionals experience the related shift to teletherapies. As in several other countries (e.g. De Luca and Calabrò, 2020; Reay *et al.*, 2020; Silver *et al.*, 2020), in Finland the pandemic generated a huge digital leap, particularly to digital therapies and online counselling, even though traditional phone calls have been in use too. Rather than pre-defining teletherapies as similar or different to traditional therapies, as a point of departure, I suggest that technological infrastructures condition and shape the affective processes of support-seeking and support-giving in diverse areas from long-term psychotherapies to anonymous one-off advice. In particular, I tap into the question of how intimacy comes to matter in teletherapy practices. As the quote above, from a research interview I conducted, indicates, experiences concerning intimacy differ: Many feel that teletherapy can facilitate or prohibit the experiences of trust, proximity, confidentiality and security. Hence, to provide substantial insights into the ways in which intimacy matters in digital therapy, I look at the socio-material constitution of intimacy and its more-than-human constituencies (Latimer and Gómez, 2019). This chapter thus traces the ways in which intimacy is being made and unmade, of and with multiple entangled materialities.

Technological infrastructures are about more-than-human worlds and the materialities that are essential parts of therapy processes. In digital therapy and counselling, technology not only 'intermediates' human–human interactions but fundamentally shapes the co-constitution of the therapy sessions. Thus, the remote sessions cannot be reduced to sessions that now only take place through video calls or other means – but rather, technology mediates therapy and has at least a potentially transformative effect on the therapy process (for the difference between intermediating and mediating, see Latour, 2005: 39). These transformations should not only be understood as disrupting therapy practice or as making it less – or more – effective, even though efficacy as a topic is regularly discussed and debated in studies concerning teletherapy and telecounselling. Rather, these transformative processes are open-ended by definition and, as my analysis will illustrate, the similar conditions and practices result in multiple experiences, having varying consequences. From this perspective, the COVID-19 pandemic and the related shift away from in-person consultations are not pre-defined as an external disruption to therapy practice, but they provide novel networks for the relational co-constitution of therapy practices.

The data entail forty-one interviews in which psychotherapists, family counsellors, crisis workers, sex therapists and other counselling professionals were interviewed about their experiences concerning the role of technology during the global COVID-19 pandemic. Seeing non-human and human intra-actions as crucial for the production of well-being, this chapter departs from individualised and psychologised notions of well-being and views well-being as always conditioned by both non-individual and more-than-human agencies (Coffey, 2020). In this vein, it seeks to contribute to such materialist analyses of COVID-19 that, as a point of departure, see it as productive of a surfeit of assemblages that require the kind of materialist analysis that attunes to agential cuts and intra-actions (Sikka, 2021). With this approach, I wish to make visible the socio-material constitution of intimacies in teletherapy practices, thus enriching our understanding of affective intimacies by stressing how intimacy is co-constituted by several dynamic processes that have capacities to affect and become affected.

I have structured the empirical discussion introduced in this chapter along two different themes, which may appear to be different. I will first discuss the rethinking of intimacies and then introduce an empirical exploration of the capacities to both bring close and to distance as facilitated by remote therapy and counselling. Whereas several accounts of disruptions in reciprocal communication, technical difficulties, concrete distance between providers and clients and the feeling of a distance were described in the data, the descriptions of a feeling of proximity, novel observations and access to spaces that were previously held private were also popular, as well as alternative ways and modalities that brought forth new entanglements.

However, the seemingly different repertoires both illustrate how mental well-being is assembled through a process of entanglements and relations (see also Coffey, 2020: 4). Their detailed analysis allows the entangled agencies that play a role in professionals' experiences concerning teletherapies to be traced, highlighting the ways in which intimacy is made and unmade, and how affective relations shape the experiences of intimacy, or lack thereof.

Rethinking intimacies

In exploring more-than-human intimacies in the approach to remote therapy and counselling, this chapter enriches the current body of work on digital intimacies that has largely focused on sexuality. In previous studies of digital intimacy, topics such as sexual content, sexual expressions and sexual rights have been increasingly examined, yet other types of intimacies and their more-than-human constituencies have remained largely unexplored. Alternative approaches are scarce but exist: while Piras and Miele (2019) consider in their insightful analysis the technologically mediated patient-provider relationships as 'digital intimacy' that is characterised by familiarity that extends the face-to-face encounters, they nevertheless stress the primary locus of creation of such intimacy in this concept, reducing 'digital' to a platform for human-human intimacies. However, intimacy should not be reduced to human-only encounters or to certain pre-defined domains (Kolehmainen and Juvonen, 2018; Lykke, 2018; Lykke, 2019). The bracketing of intimacy to certain domains, such as sexuality, private life or interpersonal relations, has made it difficult for intimacy to be a subject of importance writ large (Latimer and Gómez, 2019). It has also led to associations of intimacy with 'positive' closeness, even if this is highly problematic (Latimer and Gómez, 2019; Kolehmainen and Juvonen, 2018; Zengin, 2016). In particular, affect theory provides important insight into how proximity and closeness are not neutral practices (see Introduction, this volume; Kinnunen and Kolehmainen, 2019). Nor is intimacy only a matter of human relations, as my chapter will further demonstrate.

In the production of a suitable framework for the exploration of more-than-human intimacies, I seek to draw upon those scholars who have discussed intimacy without foregrounding sexuality, and to continue this work further. Following Lauren Berlant (2000: 4), intimacy is a matter of 'connections that impact on people, and on which they depend for living'. From this perspective, consideration of technology – and in particular the internet – is essential in studies that focus on more-than-human intimacies. Networked connectivity has grown into a matter of infrastructure, reminiscent of electricity, gas, water or heating (Paasonen, 2018a), and intimacies surface and wither in networks of human and non-human actors (Paasonen,

2018b). Thus, intimacy therefore refers not only to connections between people but to the networked environments in which these unfold and the connections that are formed with devices, apps and platforms: these all impact people, and they are all depended on for living (Paasonen, 2018a). They are, in many ways, what living depends on, but also 'worlding practices' (Tsing, 2015; Stewart, 2017) that have an effect on how living itself can take place. In the multiple processes of teletherapies and remote counselling, the networked environments and connections have an infrastructural role but they also facilitate the more nuanced (un)makings of intimacy that have at least potentially significant affective, psychic and material capacities.

Digital technologies entangle with intimacies in various ways. As we are part of technological environments, rather than individual subjects who can manage and control technology (e.g. Kember and Zylinska, 2012; Paasonen, 2018b), digital technologies have become essential, everyday non-human companionships. They are intimate in the sense that they necessitate the conditions of human living, stressing the co-dependencies between human and non-human lives. They also work as a part of socio-material practices that produce the more subjective experiences of intimacy – such as trust, confidentiality, proximity and security (or lack thereof). Further, from my point of view technology is not the platform or venue for intimacies, but is at least potentially intimate. In therapy and counselling, as my analysis will illustrate, technology cannot be separated from experiences of intimacy nor reduced to mechanistic notions where it is associated with a passive platform for human-only action. Teletherapies thus provide a fruitful site for looking at more-than-human intimacies from this perspective.

Finally, digital intimacies, in their close connections with the virtual and immaterial worlds, also remind us that intimacy does not require physical proximity nor is it limited to the material presence of (at least) two human bodies. Thus, intimacy should not be understood through physical proximity only, especially as bodies and minds have capacities to communicate – to affect and become affected – largely in immaterial ways (Dernikos, 2018). In this chapter, I am interested in the ways in which sensory, material and affective registers prove crucial for well-being, regarding the way that these dimensions further inform the conditions of possibility for well-being (also Coffey, 2020: 4). These registers can operate at least partially virtually and in immaterial ways, as my analysis will show.

Data and methodology

For the purposes of my study, I conducted forty-one thematic interviews in which psychologists, psychotherapists, family counsellors, sex therapists, crisis workers and other counselling professionals were interviewed about their experiences concerning the role of technology during the global COVID-19 pandemic. The data were collected in the summer and autumn of 2020 by me via Zoom (a cloud-based video communications app), except one interview which was conducted via phone call. The interviews lasted about one to one-and-a-half hours with a wide variance in duration. The shortest interview lasted approximately forty-five minutes. The interviewee was a busy therapist who had allocated forty-five minutes – the time they usually reserve for individual clients – for the interview. The longest one lasted over three hours (in two parts): I interviewed two professionals twice because I felt that we could not go through all the basic themes at once. Altogether I interviewed thirty-nine individuals, of which two were inter-viewed twice.

The interviewees resided and worked across the country. All the inter-views were conducted in Finnish, even though many used several languages in their work, such as Finnish, Swedish, English or Russian. Some also worked partly outside Finland, i.e. they either travelled for work or had clients abroad. The informants were both male and female; the majority of them were women, and no one identified as non-binary, for instance. The youngest interviewees were in their twenties, whereas the oldest were in their late fifties. A great deal of them had several occupational qualifica-tions, and many were also working two (or more) jobs, such as having a main job in the social and health care sector and additionally acting as a private practitioner part-time. Many were also studying at the time of the interviews, or were planning to acquire more professional competence in the future. Nevertheless, I will only use general occupational titles – such as psychotherapist or family counsellor – in this chapter, since the exact combinations of education, background and job descriptions might risk the anonymity of my interlocutors.

The interviews were semi-structured: I wanted to keep the interviews informal, yet I also had a list of themes and questions I wanted to touch upon. During the interviews, I asked, for instance, about personal infor-mation, education and work history, their current employment and job description and the clientele. I also asked about COVID-19-related topics, such as their experiences concerning remote work, the shift to teletherapies, reflections on the pros and cons of different technologies and the perceived impact of the COVID-19 pandemic on the well-being of both the profes-sionals and their clients. The interviews were transcribed verbatim by a company specialising in transliteration services.

Almost all therapy and counselling services went virtual because of COVID-19 – a shift that many of my interviewees described as a 'digital leap', either in organisational or in personal terms. In March 2020 the first wave of the pandemic hit Finland and soon the government declared a state of emergency. The state of emergency lasted for three months in 2020. During that period the authorities were granted additional powers, primarily those laid down in the Emergency Powers Act. Restrictions on social distancing were placed and recommendations concerning remote working in both public and private sectors given, which influenced the working conditions of my interviewees but also the everyday lives of their clients. Also, KELA, the Finnish State Pension Office that provides rehabilitation psychotherapy and financially supports those who have been granted access, gave specific recommendations and changed its policies, meaning that face-to-face encounters were no longer favoured but video calls and phone calls were seen to be appropriate. This all meant that single informants rarely had any say on how they should organise their work, because they were subject to employer recommendations concerning remote work and social distancing or, if they were private practitioners, they followed KELA's instructions. A few of my interviewees were already very familiar with digital therapy and online counselling to the extent that they felt the pandemic did not really cause any change in terms of work. Some had job descriptions that involved the development of digital infrastructures, and several had at least some previous experience of teletherapies. Yet for most of my interviewees, daily or otherwise intensified remote client work was an unforeseen and unexpected experience. Disruption was perhaps experienced temporarily; however, in general, the interviewees found meeting clients at a distance convenient and they got used to it, even if the majority still preferred face-to-face meetings.

In this chapter, I analyse the interviews through the lens of intra-action, arguing that teletherapy practices can be best understood from the perspective provided by this approach. The notion of intra-action is a key element of Karen Barad's agential realism, signifying the mutual constitution of entangled agencies (Barad, 2007: 33). The term does not suggest two distinct entities who interact with each other, but rather sees agency as a dynamism of forces and not as an inherent property of an individual or human to be exercised (Barad, 2007: 33, 141). It thus stresses how agents, bodies and events are 'always already entangled'. In intra-action, all designated 'things' are constantly exchanging and diffracting, influencing and working inseparably (Barad, 2007). This means that the networks of technologies, humans, discourses, animals and institutions discussed are produced in and through practices that set the conditions for the ability to study them. These assemblages are therefore not pre-determined but formed through intra-actions or agentic forces that exist only in relation to one another (Sikka, 2021).

In other words, rather than seeing therapy sessions or counselling processes as situated interactions between a therapist and a client, I argue that they could best be understood through the lens of intra-action. The remote therapy and counselling sessions are about 'becoming' with the mutually constitutive networks of several actors, bodies, events and objects such as the therapist, the client, therapy modalities, technological infrastructures, psychic conditions, particular affordances of different mediums and material venues. Those processes of becoming have a transformative effect on all the parties as well as on the process itself. Hence, the lens of intra-actions allows attention to be paid to how the conditions of possibility for well-being are produced in the manifold processes of everyday life (McLeod, 2017; Coffey, 2020). In the case of mental well-being, this kind of lens is especially useful since it enables us to pay attention to those multiple agencies that take part in the production of psychic well-being – which is inherently tied to the relational networks of care.

From a Baradian approach, technical qualities and affordances only have limited capacities to act, but rather their capacities come to matter through the intra-actions. As my chapter will demonstrate, they themselves matter in different degrees and in several alternative ways that are, for instance, technical, affective, material or psychic. In other words, the open, participatory affordances of particular media cannot be reduced to the fixed technical attributes of particular technologies, as these affordances emerge only through the relationships between different practices, values and materials: something that becomes explicit when reflecting on the significance of capacity-building practices (Giraud, 2019). For instance, an analysis of my data stresses how video calls mediate, twist, limit and expand the therapeutic processes: in certain settings, the video screen enables something novel – shared connections, new observations, a novel feeling of intimacy and trust – to happen, whereas in other cases it limits the process by fostering a feeling of emotional distance, by omitting information or by distracting. Hence, even if in what follows I discuss two seemingly different aspects provided by technology in teletherapy practice, those aspects actually both stress how intimacy works across the series of intra-actions. Professionals and their clients, COVID-19 and related policies, material conditions, technological infrastructures and applications and technical qualities and user experiences re/de/assemble in various ways.

Intimate technologies

The shift to teletherapies was also a very concrete alteration in the way in which the therapy settings changed. Some of the interviewees were able to work from their offices, but most of them started to work remotely from their homes. There were vast differences in their preparedness: some already had a spare room and suitable technical equipment, whereas others had to start from zero. Clients also had to find new venues. For many, home became the new venue for therapy or counselling. If there were alternative preferences or if home was not a potential venue for sessions, the mobile technologies still allowed clients to make (video) calls from cars, offices, saunas, walks and so on. Reportedly, there were also clients who preferred to have a break from regular meetings until face-to-face meetings were again an option, but in those cases, the reasons were almost without exception related to intense care responsibilities and had nothing to do with difficulties in accessing suitable technologies.

The interviewees used mainly video calls and phone calls in their work. Several noted that even if video calls enable access to visual information, they still omit the amount of information – from seeing the body as a whole to a variety of gestures, and from general appearance to minor facial expressions – the therapists and counsellors were accustomed to. For instance, a psychotherapist referenced a newspaper article detailing why video meetings may feel burdensome, reflecting her own experiences: 'with my clients, I'm not like half a metre away from their face. It's like you're constantly reading small clues attentively, and the whole and its message is missing'. However, the video connection also enables access to new information or knowledge. In the following, the interviewee recalls how the shift to video calls has enabled him to make novel observations:

> Video calls brought me [in]to the homes of my clients and to the circumstances they live their everyday lives in. Certainly I was able to make novel observations. [...] Especially with those who have challenges with coordination, you really could notice the change of venue. Like someone just turns a washing machine on just before the appointment or disappears from a view for a while. (Psychotherapist)

While it is important to address relationality and entanglement, Eva Haifa Giraud (2019) argues that the ethics of exclusion should also be taken into account: the entities, practices and ways of being that are foreclosed when other entangled realities are materialised. From this perspective, the shift to digital therapies provides both novel entanglements with technology as well as the potential to block the actualisation of alternative realities. The above-cited psychotherapist, for instance, noted that the foreclosure of face-to-face meetings hindered many practical tasks that he had been doing with his clients. Yet it also contributes to the materialisation of an alternative entanglement, which in turn allowed the interviewee to access the everyday living conditions of his clients in an unforeseen way and to see the activities of his clients in a new light.

As already mentioned, several interviewees stated that it was a challenge not to be able to see their clients fully and thus access the amount of non-verbal information they were accustomed to. Yet there were also experts who felt that the exclusion of visual information served their professional goals. In the following excerpt, the interviewee describes herself as an auditory person, for whom visual information is secondary. The materiality of intimacy (Latimer and Gómez, 2019) works through the headphones and the voice – in this case, physical proximity in itself does not operate as a material intimacy, but rather the proximity of human voice that the headphones carry close to the ear in a very literal sense:

> I'm an auditory person in general [...] I don't even try to get that much out of my clients with my eyes, I get more. In a way the voice comes quite close to me, especially with headphones on, I feel the clients are really close to me and I hear a lot from their voices [...] Then I also think here I can freely, I have here more means to self-regulate than in a client meeting [...] I can sway [my] legs or sit cross-legged or twiddle my thumbs. In a way I can regulate my mood and proximity and distance more, I can maintain a suitable level of alertness. Because, well I don't know if I'm a little conventional but when clients come to my office I don't sit cross-legged in my chair. (Family counsellor)

Rather than relying on sight, the sense of hearing is important for the interviewee who describes herself as an 'auditory person'. This is an important reminder of how the technical affordances always work as part of assemblages – the capacities and agencies provided by video calls are a product of different entanglements, here stressing that visual and auditory information themselves do not have the ability to influence therapy sessions in pre-defined ways. Further, the interviewee finds the opportunity of being able to partially withdraw from view as entangled with experiences of proximity or distance, making it an example of how intimacies are made and unmade, entangled of and with multiple entangled materialities.

In a similar vein another interviewee, a psychologist, mentions clients for whom technology provides a possibility to use the chat function and write, rather than verbally express themselves: 'They then wrote their replies in the chat box and they were able to express their thoughts perhaps in a more comprehensive way than here at my office'. Both examples demonstrate that the newly found technical affordances enable the mobilisation of alternative means of communication, entangling such senses and modes of communication that may become marginalised in conventional face-to-face meetings. As Giraud (2019: 66) writes, the properties of any medium emerge only through its intra-actions within a particular assemblage. Here the properties of particular media technologies have consequences for the therapy sessions and for well-being. Yet they also highlight the changing degrees of comfort brought about by the shifting intra-actions – the new opportunities for feeling at ease and secure during the remote sessions.

The next interviewee had experience working for hotlines before her current work as a family counsellor. In the following, she reflects upon the perceived strengths of a phone call, which she associates with the possibility to reach out for support without having to show one's face. This is not about COVID-19 in particular, yet still demonstrates the perceived capacities of such technologies and mediums that have been increasingly in use because of the pandemic:

> [I] learnt the pros of a phone, like a person can vent one's anxious condition and whatever feelings without having to show their face, like you can just lie on the floor curled [up] and cry [in]to the phone. And also like someone who's a very shy and timid person can benefit from having the chance to speak from here and then someone will receive it all and respond. (Family counsellor)

The interviewee mentions the ability to just vent feelings, without having to show one's face. The invisibility enabled by phone calls disentangles clients from the anticipation concerning reciprocal communication, allowing them to lie down, cry and 'vent' feelings, reminding us that intimacy in its most conventional terms – familiarity with someone – is not regarded positive or desirable for all, nor seen as beneficial in every setting (Piras and Miele, 2019). The lack of familiarity enables an affective connection with someone – as a psychotherapist who also worked as a phone counsellor explained, the clients still seek a connection. Yet she also indicated that she feels less responsibility for hotline clients, with whom she does not form a long-term professional relationship and related commitment: 'Well I don't start like, patient-relationships there because I don't have anything, like background information or else concerning this person. Then I would be skating on thin ice if I started to build a responsible relationship there'. Yet it seems that anonymity also 'frees' clients from the expectations concerning reciprocal communication and continuation. Piras and Miele (2019), in their take on digital intimacy in patient-provider relations, differentiate between 'knowing the patient' and 'knowing about the patient'. In a similar manner, the interviewees cited above seem to associate the chat function or calls with a limited capacity to enhance their 'knowing about' the person seeking support or help, even if they enable access to a certain amount of information.

However, this also brings up questions related not only to the technical affordances provided by different technologies, but also in relation to intimacy. Here the accidental, potentially one-off anonymous encounters foster the socio-material conditions for intimacy: rather than an accumulation of proximity and trust, the intimate encounter is facilitated by distance and anonymity. Similar notions were advanced by several interviewees who noticed that for some clients anonymity is a pre-condition for seeking support or help, at least in the initial first steps. For instance, a psycho-therapist working for an organisation views the possibility of seeking support or help anonymously as 'extremely important', also stating that during the COVID-19 pandemic anonymous text chats provide a feasible way of reaching out. For many who are seeking support or advice, for instance, phone calls might prove challenging since family members may possibly stay within earshot, whereas chatting is often still possible in privacy. Thus, the data also challenges the binary between personal/impersonal in several ways by disrupting any presumptions of intimacy as something that evolves over time, requires in-depth knowledge and familiarity, and that can be accumulated – and capitalised upon – in therapy and counselling. Rather, the invisibility or anonymity allows the limits of one's privacy to be overcome.

Distancing capacities

The physical distance between a therapist and client is, however, seen as a problem by several interviewees. Proximity is often seen to enable a more intimate connection between a therapist or counsellor and a client. It is also assigned an important role in serving professional work as it enables presence, which in turn is considered a significant form of support. As an interviewee describes: 'capturing the feeling through the screen, well I haven't yet learnt how to do it, like if we start to be just quiet here, you stay there quiet and I stay here quiet, we're still lacking it, some sort of connection that we would still share if we were able to sit in the same room'. The physical distance here turns into mental and affective distance, or at least to limited or partial connection. In other words, and even if it is difficult to verbalise beyond the power of presence or similar descriptions, many refer to a trans-corporeal energetic force that supports the therapy events if the human bodies share space.

In the following excerpt, the screen is seen as a concrete barrier between the therapist and a client, which also prohibits the kind of support that the interviewee considers essential in the light of developmental psychology – even if she also mentions that she enjoys the possibility of adjusting the volume on her computer and can now hear clients better. Yet the video call stills marks a 'cut', excluding many practical exercises the interviewed psycho-therapist had integrated into her therapy practice. I here understand 'cuts' as referring to boundary-drawing processes that come to matter through what they reveal or conceal (Barad, 2007) and cuts make some aspects of the phenomenon visible but other aspects less so (see also Coleman and Ringrose, 2013). Here, the screen blocks the 'co-becoming' by establishing physical distance that in turn renders the therapist and the clients separate from each other, disentangling them in a manner that rather unmakes than makes intimacy – the interviewee associates distance with being alone. In the following, she recalls some of the reasons why many of the most practical tasks, from relaxation exercises to the tasks proffered by literature therapy, have been dropped:

> if they would go lie somewhere out of my sight away from the video connection I don't have any means to know what's going on. Like if some client gets really anxious, I cannot respond immediately and help. It would be possible in principle but the point of doing things together would be missing, like it would be more about me presenting or lecturing rather than us thinking together – I consider doing things together very important from the perspective of developmental psychology and developmentally, since many of my clients have been left without when children. Like they have had to get along alone, like the mother or the father or the parent or any adult would have been holding [their] hands and advised and showed them or played – like this remote work also distances from these kinds of things. Like then we are alone and in different places. (Psychotherapist)

In the following, it is not the distance itself but the feeling of distance that twists the therapy process. The exclusion of physical proximity is also fundamental here, but from another perspective than what was described above. If it was about the concrete distance mentioned above, here the distance would have affective and psychic relevance. The interviewee associates the foreclosure of proximity with different capacities. On one hand, the distance enables the client to talk about issues that are experienced as shameful and fosters a novel connection to such sides of personality that have previously been 'closed', yet on the other hand, distance has alienating capacities that make the therapist distant. Thus, distance – especially in the case of phone connection where invisibility hides a therapist within sight – has the capacity to undo intimacy to the extent that a therapist starts to feel like a fictional character:

> People are different in this matter, like some have even themselves put it into words that distance, and of course it has to do with their personality, distance has for instance opened up some sides they have found difficult to discuss face-to-face because of shame for instance, and then it has been very significant for their processes, like now there have been new dialogical connections to such sides of their personalities that have been closed, and it has been extremely positive. And then there are clients who experience it in a manner that [...] I might feel more remote or distant [...] Yet of course the phone connection makes it possible to more easily turn a therapist into some sort of a fictional character, like if it wasn't really a person but rather just a voice somewhere, like this kind of thing might become more visible [in person] than with video connection. (Psychotherapist)

Further, the change of venue itself bears significance. The therapeutic setting has been an important topic in several psychoanalytical theories, and the interviewees reflected upon the change of venue both from a concrete, material perspective and from a more symbolic perspective which also highlights the affective and psychic relevance of the therapy venue. For instance, one interviewee ponders: 'and what is the significance of the particular therapy room one enters [in]to and brings certain issues with oneself to and where those issues are kind of left too, like traditionally at least in some therapies it is considered quite important that there is this particular space and it stays unchangeable and it is safe, but now there was no "this space" like as a third'. Here, the interviewee refers to the therapy room as a 'third', pointing out how therapeutic space is, to start with, seen to be intra-acting in therapeutic processes. Similarly, a family counsellor I interviewed argued that the changes in the therapy setting – in particular, the impossibility to access the therapy room – changes the dynamics in a way that blocks therapeutic ideals from being realised:

> Well I kind of think that something therapeutic will remain unrealised when the clients didn't come. Even though at the same time there was a lot of good in that. Now I kind of am a guest at their homes and we're not in my kingdom and in a space I conquer as they don't come to my practice. Yet there's this another side that sometimes it was difficult to generate some sort of exploratory distance because they were in their home mood. (Family counsellor)

Another family counsellor says it was surprising to see how similar the remote sessions were, but also details some exceptions. She mentions a couple with whom violence, in particular self-harm, was an issue, relating that the other half (a non-violent partner) was a little hesitant to shift to remote sessions, saying something like 'you are there so far away, at a distance'. The interviewee associates this with the lack of trust in relation to how the situation evolves, since the client is unsure whether the situation will calm down, if it reaches a critical point, when the therapist is not in the same room. The agential power of a therapy room thus seems to vanish – because either it is not a part of the therapy assemblage at all (professionals and clients all at home or elsewhere) or only to a limited degree (therapist or counsellor working from their office but clients cannot access the venue in person) – in a way that shapes the intra-actions of therapy sessions in a significant manner.

She also spoke about a couple whose mutual relation was tense, recalling how they were a little cautious of talking because 'the atmosphere – may stay at home and hang over here', explaining that because the couple then continues to reside at home in the atmosphere created by the therapy session, this might prove a challenge for them. Atmospheres, even if individually felt, always reach beyond individual subjectivities and belong to collective situations (Anderson, 2009; Seyfert, 2012). The above-mentioned cautiousness also highlights how atmospheres, even if their purposeful creation, maintenance and harnessing have limits (Kolehmainen and Mäkinen, 2021), are co-produced and intensified through entangled agencies. In other words, the clients are wary of creating such an affective atmosphere that might make it difficult for them to live out their everyday lives, and rather seek to avoid tangible tensions. Here affect, intimacy and atmosphere are central, pointing to the ways in which virtual, immaterial intimacies play a central role in the 'unfoldings' of everyday life.

Conclusion

Above, I have provided insights into teletherapy and remote counselling during the COVID-19 pandemic by utilising the Baradian concept of intra-action. Drawing upon detailed analysis of interviews with therapy and counselling professionals, I have further introduced two different sections: one which focuses on technology as intimate, and another that discusses the distancing and alienating capacities technology is perceived to have and is experienced as having in therapy settings. Contrary to what one might think, these two are not opposites: the distancing capacities are not distinct from those capacities that generate the feelings of proximity. Rather, they both exemplify the distributed agencies of entangled materialities. For Barad, it is the inseparability or entanglement of technologies, media, nature, humans and the environment that form the basis of her realist ontology (Barad, 2007). Yet from a Baradian approach, it is important to bear in mind that agency is not an attribute. From a Baradian approach, matter only becomes meaningful through intra-actions with other objects and 'matterings': matter's significance is only brought forth through ever-changing relationships with other entities. In the case of teletherapies, different technologies, software, platforms, applications and affordances come to matter in new ways – but various other matterings also come from homes and family settings, and from national COVID-19 restrictions to the different therapy approaches. Affects here are products of intra-actions but they also intra-act within particular assemblages, further contributing to the makings of intimacies (or lack thereof).

While in this chapter I have focused on technology, different phenomena from COVID-19 in itself and related policies (such as restricted access to therapy venues and other office spaces) to those particular issues that are special to therapy and counselling sessions and processes (such as psychic conditions) all come to matter in teletherapy practices. Yet as I have illustrated above (often mobile) technologies, platforms, software and applications in particular have been transformed into essential agents in the maintenance and implementation of mental health care. COVID-19 has enacted the agency of mundane, everyday objects in remarkable ways (Sikka, 2021) and this also is evident in teletherapies. However, the increased reliance on technological infrastructures in the health care sector is not a random nor a top-down process, but workers engage in the processes of making technologies work in a situated manner (Schwennesen, 2021). This becomes very visible in the ways in which the socio-material constitution of intimacy is 'coordinated' by my interviewees: they, for instance, invest in regulating proximity and distance by adjusting the volume or screen view and try to make the technology accommodate their specific preferences by favouring either video calls or phone calls, or make attempts to consider what the differing personal characteristics of their clients might mean when the settings change.

Last but not least, my chapter also valorises several aspects concerning the more subjective feelings for and of intimacy, like the affective experiences of trust, proximity, confidentiality and security. These have to do with care and caring relations. Piras and Miele (2019) summarised their findings by arguing that one essential dimension of remote provider-patient relationships is that intimacy is experienced by patients as a feeling of being taken care of. My study indicates that the feeling of being taken care of – as well as the feeling of being able to care for clients – can be both intensified and heightened through technologies. For instance, rapport building is experienced as being both facilitated and undermined by different teletherapy practices. Further, my study highlights that in mental care, agency is distributed across various human and non-human actors: from professionals and clients to therapy venues, from psychic conditions to legislation, from technological equipment and software apps to economic factors. Hence, it departs from the more traditional notions of care, where care is seen as a human matter only and where the categories of caring- and cared-for play major roles (see Puig de la Bellacasa, 2012, 2017). Technological solutions might carry caring qualities with them, but not in any straightforward way. Different intra-actions iteratively constitute different phenomena and exclude others (Juelskjær and Schwennesen, 2012: 79–80). My study shows how exclusion has open-ended consequences for therapeutic processes, materialising alternative entangled realities (Giraud, 2019). The foreclosure of in-person meetings, and the related shift to teletherapies, materialise new entanglements that constitute more-than-human care in ways that can also enrich therapy and counselling practices.

Note

1 Marjo Kolehmainen's work was supported by 'Intimacy in Data-Driven Culture', a research consortium funded by the Strategic Research Council at the Academy of Finland (327391).

References

Anderson, B. (2009), 'Affective Atmospheres', *Emotion, Space and Society*, 2, 77–81.

Barad, K. M. (2007), *Meeting the Universe Halfway: Quantum Physics and the Entanglement of Matter and Meaning* (Durham, NC: Duke University Press).

Berlant, L. (2000), 'Intimacy: A Special Issue', in *Intimacy*, L. Berlant (ed.) (Chicago, IL: University of Chicago Press), 1–8.

Coffey, J. (2020), 'Assembling Wellbeing: Bodies, Affects and the "Conditions of Possibility" for Wellbeing', *Journal of Youth Studies* (online, 2020). doi: https://doi.org/10.1080/13676261.2020.1844171

Coleman, R., and Ringrose, J. (2013), 'Introduction: Deleuze and Research Methodologies', in *Deleuze and Research Methodologies*, R. Coleman and J. Ringrose (eds) (Edinburgh: Edinburgh University Press), 1–22.

De Luca, R., and Calabrò, R. S. (2020), 'How the COVID-19 Pandemic Is Changing Mental Health Disease Management: The Growing Need of Telecounseling in Italy', *Innovations in Clinical Neuroscience*, 17:4–6, 16–17.

Dernikos, B. P. (2018), 'Reviving Ghostly Bodies: Student-Teacher Intimacies as Affective Hauntings', in *Affective Inequalities in Intimate Relationships*, T. Juvonen and M. Kolehmainen (eds) (London: Routledge), 218–30.

Giraud, E. H. (2019), *What Comes After Entanglement?* (Durham, NC: Duke University Press).

Juelskjær, M., and Schwennesen, N. (2012), 'Intra-Active Entanglements – An Interview with Karen Barad', *Kvinder, Køn & Forskning*, 1–2. doi: https://doi.org/10.7146/kkf.v0i1-2.28068

Kember, S., and Zylinska, J. (2012), *Life After Media: Mediation as a Vital Process* (Cambridge, MA: MIT Press).

Kinnunen, T., and Kolehmainen, M. (2019), 'Touch and Affect: Analysing the Archive of Touch Biographies', *Body & Society*, 25:1, 29–56.

Kolehmainen, M., and Juvonen, T. (2018), 'Introduction: Thinking With and Through Affective Inequalities', in *Affective Inequalities in Intimate Relationships*, T. Juvonen, and M. Kolehmainen (eds) (London: Routledge), 1–16.

Kolehmainen, M., and Mäkinen, K. (2021), 'Affective Labour of Creating Atmospheres', *European Journal of Cultural Studies*, 24:2, 448–63. doi: https://doi.org/10.1177/13675494198860218

Latimer, J., and López Gómez, D. (2019), 'Intimate Entanglements: Affects, More-Than-Human Intimacies and the Politics of Relations in Science and Technology', *The Sociological Review*, 67:2, 247–63.

Latour, B. (2005), *Reassembling the Social: An Introduction to Actor-Network-Theory* (Oxford: Oxford University Press).

Lykke, N. (2018), 'When Death Cuts Apart: On Affective Difference, Compassionate Companionship and Lesbian Widowhood', in *Affective Inequalities in Intimate Relationships*, T. Juvonen and M. Kolehmainen (eds) (London: Routledge), 109–25.

Lykke, N. (2019), 'Co-Becoming With Diatoms: Between Posthuman Mourning and Wonder in Algae Research', *Catalyst: Feminism, Theory, Technoscience*, 5:2, 1–25.

McLeod, K. (2017), *Wellbeing Machine: How Health Emerges from the Assemblages of Everyday Life* (Durham, NC: Carolina Academic Press).

Paasonen, S. (2018a), 'The Infrastructures of Intimacy', in *Mediated Intimacies*, R. Andreassen, *et al.* (eds) (London: Routledge), 103–16.

Paasonen, S. (2018b), 'Networked Affect', in *Posthuman Glossary*, R. Braidotti and M. Hlavajova (eds) (London: Bloomsbury Academic), 283–5.

Piras, E., and Miele, F. (2019), 'On Digital Intimacy: Redefining Provider–Patient Relationships in Remote Monitoring', *Sociology of Health & Illness*, 41:S1, 116–31.

Puig de la Bellacasa, M. (2012), '"Nothing Comes Without Its World": Thinking with Care', *The Sociological Review*, 60:2, 197–216.

Puig de la Bellacasa, M. (2017), *The Matters of Care* (Minneapolis, MN: University of Minnesota Press).

Reay, R. E., Looi, J. C., and Keightley, P. (2020), 'Telehealth Mental Health Services During COVID-19: Summary of Evidence and Clinical Practice', *Australasian Psychiatry*, 28:5, 514–16. doi: https://doi.org/10.1177/1039856220943032

Schwennesen, N. (2021), 'Between Repair and Bricolage: Digital Entanglements and Fragile Connections in Dementia Care Work in Denmark', in *Socio-Gerontechnology: Interdisciplinary Critical Studies of Ageing and Technology* (1st edition), A. Peine, B. L. Marshall, W. Martin, and L. Neven (eds) (London: Routledge), 175–89. doi: https://doi.org/10.4324/9780429278266

Seyfert, R. (2012), 'Beyond Personal Feelings and Collective Emotions: Toward a Theory of Social Affect', *Theory, Culture & Society*, 29:6, 27–46. doi: https://doi.org/10.1177/0263276412438591

Sikka, T. (2021), 'Feminist Materialism and COVID-19: The Agential Activation of Everyday Objects', *NORA – Nordic Journal of Feminist and Gender Research*, 29:1, 4–16, doi: https://doi.org/10.1080/08038740.2020.1825119

Silver, Z., Coger, M., Barr, S., and Drill, R. (2020), 'Psychotherapy at a Public Hospital in the Time of COVID-19: Telehealth and Implications for Practice', *Counselling Psychology Quarterly* (online, 2020). doi: https://doi.org/10.1080/09515070.2020.1777390

Stewart, K. (2017), 'In the World that Affect Proposed', *Cultural Anthropology*, 32:2, 192–8.

Tsing, A. (2015), *The Mushroom at the End of the World* (Princeton, NJ: Princeton University Press).

Zengin, A. (2016), 'Violent Intimacies: Tactile State Power, Sex/Gender Transgression, and the Politics of Touch in Contemporary Turkey', *Journal of Middle East Women's Studies*, 12:2, 225–45.

Part II

The politics of affect: Spatial and
societal entanglements

4

The empathiser's new shoes: The discomforts of empathy as white feminist affect

Andrea Lobb

A local preface to discomfort

There is a bad smell in here. It wends its way down the length of the carriage, passing over the faces of the patrons of the No. 86 tram in whose company I'm travelling through the heart of my home city of Melbourne on this late autumn afternoon in the year 2019. As we move down Bourke Street, circle past the grand Victorian Parliament House, there is no escaping it. No averted gaze or phone-riveted stare can block the powerful, olfactory truth: here we are bound together in an unpleasant fug. Someone (but who?) has breached the unspoken rule of public transport: do not trespass on another's personal space, and never, but never, get up their nose. Yet, Lord, now here we are, sitting or standing in close confinement; necks craned, heads choreographed in the delicate art of not noticing a thing – what the sociologist Erving Goffman once called the 'civil inattention of modern public space' – some rearing back with a trace of disdain, just so it's clear: 'mistakes were made … but not by me!'

At this moment, I'm assuming the collective awkwardness will dissipate as such moments usually do, along with the unedifying air that provoked it. But then, unexpectedly, a woman starts speaking, and I glance over. The first thing that I register is that she is black, an Indigenous woman – in her fifties perhaps. I'm startled by her presence, and then surprised at how taken aback I am at seeing a member of a First Nations people on a tram in the Central Business District. (What is she doing here?) Notwithstanding the decades of avowed multiculturalism in Australia, I actually can't remember the last time I saw an Indigenous person on a tram like this, crammed full with the regular city commuter crowd. On what passes for an average day, the Melbourne metropolis rises up along the Yarra River sparkling like the Lethe, and there are few prompts to sting the white 'quiet majority' into awareness of the original peoples of the land upon which this city was brutally, at times murderously, 'settled'. It is not that I forget this fact, exactly. I neither remember, nor forget. Most days, in much the same way, I neither forget nor remember that I am white. But the unexpected proximity of an Indigenous woman shifts something in my awareness of where and who I am, and I shift uncomfortably in my seat.

Perhaps it is this awkward shuffle that attracts her gaze. Because now she looks me right in the eye and declares out loud, for all to hear: 'Ewwwwwwww, she *farted!* What a *stink!*' 'No, no', I think in some desperation: 'but it wasn't me!' I don't want this public exposure, this embarrassment. I scramble to recover equilibrium while split-second judgments flash through my mind as likely facts-of-the-matter before I even know I'm party to them, let alone signed on for them. Who is this woman? She looks rough, poor, unkempt, down-and-out, definitely out of place (!) in this crowd of business and office workers. As the tram lurches forward, a heavy silence of shared/unshared history sways between us: an amalgam of accusation, shame, and, yes, this stink. It could cling to a body as it passes by – but to whose body exactly? Hers? Mine?

Only at this point do I notice that, without being conscious of it, I've drawn my knees tightly together. Folded my hands neatly atop my smoothed and skirted lap. Suddenly, I feel very white and ultra-respectable. Who could possibly mistake me as the source of an unpleasant smell? Or any unpleasantry at all? Heaven forfend. No, I can be pretty confident this accusation will not stick, not to this white body, not to this gentle hand. The hidden force field of white, middle-class privilege has an automatic sensor and I feel how it has activated spontaneously now and is humming unobtrusively all around me: my halo. My body knows this before I do, and it has adopted the position of respectable white femininity like a call to arms. And here's the thing: once restored to a sense of (relative) safely that is the assumed entitlement of 'commuting while white', I realise I've really got nothing to worry about here. Balance returned, I start to feel sorry for the woman opposite me, who's probably worried (not without cause) that everyone will assume that it is *she* who is the trouble here; the cause of unruly disruption, the break in civility, the source of the stink. My response to her now takes a decidedly compassionate turn. I feel concerned. Tolerant. Poor thing. 'It must be really awful for her, to have to constantly face racial prejudice in this country', my good, empathetic self is eager to announce – and not without sincerity or genuine solidarity either. And yet, it flickers unsteadily, uneasily – this empathic identification – and before I know it, it has ricocheted, turned back, and coiled itself around my nostrils with a distinct whiff of offensiveness all its own.

Introduction

I begin with this scene – inviting you, dear reader, to lurch alongside me for a few moments on a crowded tram – because in this everyday encounter lies something of the living entanglements of empathy, race and intimate affect that the following contribution attempts to theorise. The central aim of this chapter is to discuss how and why the capacity for empathy – so long celebrated in Anglo-American feminism – no longer appears to be such a straightforward ethical or epistemic virtue when read through the double lens of affect and critical race theory. A fortiori, it loses, I suggest, its secure tenure as a feminist virtue. Drawing on the critical insights of cultural theorists of affect who take a special interest in empathy (Pedwell, 2014, 2016; Hemmings, 2012), the argument foregrounds the empathy of the white feminist as an acutely ambivalent affect tied up in complex ways with the asymmetrical power relations of race.

With a focus on how inequalities are both reproduced and disrupted through circulations of affect, this chapter offers a reading of (white) empathy as a striking example of an affective practice that can re-entrench, as much as resist, the dynamics of race privilege and oppression. This ambivalent potential, I argue, escapes proper critical attention when the intimacy of empathetic relationships (like intimacy in general) is afforded an unexamined normative positivity (i.e. when both empathy and intimacy are automatically deemed, by default, to be 'good'). In challenging this monochromatic view of empathy, this chapter aims to contribute to the general remit of this collection to mobilise affect theory in the service of reassessing some of the hardier pre-conceptions (such as 'positive closeness') that attend notions of intimacy in the standard sociological and psychological literatures (see Kolehmainen, Lahti and Lahad's Introduction to this volume, p. 1).

To that end, the opening section diagnoses a specific form of 'empathy trouble' that haunts the feminist consciousness of white-settler societies like my own in Australia. The chapter then explores why disquiet and moral ambivalence come to permeate the efforts of the white feminist subject who wants to maintain her empathetic identifications with the victims of racial oppression, yet must divest herself of wilful ignorance regarding the potential for a white woman's empathy to reproduce race privilege and myths of 'white innocence', and to further ingrain the affective dynamics of colonisation. Attention to the imbrications of racial domination and the intimacies of affect,[1] I argue, dislodges the taken-for-granted normative 'goodness' so often ascribed to empathy within feminist theory. To explain why such a dislodgement is called for, the next section delineates the contours of this specific 'empathy trouble' in closer detail.

Empathy trouble

Men [*sic*] make their own history, but they do not make it as they please; they do not make it under self-selected circumstances, but under circumstances existing already, given and transmitted from the past. The tradition of all dead generations weighs like a nightmare on the brains of the living.

Karl Marx (1852)

We make our own history of affective intimacy, but of course we don't make it just as we please. If the feminist reception of affect theory partakes of the joyful potential conveyed in Spinoza's observation that 'we do not even know of what affections we are capable, nor the extent of our power' (quoted in Deleuze, 1990: 226), it must also engage with what we might call (after Ahmed, 2017) the darker 'killjoyful' apprehension of how affect also constitutes and endlessly re-animates the force-fields of social power and oppression. This latter critical impulse bears witness to how living bodies affect each other in ways that can transmit, as much as they can transform, inherited nightmares from the past. In the following discussion, I examine how the trope of empathy in white feminist theory offers a particularly rich site for interrogating this duality of promise and peril; of affective transmission and transformation.

At the core of my argument is a claim that white feminists in colonised-settler nation-states, like my own in Australia, have serious trouble with empathy in relation to their non-white and Indigenous 'sisters'. This empathy trouble, however, is not appropriately understood by the diagnosis of a lack of empathetic capacity. It is not (simply) that white women fail to empathise with bla(c)k women (although they can fail in this sense too, and often do). Rather, the kind of trouble I am concerned with here is often found right at the heart of explicit 'empathy projects' proposed as humanitarian and anti-racist agendas; paradoxically, it can be present alongside the most fervent enthusiasm for 'walking a mile in another person's shoes'. For this reason, it does not reveal itself to critical scrutiny when the only place we dare look is under the spotlight thrown by the category of 'empathy deficits' (on this point, see Pedwell, 2014).

White feminist theory has never been exactly lacking in empathy. Many Anglo-American feminist thinkers explicitly identify the cultivation of the empathetic imagination (see Nussbaum, 1997), or the capacity to empathise sensitively with the plight of others, as integral to social, political and moral progress and the ethics of care (see Meyers, 2016; Noddings, 2010). Yet, I will argue here, when it comes to forging intimate-political affective bonds of feminist solidarity with bla(c)k, Muslim, Indigenous or 'third world' women, we white feminists not only have serious trouble with our empathy; there is also a certain sense in which we 'must' have trouble with it.

To get an intimation of this paradoxical trouble you can get into even though – or even because – you have empathy in spades, we might turn to some of the problematising genealogies of Western moral affects and sentiments offered by scholars such as Amit Rai (2002), Kyla Schuller (2018) and Carolyn Pedwell (2014, 2016). In each of these careful works of genealogical reconstruction, Western discourses of moral affect and sentiment are revealed to have a deep, if disavowed, connections with the history of white and European imperialism. They get deployed as discourses of legitimation for the colonisation of Indigenous peoples under the guise of fulfilling the project of moral and civilising human 'development' (even if the notion of 'sympathy' also serves progressive agendas such as the Abolitionist movement in the United States (on this point, see Rai, 2002: xi)). What these critical genealogies of sentimental affect show is the extent to which humanist (and avowedly 'anti-racist') agendas can function, paradoxically, as the sentimental 'arm' of a white racist social imaginary. This has led critics such as Pedwell to conclude that the cultural politics of empathy within Western liberal-style democracies is itself in urgent need of decolonisation (Pedwell, 2014, 2016).

In this context, there is likewise something problematic when white feminists call for more empathy for 'poor, brown women', for Indigenous women, or the 'average third world woman'[2] in the absence of any critical interrogation of how colonising power and supremacist assumptions can travel within the discourses and practices of white empathy itself.

For Schuller, contemporary feminist theories of affect need to look more closely at the ambivalent roots of the Western genealogies of sentimental affect in order to note that these were not automatically or always on the side of the subaltern or resistance to racism: they are also found to be internal to the discourse of white supremacy (Schuller, 2018). The prospect that a well-cultivated capacity for empathy can operate as a technique of white privilege and power intimates the kind of empathy trouble that haunts white feminist thought today. To place the affirmations of empathy as a virtue – such as we find in Nussbaum (1997), Noddings (2010) and Meyers (2016), among many others – alongside the problematisation of empathy by feminist 'trouble-makers' – such as Pedwell (2014, 2016), Hemmings (2012), Ngo (2017) and others – reveals the degree to which empathy is a sort of normative 'duck-rabbit' in contemporary Anglophone feminist theory. What appears from one angle to be an anti-racist, humanitarian, ethical and epistemic feminist virtue, from the other looks closer to a white feminist vice par excellence.

But how can the affective response of empathising with others be guilty of reinforcing (rather than redressing) oppressive power structures? Consider, by way of example, the phenomenon of 'himpathy' identified by philosopher Kate Manne as a feature of the affective landscape of misogyny. 'Himpathy', Manne contends, occurs when pre-existing sexist ideology effectively derails or hijacks the affective response of concern owed a victim of sexual assault or harassment. Rather than empathy and support flowing to the (usually female) victim, it can instead flow to the (usually male) perpetrator when, say, the latter is a 'golden-boy': one of the privileged young men in prestigious institutions whose promising careers (as lawyers, high court judges, etc.) would be imperilled (and their lives 'ruined') by a rape charge, for example (Manne, 2017).

An analogous misdirection of empathy from victim to perpetrator can also occur in the intimate affective landscape of racism. Ruby Hamad's critique of 'white woman's tears' points precisely to such a pattern of mis-allocation of empathy in the affective dynamics between white and black women. She contends there is a predictable sequence that unfolds in those intense moments when a white woman is pulled up or confronted on her racism by a woman of colour, particularly when this occurs between women who understood themselves to be intimates, or allies. The former declares she is misunderstood, hurt by the accusation of being a racist and cries 'white tears'. Reacting to those tears, the (white) bystanders who witness the interaction respond with a flood of sympathy to the distressed white woman, and offer her their emotional support and comfort, chastising the black woman for her 'aggression'. For Hamad, this mobilisation of collective feeling (through the stimulation of empathy for fellow white women) is a secret power ploy that reasserts racial domination. The trouble here cannot be described as an empathy deficit because the racism is not enacted through an absence of empathy, but rather through its presence. It is not that empathy is missing from the scene, but rather that a subterranean racism has already pre-determined the channels that this transmission of affect will most readily take, reconfirming those 'proper' assemblages forged by (white) intimates through the strategic mobilisation and (mis-)direction of affect. The reinforcement of intimacy between the white women is a circulation of affect that simultaneously reinforces the exclusion of the black woman. While the empathetic response in question (to white tears) is, arguably, responsively attuned in one sense, it is also mis-attuned by the racial power dynamics in play. As a channel through which affective states are transmitted from one subject to another, the mobilisation of empathy does not always or necessarily bridge racial divides: it can, as in this case, deepen them.

Black skin, white empathies

To further explore the ambivalence of white empathy and the affective intimacies that it can reinforce and refuse, I turn now briefly to a discussion by feminist philosopher Miranda Fricker on the relationship between empathy, racism and testimonial injustice (Fricker, 2006). Fricker describes how a central element of the injustice of racism is that it deflates the credibility granted to the testimony of black people. By way of illustration, she invokes the case of the fictional character Tom Robinson, the black man falsely accused of raping a white woman in Harper Lee's classic novel *To Kill a Mockingbird*.

Giving testimony before the jury as to what he was doing in the yard of a white woman, Tom explains that he sometimes helped Mayella out with her chores 'because her life seemed hard to him and he felt sorry for her' (quoted in Fricker, 2006). That a black man should express sympathy for the misery of a white woman or empathise with the hardships of her life has an abrupt and explosive effect on the white audience. It triggers currents of outrage in the white courtroom, and Tom himself 'immediately realises his "mistake"'. But what mistake, exactly, has he committed? Why does the prospect of a black man empathising with the unhappiness and bleak circumstances in the life of a white woman – and his expression of concern for her – create such blank fury in the white subjects who witness it? For Fricker, what this indicates is the racist jury's 'perverted' reading of the expression of 'natural sympathy' that one person might feel for the hardships of another. But in my view, this misses something: by confirming the 'innocence' of empathy as a 'natural response to suffering' this interpretation makes it impossible to recognise that the imbrications of empathy and racial power are not, in fact, innocent at all.

What unfolds in the courtroom in the face of a black man's empathy might also be read as an illustration of how thoroughly context-dependent the meaning of empathy is. Rather than a 'simple' goodness untouched by power relations, every empathetic response is embedded in the social and affective fields of power. When a black man empathises with the plight of a poor white woman, he actually commits a serious breach of the 'feeling rules' (Hochschild, 1979) of white supremacy: these rules insist that empathy and 'feeling sorry for' is a prerogative of white privilege. Empathy belongs here to the white man (arguably, even more so to the white woman), if such a white subject deigns to feel it 'downwards' for the racially inferiorised other. If a black man empathises with a white woman, he has overstepped the mark and forgotten his 'proper station' in the social world. Paying attention to the rules of the social field, we might say that he goes against the 'natural order' as defined by the ideology of white supremacy: he is empathising 'up' and hence showing himself to be 'uppity'. By feeling empathy for Mayella, Tom is acting as a black subject who can recognise and respond with concern to the vulnerability of a white subject. To the white supremacist, for a black man to hold (and, even worse, publicly declare) that he has such knowledge of white vulnerability amounts to an act of seditious rebellion.

What does this fleeting glimpse of 'forbidden' empathy felt by the black subject for a white woman do to the proposal that empathy be conceived as an epistemic virtue that can correct the wrongs of testimonial injustice caused by racial prejudice? To my mind, it helps make more explicit whose empathy exactly is being envisaged here. It only makes sense to grant empathy such corrective power if in fact the empathy we are talking about is allocated as a virtue of the dominant subject. In other words, it is not the cultivation of Tom's empathetic imagination that is the focus of attention. It is not the subordinated subject whose ethico-epistemic virtues are to be the object of any cultivation, but the more powerful subject who can engage in 'empathetic listening'. The risk here is that this empathetic relation, even as it promises to restore epistemic agency to the other, subtly reproduces an implicit power asymmetry that takes away with one hand what it gives with another. Here is the paradox: Tom Robinson could exercise all the empathy in the world, but it is not his practice or capacity for empathy that is being proposed as the lever with which to effectively shift the scene of epistemic injustice resulting from racism. The agency still lies disproportionately with the empathising disposition of the dominant white subject. Affirming the epistemic virtue of the (white) empathetic listener as the chief strategy to combat the testimonial injustices of racism risks inadvertently re-inscribing the power dynamic of inequality between black and white subjects. Empathy (as virtue) still 'belongs' to the dominant white subject.

Wilfully ignorant empathy

Sandra Bartky has noted the presence of 'powerful ideological systems that serve to reassure whites that the suffering of darker-skinned Others is not of their doing' (Bartky, 2002: 154). In this section I explore whether it might be possible for white subjects to respond empathetically to the suffering of racialised others, yet in ways that establish powerful affective systems that likewise bolster their reassurance that this suffering is not 'of their doing'? Here I propose that one serious risk in framing empathy as a virtue in feminist and moral theory is that it may offer the affective correlate of the ideological reassurance of which Bartky warns. The subject who takes her empathy for another's suffering to be evidence of ethical practice and epistemic virtue thereby sets up an affective reticulation of 'good feeling about being good' – thereby garnering an implied reassurance of moral rectitude with regard to the plight of the other (with whose suffering she empathises). The virtuous white empathiser gets both character reference and moral alibi that can facilitate 'not knowing' about the viciousness of the structural location she actually occupies as a privileged beneficiary of a racist society. The trouble I am attempting to flag here is that when 'we' white feminists conceptualise empathy as a humanist and anti-racist virtue in the specific context of a colonised white-settler society, this comes perilously close to affording just the sort of reassurance through which the myths of white innocence gain their ideological purchase.

In such a context, the affective system of wilfully ignorant empathy – like all forms of wilful ignorance – requires a careful maintenance of strategic not-knowing at the heart of any explicit commitment to know or under-stand (in this case, about the suffering of the other). In common with exam-ples of the misallocation or mal-distribution of empathy (described above in the case of Hamad's 'white tears' and Manne's 'himpathy'), the trouble here is not a matter of empathy being absent or missing from the scene. However, in contrast to those manifestations of empathy trouble, the harms of wilfully ignorant empathy don't come about through the misallocation of empa-thetic attention, resources or concern to the 'wrong' object. Rather, insofar as the capacity to empathise with suffering is taken by itself to be demon-strative of moral character, it offers license to the virtuous white empathiser to not know something essential about the very suffering to which her empathy gives her some (however limited or distorted) phenomenological access: namely, it blocks knowledge of how she stands (as a participant and beneficiary, if not an active signatory, of white racism) in some structural complicity with the causes of that suffering.

This is not to rule out that a white feminist might get some phenom-enological insight into what it 'feels like' to live under the weight of rac-ist oppression by cultivating her empathetic identification with black, Indigenous women or women from the so-called 'third world' (although for an incisive dissection of the limits of this knowledge, see Ngo's essay (2017) on 'embodied empathy and political tourism').[3] Yet, while she might be empathetically attuned to such experiences of suffering, where this empathy simultaneously generates a feedback loop of good feelings about herself, this reassurance can affectively reinforce the maintenance of wilful ignorance regarding her structural complicity in the racist system responsible for that suffering.

I don't mean to suggest here, of course, that all empathy of white peo-ple is wilfully ignorant in this way. What I want to draw attention to is the potential for white empathy to be wilfully ignorant, and to warn that may be quite possible to manifest both a highly sensitive, affective respon-siveness to the lived experience of another's suffering, and yet still main-tain a blank disavowal of any implication or complicity in the structural or systemic situation that lies at its causal root. Even worse, by framing empathy as the sort of thing good and virtuous people do, the affiliation with the project of cultivating empathy might even increase the ease of the latter's denial. In short, where it operates as a confirmation of the white empathiser's 'reassurance that this suffering of the darker-skinned Others is not of her doing' (Bartky, 2002: 154), we white feminists are still deep in empathy trouble.

The white feminist's two empathies

What else might a white-settler Australian feminist come to know, if her empathy with Indigenous women were not of the wilfully ignorant sort described above? And what remains of the 'empathy projects' of white feminism if the white, middle-class investment in empathy as a virtue is potentially complicit in the affective 'habitus' of white racism itself, and particularly of privileged white womanhood?

Several Anglo-American feminist moral philosophers have endorsed empathy as a method of 'de-centring' from the narcissistic preoccupations with the needs and perspective of the self in order to become receptive and attentive to the experience and vulnerability of others (Noddings, 2010). Yet, this de-centring has arguably not been extended radically enough to include the normative decolonising of Western empathy itself (as revealed in the problematising genealogical constructions of the discourses of affect and sentiment in Pedwell, Rai and Schuller). Were it to be deployed as a more radically de-centring force, then 'walking a mile in the shoes of the other' may well include an unscheduled encounter with an uncanny double of the good and civilised white self, but this time perceived afresh from the 'elsewhere' of the oppressed social margins. Such a shock-inducing swivel of perspective was, arguably, demanded of white Australian feminists of the academy when in 1994 Indigenous feminist Aileen Moreton-Robinson first published *Talkin' Up to the White Woman*. There, Moreton-Robinson observed how

> White women participated in gendered racial oppression by deploying the subject position [of the] middle-class white woman both unconsciously and consciously, informed by an ideology of true white womanhood, which positioned Indigenous women as less feminine, less human and less spiritual than themselves. Although the morphology of colonialism has changed, it persists in discursive and cultural practices. (Moreton-Robinson, 2000: 24)

The 'empathy trouble' of white post-colonial feminism, as I have attempted to formulate it here, comes out of the uneasy confrontation with the following question: to what extent do the ongoing attachments to empathy as a (white) feminist virtue still operate 'informed by the ideology of true white womanhood, that by implication positions its target – the Indigenous woman – as less'? When do the affective habits of 'whiteliness' (to recall Marilyn Frye's memorable phrase (Frye, 1992)) intermingle with the 'feeling rules' of middle-class femininity to cultivate a particular mode of white empathy that reinforces the inequalities of race relations, even in the moment of expressing a passionate humanist solidarity with its victims? And how deep does this current of 'empathy trouble' run as a tension that disrupts (even as it aspires to build) any meaningful solidarity between white and Indigenous feminists? Consider, for example, the repudiation and fierce reproach to white feminists sounded by the Australian Indigenous writer Melissa Lucashenko:

> because you insist on burying your own racism under an avalanche of pseudo-solidarity; because you do not know whose traditional land you stand on; because you are baffled by the idea that Black women are justified in fearing you; because you want to 'help' Black women; because you presume that having attempted our genocide you can attempt our ideological resurrection; because you think that Indigenous culture survived for millennia in this country *without* Black feminists, and because of your imperialist attitude that you alone hold a meaningful concept of female strength and solidarity, for these and for many other reasons, we Black feminists are not a part of the Australian women's movement. (Lucashenko, 1994: 24, original emphasis)

Given the extent of the trouble discussed above, should a white feminist still persist in cultivating her empathetic identifications (with her non-white, Indigenous 'sisters') at all, let alone in the name of a commitment to anti-racist politics? While it seems essential to deconstruct the positive account of empathy as virtue in white feminist theory, the deeper purpose of making empathy trouble in this way is not, ultimately, to abandon the idea of empathy as a site of feminist investment altogether. It is instead to accept the necessity for a continual problematisation of that investment.

If wilfully ignorant empathy can sustain racism under a rhetoric of a civilising humanism, this does not preclude it from also having the potential to function differently: it can also be a method of a deflation and 'unlearning' of the affective habits of white racism. This is why it remains both 'indispensable and dangerous' (see McCarthy, 2009: 8). This duality in normative potential is reflected in the fact that 'taking the perspective of the other' can be undertaken in either a 'thin' or a more profoundly transformative or disruptive way. When de-centring is sufficiently radical it can generate affective states that dislocate and prime the deflationary unlearning of the habits of white privilege and narcissism. 'Empathising while white' in this more radical way means relinquishing the reassurance of feeling virtuous. Instead of that moral reassurance, the empathiser is displaced from the centre of goodness by the affective force of 'feeling her way out' of an identification with the white virtuous self.

Clare Hemmings (2012) has proposed that an 'affective solidarity' that includes dissonance, disunity and difference between women across different social locations offers a much better model for feminist solidarity than one rooted in the feminist investment in empathy (with its emphasis on finding union, sameness and harmony). While I am sympathetic to this view that affective dissonance (rather than unity and harmony) is a productive generator of feminist reflexivity and critique, what I'm proposing here is that empathy, where it functions as a centrifugal force that allows one to 'feel one's way out' of one's own perspective, is not necessarily an affective state of harmony and consonance at all. Rather, empathy can itself be a source of critical 'affective dissonance' within the white subject. Such dissonant and disquieting empathy is conducive to a kind of self-critical, self-reflexive consciousness in the sense that it involves a way of experiencing the relation of the self and other 'twice over'; from both 'here' and 'elsewhere'. Its particular nature might be usefully illustrated by contrasting it with another well-known critical doubling of perspective that American feminist Patricia Hill Collins ascribes to the American black woman as the figure of the 'outsider-within'. Hill Collins observes:

> Domestic work fostered U.S. Black women's economic exploitation, yet it simultaneously created the conditions for distinctly Black and female forms of resistance. Domestic work allowed African-American women to see White elites, both actual and aspiring, from perspectives largely obscured from Black men and from these groups themselves. In their White 'families', Black women not only performed domestic duties but frequently formed strong ties with the children they nurtured, and with the employers themselves. Accounts of Black domestic workers stress the sense of self-affirmation the women experienced at seeing racist ideology demystified. But on another level these Black women knew that they could never belong to their White 'families'. They were economically exploited workers and thus would remain outsiders. The result was being placed in a curious outsider-within social location, a particular marginality that stimulated a distinctive Black women's perspective on a variety of themes. (Hill Collins, 2000: 10–11)

As Hill Collins tells us, because the material and economic exploitation endured by black women occurs in the sphere of the affective intimacy of the elite white family, it also gives them a unique standpoint of privileged insight and knowledge. Privy to, and participating in, the close and intimate caregiving relations in the white household (with which, we might say, she also 'empathises' – including practising a kind of (allo-)maternal empathy with the white children she cares for), the black woman nevertheless does not belong to that elite white world; she is exploited by it. The white world she knows intimately, she also knows 'from elsewhere'; from the marginalised position of the permanent outsider as a black woman. This simultaneous 'insider' and 'outsider' positioning or standpoint is, for Hill Collins, key to the epistemic friction (and epistemic privilege) integral to critical black consciousness and black feminist thought (Hill Collins, 2000).

The 'doubling' of perspective open to a white subject that I'm proposing here as the potential of radical empathy is not, of course, the unique 'double-vision' of the 'outsider-within' that Hill Collins ascribes as the source of the critical reflexivity of the black woman. The empathy of the white subject in a racist world still starts, we might say, 'from above' – from a social location of privilege – not 'from below'. The critical reflexivity of the black 'outsider-within' (born from being both inside the circle of white familial intimacy and yet excluded from it and exploited by it) is therefore very different from the affective dissonance of the white 'insider-without' (whose 'taking the perspective of the other' allows her to catch a critical glimpse of herself from the outside as a beneficiary of the oppression and exploitation of the woman whose intimate-political solidarity she may also seek in the name of feminist solidarity).

Kimberly Davis (2004) has described this more radical potential of a white woman's empathy for black women as one of 'reflective self-alienation' (Davis, 2004: 410); Kaja Silverman calls it 'spectatorial self-estrangement' (quoted in Davis: 411). What affect theory allows us to add here is that this self-alienation is not just experienced from afar in a distanced register of spectatorship, but rather is also felt in the body; in an affective, as much as a reflective, register. The felt estrangement from the racist embodied 'habitus' is experienced as affective dissonance: as an embodied sense of not being at home in one's white body.

Conclusion

As I described in the opening vignette of this chapter, the movements and responses of one's own body can provide an uncanny opportunity to literally feel the legacy of racism move in and through the body. This legacy persists in the way one affects and is affected by other bodies, operating below and above the level of conscious awareness in ways that are both deeply alien and alarmingly familiar. The affective oscillations of empathising as a white 'insider-without' may at times allow one to catch those embodied habits of white racism in motion, and, if not to master them, at least to feel at odds with them and to begin to deflect them into a different iteration. The living encounter with the presence of the other's body can be the impetus to an empathetic 'self-estrangement' from one's own embodied 'habitus'.

My contention here has been that to confront the 'empathy trouble' that haunts it, white feminism needs to be prepared to relinquish the attachment to feeling virtuous and good, and the misplaced moral reassurance this can provide. By working instead with the affective dissonance of ambivalent empathy available from the location of the white 'insider-without', it also becomes possible to fathom why the most heartfelt expressions of virtuous 'whiteliness' at times arouse acute impatience and irritation in the Indigenous women who become its chosen 'object'. As Clare Hemmings observes, 'feminists [who] acknowledge that the other, the object of empathy, may not wish to be empathised with when the empathy is "bad" tend to assume that "good" empathy will always be appreciated'. 'But what if', she muses, 'the other refuses the terms of the empathetic recognition?' What if 'the subject [...] may already consider your position as part of the epistemological terrain rendered problematic by their own experience' (Hemmings, 2012: 152–3)?

It is striking that while the texts of black (and blak) feminists have invoked the power of empathy as a source of solidarity, it is rarely the 'vertical' empathy of privileged white women (flowing 'down') to oppressed black women that they have in mind. Where there is active endorsement of practices of empathy, this is the 'horizontal' empathy that black women feel and express for each other, and the powerful internal support this gives to sustain them in the face of white oppression. There is, understandably, much less enthusiasm on the part of black and Indigenous women to find themselves located as the grateful objects of virtuous white empathy, and certainly far less enchantment shown with such a relational dynamic than is likely to be expressed (or assumed) by white feminists themselves (including those keen to thereby 'rehumanise' the dehumanised Indigenous woman).

It is perhaps this that impelled Gomerei woman, lawyer and Indigenous activist Alison Whittaker to declare in a recent Melbourne public lecture that First Nations people have 'had enough of calls for more education and for more empathy with their situation' (Whittaker, 2019). What is behind this black feminist irritation with always needing to appeal to white empathy? And what kind of moral failing would it be – even, what kind of failure of empathy would it amount to – for a white empathiser to insist the other enter this empathetic relation, even when the supposed beneficiary of it has grown weary of finding herself on the supplicating end of it?

The more radical kind of 'walking in the shoes of the other' (of the 'insider-without') proposed here, means reckoning with the possibility that this 'perspective-taking' does not return the white feminist to herself as a good woman: instead, it can deliver the full-blown discomfort of coming face to face with herself as a structural incumbent of white racism, and this regardless of whatever individual disposition or character trait she might seek to cultivate. This racism is embedded in the affective responsiveness of her body to other bodies, not just what she consciously thinks about racism. If transformative empathy only comes with 'struggles and loss of authority' (Hemmings, 2012: 152), then part of the package deal may also include having to accept the loss of moral authority that empathy has traditionally secured for the white feminist.

The contribution that the empathy of white Australian feminists might make to cross-racial solidarity does not lie, then, in the promise of harmonious unity or a universal sameness of shared humanity with Indigenous peoples (who may not even want or welcome that white empathy, given its propensity to re-inscribe power asymmetries). If a white feminist hopes to become otherwise through 'feeling her way into' the Indigenous experience of dispossession and grief, this must also be a 'feeling her way out' of self-identifications with virtue, benevolence and white innocence that identifying with the role of a good empathiser once confirmed. The alternative potential of 'post-virtuous' empathy is the 'unbecoming' of the white subject that disrupts what it means to be at home in a white body.

If affect theory rightly alerts us to the fact that 'no one has yet determined what the body can do' (Spinoza, quoted in Gregg and Seigworth, 2010: 3) – thereby honouring the transformative potential of affect – it also demands that we be prepared to ask: what has this body and (white) bodies like mine done, of what intimacies has it been (in-)capable, and how does this still operate as an affective force-field on the bodies of the living? Perhaps this is what the white double-consciousness of an 'insider-without' most usefully reveals: for a white-settler feminist living on stolen Indigenous lands, empathising may well mean accepting that empathy becomes an impossible virtue to claim as her own – not for her, not from here – without once again courting some degree of wilful white ignorance. If, under these conditions, you still want to take a walk in the empathiser's new shoes then you had best prepare, at the very least, for a long and unsettling mile.

Acknowledgement

I would like to thank Dr Miriam Bankovsky for her helpful comments on this chapter. This work was supported by an Australian Government Research Training Program Scholarship.

Notes

1 When read through theories of affect, what is meant by 'intimate life' and 'intimacies' becomes a much more polymorphous conception of 'connections that impact on people' (Berlant, 1998: 284) than ever dreamt of, for example, in the canonical works of the modern sociology of intimacy (such as Giddens (1992) and Beck and Beck-Gernsheim (1995)). Affective intimacies can be understood to extend to those 'modes of attachment that make persons public and collective and that make collective scenes intimate spaces' (Berlant, 1998: 288). What

affects (and moves) us in intimate ways, then, might involve the unscheduled intensity of bumping up against the living presence of others (and other bodies) with whom we share the world, and involve currents of material-affective transmission that penetrate and crisscross the boundaries of our individual 'selves' (even, for example, via the smells that 'get up our nose'), as much as they demarcate what we consciously embrace. So too, the conceptualisation of empathy as a 'component part of intimacy' (Jamieson, 2011: 3) morphs in curious ways if we take the plunge and follow the blandishments of affect theory to drop 'below' or move 'above' the humanist self.

2 Mohanty uses this term to convey how Western feminism often constructs 'third-world women as a homogeneous, "powerless" group located as the implicit victims of a particular culture and social-economic system' (Mohanty, 1988: 66). How problematic, we might add, to then proceed to 'empathise' with this imago because such empathy results in a 'closed-circuit': namely, a circulation of affect with the empathiser's own projections, not with the actual other.

3 Helen Ngo offers a critique of empathy-projects like the 'wear a Hijab for a day programme', and online 'empathy apps' that invite white people to virtually simulate the experience of racist abuse. As Ngo points out, there is a fundamental difference between donning an oppressed subject position (at will, for a designated time period) and then shedding it with the same ease, and what it means to be black or Muslim in a racially hostile world. Indeed the 'donning and doffing' of oppressed identities re-enacts the disparity in freedom to move at will in and out of spaces and identities that is the marker of (white) privilege (see Ngo, 2017: 115–16).

References

Ahmed, S. (2017), *Living a Feminist Life* (Durham, NC: Duke University Press).

Bartky, S. L. (2002), *'Sympathy and Solidarity' and Other Essays* (Lanham, MD: Rowman & Littlefield).

Beck, U., and Beck-Gernsheim, E. (1995), *The Normal Chaos of Love* (Cambridge: Polity Press).

Berlant, L. (1998), 'Intimacy: A Special Issue', *Critical Inquiry*, 24, 281–8.

Blackman, L. (2012), *Immaterial Bodies: Affect, Embodiment, Mediation* (Los Angeles, CA: SAGE Publications).

Davis, K. C. (2004), 'Oprah's Book Club and the Politics of Cross-Racial Empathy', *International Journal of Cultural Studies*, 7:4, 399–419.

Deleuze, G. (1990), *Expressionism in Philosophy: Spinoza* (New York, NY: Zone Books).

DiAngelo, R. (2018), *White Fragility: Why It's So Hard to Talk to White People About Racism* (Boston, MA: Beacon Press).

Fricker, M. (2006), *Epistemic Injustice* (Oxford: Oxford University Press).

Frye, M. (1992), *Willful Virgin* (Freedom, CA: Crossing Press).

Giddens, A. (1992), *The Transformation of Intimacy: Sex, Love and Eroticism in Modern Societies* (Cambridge: Polity Press).

Gregg, M., and Seigworth, G. J. (eds) (2010), *The Affect Theory Reader* (Durham, NC: Duke University Press).

Hamad, R. (2019), *White Tears/Brown Scars* (Melbourne, Australia: Melbourne University Press).

Hemmings, C. (2012), 'Affective Solidarity: Feminist Reflexivity and Political Transformation', *Feminist Theory*, 13, 147–61.

Hill Collins, P. (2000), *Black Feminist Thought* (New York, NY: Routledge).

Hochschild, A. R. (1979), 'Emotion Work, Feeling Rules, and Social Structure', *American Journal of Sociology*, 85:3, 551–75.

Jamieson, L. (2011), 'Intimacy as a Concept: Explaining Social Change in the Context of Globalization or Another Form of Ethnocentrism?', *Sociological Research Online*, 16:4, 1–13. Available at: www.socresonline.org.uk/16/4/15 .html (Accessed: 30 May 2021).

Lucashenko, M. (1994), 'No Other Truth? Aboriginal Women and Australian Feminism', *Social Alternatives*, 12:4, 21–4.

Manne, K. (2017), *Down Girl: The Logic of Misogyny* (Oxford: Oxford University Press).

McCarthy, T. (2009), *Race, Empire, and the Idea of Human Development* (Cambridge: Cambridge University Press).

Meyers, D. T. (2016), *Victims' Stories and the Advancement of Human Rights* (New York, NY: Oxford University Press).

Mohanty, C. T. (1988), Under Western Eyes: Feminist Scholarship and Colonial Discourses, *Feminist Review*, 30, 61–88.

Moreton-Robinson, A. (2000), *Talkin' Up to the White Woman: Indigenous Women and Feminism* (St Lucia, Australia: Queensland University Press).

Ngo, H. (2017), 'Simulating the Lived Experience of Racism and Islamophobia: On "Embodied Empathy" and Political Tourism', *Australian Feminist Law Journal*, 44, 107–23.

Noddings, N. (2010), *Maternal Factor: Two Paths to Morality* (Berkeley, CA: University of California Press).

Nussbaum, M. C. (1997), *Cultivating Humanity* (Cambridge, MA: Harvard University Press).

Pedwell, C. (2014), *Affective Relations: The Transnational Politics of Empathy* (Basingstoke: Palgrave Macmillan).

Pedwell, C. (2016), 'Decolonizing Empathy: Thinking Affect Transnationally', *Samyukta: A Journal of Women's Studies*, 26:1, 27–49.

Rai, A. S. (2002), *Rule of Sympathy: Sentiment, Race, and Power 1750–1850* (Basingstoke: Palgrave Macmillan).

Schuller, K. (2018), *The Biopolitics of Feeling: Race, Sex, and Science in the 19th Century* (Durham, NC: Duke University Press).

Whittaker, A. (2019), Public Lecture Held at the Wheeler Centre in Melbourne (May). Podcast 'The F-Word Address: Alison Whittaker'. Available at: www. wheelercentre.com/broadcasts/podcasts/the-wheeler-centre/the-f-word-address -alison-whittaker (Accessed: 30 May 2021).

5

Neighbouring in times of austerity: Intimacy and the 'noikokyrio'

Ilektra Kyriazidou

'We feel the crisis on our skin' was often used by female residents of a low-income neighbourhood in Thessaloniki, a city in northern Greece, to sum up their experiences of austerity. This popular phrase described the way austerity was lived, perceived and objected to by the residents as a form of daily crisis. It was a characteristic way through which they narrated and shared their experiences of being precarious, insecure and bodily exhausted through a feeling that was personal, collective and public at the same time; an appeal to a shared feeling of precarity as their bodies were overwhelmed by daily obstacles and commitments.

The 'skin' – the bodily skin and the social skin – offers a symbolic sense of the material and affective effects of austerity; it expresses a sense of embodied austerity, how it is felt as a blow to the body. This singular feeling – expressed, shared and articulated through a plural subject – marks relational milieus that correspond to forms of collective intimacy in living with the disastrous effects of austerity. But what is the qualitative order of this collective intimacy and what does it describe? What are its limits and thresholds? How are the boundaries of inclusion and exclusion demarcated each time people express and observe commonalities and differences of living in precarious conditions?

In this chapter I document and analyse the intimacies that affectively emerge in the everyday construction of meaning and belonging in urban austerity Greece. I focus on collective and gender-based forms of intimacy in neighbourly relations and explore how these are mobilised by embodiments, sentiments and interpretations of austerity experiences and cultural practices and meanings. I approach intimacy through the particular context of neighbourliness and at the level of affective emergences and dispositions, looking at the patterns and thresholds that direct the movements and shifts of collective intimacy.

Intimacy portrays a general realm of relationality and connection commonly associated with familiarity and wrought with continuity and unpredictability (Berlant, 2000). It has received considerable attention in scholarly work as an analytical framework and a subject of exploration, but also as a concept that indicates new realms of study that allow for novel descriptions of a dynamic array of relations (Wilson, 2012). Scholars have employed intimacy as an approach to critically think about the subtle operations of power amongst daily relations, exploring the ways intimacy links to national ideologies (Herzfeld, 2005), gender normativity, the hegemonies accepted in the mainstream culture (Berlant and Warner, 2000), the biopolitics of colonial powers (Stoler, 2002) and the hegemonies of liberal capitalist democracy (Povinelli, 2006). These studies present excellent examples of how the boundaries between the public and the private rearrange, as they examine the intimacy of public institutions, policies and large cultural, economic and political processes and the way these processes are embodied in everyday relations that often correspond to unequal social arrangements.

In line with this approach, this chapter examines the austerity policies implemented in Greece in intimate realms of everyday life. Greece was at the epicentre of the European sovereign debt crisis and has undergone major social, political and economic changes under the violent neoliberal restructuring that was implemented, which produced generalised precarity. This chapter explores the way in which austerity economies become intimate and the forms that intimacy takes in the effects of austerity in urban Greece. Drawing from twelve months of ethnographic research between 2015 and 2016 in a low-income neighbourhood in a western area of Thessaloniki in northern Greece, the chapter attempts to map the affective gendered everyday makings of intimacy between neighbours who face precarious conditions and forms of daily crisis. The neighbours are of different ages (forty-five to sixty-five years old), are mothers and a few are grandmothers, and are unemployed, precariously employed or low pensioned. Some live with their spouses and children, and a few are widowed or separated and live with their children or near their children's households. The examined intimacy between them is contingent on the power dynamics, histories and locality of realms of neighbourly sociality they share in the everyday. It is shaped by dwelling in proximity and the Mediterranean climate conditions that bring them into public, random encounters at the local open street market, corner shops, Sunday church liturgies, public squares, cafeterias, small gatherings in each other's houses and fleeting dialogues between them across apartment balconies.

Drawing from ethnographic analysis of data derived from participant observation, semi-structured interviews and informal discussions, I ask how austerity intervenes in the livelihoods of intimate relations and how it is contested and performed from below. To this end I explore two distinct occasions of intimacy between female neighbours, shaped by diverse affects and narratives. I examine how they link to austerity and to the local dominant model of the family household, the 'noikokyrio'. By 'noikokyrio', I refer to a domestic arrangement, the conjugal household, but also to a historical and cultural view of domesticity that orients gender and relationality according to the hegemonic model of heterosexual marriage and procreation, and prioritises conjugal domesticity over any other form of sociality (Papataxiarchis, 2012). I focus on the way that collective intimacy happens in neighbourhood sociality, the form it takes and the traces it leaves behind, and thus I call attention to the narratives and affective compositions and dispositions that condition its emergence.

Affect points to the intensity and the bodily feelings sensed when bodies meet. It evokes the way relations and institutions can become sedimented little by little and how bodies intervene to occasion new emergences of relational realms. In this case, the concept of affect is mobilised in order to attend to scenes unfolding in the precarious conditions of urban austerity Greece, and particularly to the way they channel and mediate embodied life and interaction, composing planes of emergences, thresholds and entrenchments (Stewart, 2007). Hence, the study of intimacy in terms of affect exposes the configurations, discontinuities, contingencies and sedimentations that occur in everyday realms of relationality.

I treat affect in the dimension of the body, in Spinozian terms, as the ability to affect and be affected and thus as an ability to connect with others (Massumi, 2015: ix). Based on this understanding, affect is seen through a political lens as open and incomplete, which expresses a field of possibilities (Avramopoulou, 2018). More specifically, as a potential for collaboration, founded on the relational nature of our being in the world (Ruddick, 2010: 25), and a potential for change sketched in the way bodies affect each other and connect (Massumi, 2015: viii). For example, studies have demonstrated the crucial role of affect in motivating collective responses to inequality and organising forms of resistance (Alexandrakis, 2016). Affect can also reveal self-structuring processes of power relations and institutions and the many ways 'relations become entrenched' (Stewart, 2007: 15) and their effects can be translated inequalities (Massumi, 2015: 85–6). Affect thus suggests scenes and events of change but also of solidification (Massumi, 2015; Stewart, 2007; Kolehmainen and Juvonen, 2018). This study offers ways to recognise and understand emergent forms of collective intimacy in austere conditions and subtle reconfigurations in the everyday, but also how forms of living and relating are built up piecemeal and become established.

This chapter contributes to anthropological studies of austerity capitalism and critical discussions on intimacy and affect. It focuses on a particular ethnographic context – gender-based experiences of low-income family households and neighbourhood sociality in urban austerity Greece – and explores manifestations of affect and intimacy and the dynamics of their entanglements. It shows that forms of intimacy between female neighbours, who are trying to cope with the increasing deterioration of life, entail significant affective dimensions and dispositions that paint coalesced relations of solidarity and antagonism, entangled with austerity conditions and the affective and discursive register of the 'noikokyrio' in neighbourhood sociality. The distinct forms of intimacy map the intersections of different scales and social contexts, such as the household, austerity state and global neoliberalism, and complicate clear-cut distinctions between resisting and accepting austerity reforms.

Hence, affective intimacies in this chapter entail both affective economies and affective fluid passages that provide us with insight into the political operations of socio-cultural phenomena and into the intimate cost of global policies and their complex entwinement. They touch on deep-seated political questions on the ethics of solidarity and antagonism, as well as on anthropological queries about sociality and the embodiment of institutions and economic programmes.

I now present a neighbourly encounter in which my interlocutors share and discuss the way they feel and experience austerity. In the following section, I ethnographically approach the way their experiences and feelings derive from the changes in the social reproduction of livelihoods in austere times and how these create precarious conditions for them.[1] The next two sections then examine how these conditions shape forms of collective intimacy and distinct relations of solidarity and antagonism between the neighbours. The fifth section looks at the affective and discursive role of the 'noikokyrio' in the making of collective intimacy. Finally, the last section concludes with some final thoughts on the relations between austerity, gendered precarity and the 'noikokyrio'.

A neighbourly encounter

It is a spring evening.

We are sitting around the kitchen table, freshly baked sponge cake on plates, cups of coffee and the TV remote control on top of a pile of supermarket sale flyers. The TV is playing in the background.

A wooden cross and an icon of Jesus are hanging above the kitchen counter, and below the icon of Saint Mary.

On the wall to one side there is a credenza, on its long surface there is a whole gallery of our hostess's family in gold and brown frames.

There is talk between female neighbours. We discuss the latest political news and the daily chores completed, feelings of tiredness and pride resonate in the bodies of my interlocutors as they talk.

The discussion is interrupted when another neighbour comes walking in with a limp and flings herself into a chair. She has taken a short break from caring for her bedridden sick mother next door.

She lets out a long-drawn sigh of pain and irritation. She points to her swollen knee and explains that it is a painful meniscus tear.

Others scold her for continuing to do care work 'in this condition'. She explains while massaging her knee that is impossible to avoid all the daily activities aggravating the knee injury. 'Who is going to do them?' She draws in a breath and raises her brows. Her words set in motion other similar stories. Our hostess recounts her recent experience of continuing to do care work with a broken wrist after tripping on a pavement.

There is an atmosphere of anger as the neighbours talk about feeling over-worked and physically exhausted. They talk about the support they offer to their families as something unassailable, but in their statements there is a visceral criticism of continuing working even when ill, tired or injured. They blame the 'crisis'.

The injured leg is straightened out on the floor as tales are told about the increase of daily housework, about how lives are rearranged around the obstacles and difficulties other family members face, grandchildren's and parents' care demands, pension cuts, precarious work and unemployment.

The gendered impact of austerity

I attended this unanticipated meeting with one of my main research participants, who was fifty-eight years old and had been unemployed for two years at the time I got to know her. She was dismissed from her job as a production line worker at a clothing company under new elastic austerity laws regulating lay-offs in the private sector. Faced with a collapsed labour market, she was battling with intersecting forms of precarity and occasionally received municipal support and food from the area's main church soup kitchen. Yet, even with limited resources, she helped in the reproduction of domestic labour in her two children's indebted households by cooking, cleaning and caring for the dependent members. In 2016, after six years of ongoing austerity, she was diagnosed with heart disease and suffers from pain and sleeping problems.

Austerity, which has been shown to have a long history across geographies (Rakopoulos, 2018), is a way of managing sovereign debt 'by the value systems of financial markets' (Bear, 2015: 192). By austerity I refer to the conditions generated by national policies implemented to reduce the deficit through aggressive fiscal tightening and cuts in public spending, wages and pensions (Blyth, 2013). Greek austerity is a deepening of the neoliberal reforms introduced in the 1990s and is largely known to people in Greece as 'mnimonia', the Memoranda of Understanding (MoU) signed under rescue deals and in exchange for loans provided, which produced high unemployment, poverty, homelessness and the precarisation of life and labour. Yet, as studies show, the dire consequences of austerity in Greece were unevenly distributed across contexts of inequality and further increased exploitation and xenophobia (Athanasiou, 2012; Athanasiou and Alexandrakis, 2016; Karamessini, 2013; Vaiou, 2016).

Conducting ethnographic research in a neighbourhood in western Thessaloniki, an area with a high number of households living below the poverty line and widely viewed as working class (laiki sinikia), I encountered the disastrous effects of the intersections of social inequality, austerity capitalism and nationalist institutions that shaped every aspect of people's lives, their income, health and intimate relations. When I arrived in the field in 2015, it had been five years of continuing austerity and the residents of the neighbourhood referred to 'crisis' to describe the political period of a financial meltdown, but most importantly, how they found themselves in a state of profound daily crisis generated by austerity reforms crosscut by unequal structures. The focus here is on the gender aspects of this crisis and how it burdened the lives of my interlocutors who tried to adjust the social reproduction of life to the changing conditions of austerity. As their lives were constantly organised according to the imperatives of reforms and debt repayment, their daily practices of social reproduction intensified in order to fill the gaps created by the reforms (Feminist Fightback, 2011; Hall, 2020).

Greek austerity had a hard impact on low-income family households, with significant gendered dimensions. The drastic household income reduction, the welfare state's withdrawal and widespread labour precarity called for an increasing participation of female family members in their children's or parents' reproduction of livelihoods. We can say that the accelerating precarity strengthened the local model of the 'functionally extended' family household, which refers to the family households linked through kinship in the context of a common intergenerational allocation of housework (Papataxiarchis, 2012: 229), and intensified gendered unpaid care work.

My interlocutors were greatly affected by these changes, disproportionally bearing the growing workloads in life's reproduction. They faced increasing responsibilities in paid and unpaid work, as they struggled to support their families in multiple sites and in ways that often merged production and reproduction. For example, my main interlocutor was trying to earn some money to help her children's family households by producing home-made spirits, jams and fruit preserves from materials she received from the area's open street market in exchange for work, which she unofficially sold to her neighbours and the open market. Her closest neighbour worked 'off the books', providing in-home senior care to another family household in the neighbourhood, trying to make some money and help her unemployed son. Our hostess in the neighbourly encounter assisted her sister's bakery business in return for a small unofficial payment that complemented her pension and allowed her to support her children's families. The spaces and temporalities of production and social reproduction often overlapped and realigned the taken-for-granted boundaries between the private and the public, the economic and the intimate (Wilson, 2012).

At the same time, my interlocutors tried daily to redraw the borders between paid labour and household life, in their attempts to offset the insecurity of the precarious work they and other family members faced. They managed affective and financial economies and temporalities with more work and less income, and often felt anxiety under the pressure to organise expenses and careful spending, prioritising the needs and desires of other family members. This form of self-giving to their families – even if not a disinterested gift as it often accomplished other interests, such as securing the loyalty of children – was precarious and emotionally conflicting. I thus approach their practices of everyday social reproduction under austerity not solely as ways of surviving crises and fields of everyday struggle but also as realms of precarity. They evoke the ordinariness of austerity crises and show how austerity economies depend on gendered unwaged labour. Most importantly, they name anxiety and physical exhaustion as core gendered embodiments of austerity in low-income households.

Collective intimacy and relations of solidarity in precarious situations

Let us return to the neighbourly encounter described. In this unplanned meeting the participants talked about their troubles in coping with the intensification of physical and emotional work that goes into supporting their families. During the talk there was a palpable sense of anger and frustration. Troubles registered in emotions and emotions begot emotions that made the precarity experienced alongside the difficulties and anguish in everyday social reproduction affectively apparent. Yet, the talk delivered a contradictory feeling of frustration, anger and pride in dealing with daily forms of crisis.

As I accompanied my main interlocutor around the neighbourhood, a few more similar events unexpectedly followed. Each event happened differently, yet each time female neighbours complained about the increasing troubles they faced in their efforts to help and care for their families. Every time I wrote the content of the stories told and the feelings felt in my fieldwork notes. I tried to map the form and potentiality of the emergent intimacy between the participants in these events and the entangled emotional landscapes: the anxiety, insecurity, pride, frustration and anger.

The collective anger and lament unfolding in these meetings brought to attention a situation and, in that sense, made visible the hidden practices and relations that are involved in the sustenance of family households and interrupted the invisibility of the gendered impact of austerity. This brought about yet further implications, i.e. the undermining of the nationalist framed narratives of the Greek debt crisis, which assumed a homogenous social body equally affected by austerity. Above all, they generated a common sphere for thinking and feeling the experienced conflicts and troubles in the everyday that gave way to a gender-based solidarity, as we will see.

Taking into consideration the affective aspect of this realm of relationality allows us to understand the way intimacy happened, what form it assumed. Candace Vogler's (2000) affective approach to 'troubles talk' between women is extremely relevant here. As she describes, 'troubles talk' (women talking about their troubles) is 'a kind of collective lament' (Vogler, 2000: 79) that does not re-inscribe the borders of selfhood but shapes a 'depersonalising' intimacy that is 'beyond an affair of the self' (Vogler, 2000: 81). The aim of these conversations is not so much to find solutions to the problems discussed but to immerse oneself in the talk (Vogler, 2000).

The meetings between female neighbours described here did not resolve the problems voiced but fashioned a larger affective setting through which they expressed their stories and conflicting feelings. The talk did not seek solutions, nor did it end with giving final answers, but flagged something that could no longer be suppressed. It raised the problem of the intensification of gendered unpaid work and the precarity it causes at the level of affect. This is a key aspect of the form of intimacy between the neighbours in these events. A kind of intimacy, as Vogler (2000: 81) insightfully describes, that allows one to 'feel like the most personal things do not mark one off as unique'.

This central feature of the intimacy during the 'troubles talk' generated and sustained the potential to rethink personal experience in relational and political terms (Vogler, 2000). It revealed how relationality can constitute a politically important act in itself (Ruddick, 2010), more so in austerity times (Hall, 2020), that can take the shape of a gender-based solidarity. Focusing on affect helps us to recognise this solidarity, which was not claimed nor named – a solidarity that corresponded to an affective bond built amidst resonating patterns of experiencing, thinking and feeling. A solidarity that just happened in the sharing of troubles and emotions and that constituted a political relation that did not operate at the level of feminist political action but registered as an affective and active passage and interaction. A solidarity that charted a potentiality in the way bodies can relate to each other in the daily life of the neighbourhood.

The solidarity described here is thus a political relation and affect that could not be formulated as a strategy. Ways of relating in the neighbourhood can generate solidarity but cannot, however, plan or organise it. They can shape matrixes of words, intensities, connections and feelings that can generate a relation of solidarity that can re-arise but cannot be mastered. However unpredictable and unstructured, this relation is important in bringing bodies together against the individualisation of their experiences that tends to hide their anguishes and experienced conflicts. Moreover, it seems to challenge the rationality of austerity that is founded to a great extent on the responsibilisation of citizens, which displaces welfare into the ethics of personal responsibility and tends to convert widespread precarity into fragmented individualised experiences. This kind of collective intimacy therefore constitutes a potent example of the political possibilities of creating sites of recognised relationality amidst commonalities of feeling precarious (Butler, 2004).

Antagonism and the austerity state

The instances of solidarity described above coexisted with different events and forms of sociality in this group of neighbours. I am referring here to events that were marked by hostility and conflict between my interlocutors and that in distinct ways shaped the dynamics of collective intimacy in the neighbourhood. In these moments, the neighbours engaged in a kind of antagonistic relationality, manifested in insinuations and adverse comments expressed towards each other and in scenes of tacit hostility and mistrust. In what follows, I give two examples that portray the content and the subtleties of such events of antagonism between them.

Two neighbours, with whom I was conversing at a local café one evening, interpreted the difficult circumstances experienced by another neighbour (my main interlocutor) as her own failing as a single mother to make sensible financial management in the past. They also accused her of previously spending money recklessly in what is considered an anti-domestic practice, partying at local live music nightclubs (mpouzoukia). Her problems were contrasted with the difficulties they unjustly faced with the austerity policies. In another instance when I was with my main interlocutor at the open local market and met them again, we all started discussing the problem of another neighbour who worked informally as an in-home senior carer and had been unpaid for three months. While we all agreed on the grim effects of her situation, I was surprised to hear my three discussants commenting that she was 'also lazy' and 'not good at her job'.

There have been previous observations of gender-based antagonism in Greece (Cowan, 1990; Herzfeld, 1985).[2] Yet, in the specific context of austerity, antagonism is shaped by the situation of living in precarious conditions and with low income. It entails an antagonistic position taken across experiences of national austerity. Antagonism is thus not so much the result of individualism but of a distressed reflection of one's position vis-à-vis precarity and the austerity state. It involves emotional elaborations of disregard and indifference towards others and their hard struggle to reproduce the labour of daily life amidst impediments and the uncertainty of precarious work. This resonates with the 'affective formation of indifference' by the politics of exclusion enacted by the austerity state towards those bodies that were presented as a threat to the national order in crisis (Kyriakopoulos, 2016: 97).

The allegations even seemed to propose that those to whom they were directed were the agents of their own precarity due to previous excess, laziness and irresponsible behaviour. They were not simply expressions of a negative view but negative definitions that pronounced what the other female neighbours were not: good carers, housewives and mothers. The figures of the irresponsible mother and lazy carer were juxtaposed with the way that caring, mothering and managing the family household is expected to happen. I propose thus to see these acts of accusing and antagonising other neighbours not solely as expressions of power dynamics in everyday sociality, but also in terms of the gender normativities they reanimate and the effects of inequality they affirm.

In austere conditions, the antagonism seemed to pit neighbour against neighbour and tended to become a way through which neighbours disciplined each other. What strikes me is that the moral narratives employed by my interlocutors resemble the morality of shaming of debt (Graeber, 2011), central in the negotiation and management of the Greek debt crisis, which not only shaped popular views but also influenced policy. They recall the demonisation of the local population in Greece (Shore and Raudon, 2018), portrayed in orientalist terms as lazy, irresponsible and unruly, that influenced the national imagination (Kalantzis, 2015).

We see therefore how antagonism offers the medium through which global policies fasten into deeply embedded local meanings and relations (Herzfeld, 2016); the way it organises a moral sociality in which austerity is performed from below. Let us not forget that austerity was presented by policy makers as a necessary response to previous excess and a form of self-discipline (Muechlebach, 2016), which suggests reverberations and overlaps with accusations of previous overspending towards my main interlocutor.

The tensions and divisiveness I witnessed in these moments of antagonism evidenced that solidarity was overridden by conflict and collective intimacy shifted into a matter between antagonistic selves. The co-presence of these diverse instances and the conflicting and ambiguous emotional entanglements, gathered up in everyday scenes of neighbourhood sociality, complicated my inquiry into the relations between female neighbours afflicted by austerity and prompted me to think further on this messy ecology of intimacy.

Seen in the context of previous ethnographic references, solidarity and antagonism are not contradictory relations but moments of a constantly changing sociality that can easily shift from affinity to hostility (Herzfeld, 2016).[3] Yet, what interests me here is the affective and discursive role of the local model of the family household, the 'noikokyrio', in these tangled compositions of intimacy.

The 'noikokyrio' as ethos and affect disposition

As I followed my interlocutors in their everyday routines and interviewed them about certain aspects of their lives, I came to realise the affective subjective dispositions of their statements and practices which included: regular comments on how others – relatives, friends and neighbours – attended to the project of 'noikokyrio', the local model of family domesticity based on heterosexual marriage, and a persistent pursuit of recognition for being 'good' housewives, mothers, grandmothers, spouses by demonstrating how 'well' they inhabited these gendered realms of identity. This aspect of demonstrating excellence in embodying and reproducing the 'noikokyrio' is central to the sense of belonging it promises. And it is this promise of inclusion and belonging that colonises the affective ecology of collective intimacy.

I want to argue that the collective intimacy in this group of neighbours that continuously interfolds solidarity and antagonism, however idiosyncratic, is linked to the 'noikokyrio'. I do not refer here to the 'noikokyrio' as an unchanging structure that reigns over all of local social life. There have been important changes and novel forms of kinship and domesticity (Kantsa, 2006; Kantsa and Chalkidou, 2014).[4] Most importantly, I do not approach the 'noikokyrio' solely as a domestic arrangement, but as a cultural background that organises kinship, gender and sociality (Papataxiarchis, 2012). There is a deep-seated competitive and conservative 'ethos' that is shaped by the way the 'noikokyrio' is positioned as an independent economic and social unit that must constantly defend itself against external real and imagined threats and struggle for its conservation (Papataxiarchis, 2020). This ethos informs all aspects of Greek society, a society fundamentally of the 'noikokyreous' (people of the 'noikokyrio') (Papataxiarchis, 2020: 70). It is an ethos that tends to enforce heteronormativity in the everyday (Papataxiarchis, 2012), affectively as a sense of rightness based on the norm of heterosexuality, in all aspects of different forms of social life (Berlant and Warner, 2000: 312). It corresponds to a reality people affectively shape and whose shape they acquire (Ahmed, 2014: 148). But let me first outline some key aspects drawn from previous anthropological accounts that outline what is culturally distinctive in the ethos of the 'noikokyrio'.

First, we must take into account that the 'noikokyrio' is promoted by the state and the church and widely adopted by the local population in Greece (Papataxiarchis, 2012). Its strength is depicted in several indicators, such as the high number of conjugal family households and the absence of state policies in support of other family and domestic arrangements (Kantsa and Chalkidou 2014; Papataxiarchis, 2012). It is founded on a set of normative meanings and associations between kinship, gender and sexuality, that provide what Herzfeld (2005) calls the 'cultural intimacy' of the Greek state, the representations of the essentialisms of nationalism and 'national heterosexuality' (Berlant and Warner, 2000), in popular culture, law and economy. Motherhood, for instance, is rife with normative meanings of life, gender (Athanasiou, 2006) and sexuality (Kantsa and Chalkidou, 2014); it is seen as a moral attribute (Paxson, 2004: 18) and a duty to the family, God and the nation (Georgiadi, 2013), and underscored by Christian beliefs and identifications with the image of Saint Mary as a devoted mother (Rushton, 1998). Being a housewife (noikokyra) is a source of status in successfully reproducing the household in managing economy and order (Salamone and Stanton, 1986).

During periods of crisis the link between the nation and the 'noikokyrio' is strengthened. The nation in crisis threatened by others (the foreign powers that manage austerity, the immigrants that enter the country, the undisciplined bodies), must protect and defend the 'noikokyria' against the hostile others (Athanasiou, 2012; Papataxiarchis, 2020). The defensive nationalism that was cultivated (Kotouza, 2019) intensifies the conservative ethos of the 'noikokyrio'; in times of crisis 'the insecure nation corresponds to the insecure "noikokyrio"' (Papataxiarchis, 2020: 70).

The 'noikokyrio' operates as a regime of belonging; it acts as a central organising principle of inclusion. 'It presents to individuals the most viable cultural option according to which the self as a member of a corporate conjugal group is entitled to a place in the wider community' (Papataxiarchis, 2012: 223). And while it can function as a medium of integration (Rozakou,

2006), a refusal to reproduce it brings stigmatisation and othering (Athanasiou, 2006). Those who do not match the privileged ethos of the 'noikokyrio' and don't feel part of the belonging in a normal way are confronted with the exclusionary aspects of this ethos (Kantsa and Chalkidou, 2014). While those who invest in it must constantly demonstrate compliance in performing and embodying the ethos of the 'noikokyrio' (Papataxiarchis, 2020). This can take cruel and violent dimensions.[5]

Thus, the issue here is how ordinarily hostile the antagonistic ethos of the 'noikokyrio' can become. How do investments in the 'noikokyrio' and belonging move into and through the regeneration of exclusion? How do gendered patterns of responsibility and support of the 'noikokyrio' exhaust the gendered body in austere times? But also, how does the ethos of the 'noikokyrio' become compatible with neoliberal global policies? The case examined here of gender-based experiences of exhaustion during austerity in the context of reproducing the 'noikokyrio', entwined with solidarity and hostile antagonism between female neighbours, articulates exactly these concerns. It expresses certain implications of the austerity experience in relation to the ordinariness of crisis, exhaustion and indifference and to the complicity of culturally-oriented feelings and relations with a neoliberal logic.

Approaching the 'noikokyrio' as an ethos, I believe, helps us to understand its affective reach in everyday local sociality: how it orients the affective into privileged realms of gendered meaning and action and draws boundaries of communication that guide everyday makings of intimacy. How, in short, it organises gender and intimacy not through a set of demarcated norms but on an affective everyday level. From this point of view, antagonism depicts what Sara Ahmed (2014: 8) calls 'affective economy', a feeling produced as an effect of 'circulation' that is culturally and socially oriented and that, in this case, forms part of the conditions of the emergence of neighbourly intimacy. Solidarity is thus a passage of intimacy that follows a series of affective transformations worked upon antagonism. In this case, it comes with the sharing of troubles felt within the 'noikokyrio' between female neighbours. And although it does not challenge the premise of the 'noikokyrio', it marks a realm of relationality that does not work through exclusion and indifference. I propose to see the antagonism between the neighbours thus as an ambivalence that describes how gender-based conflicts can give way to bonds and how alliances often entail conflicts (Vlahoutsikou, 2003).

Conclusion

In this chapter I focused on diverse couplings of intimacy and affect in the sociality of a group of female neighbours who face difficulties in reproducing the daily labour of life under the restrictions of low income in urban austerity Greece. I looked at the discontinuities, concretions and eventualities that were taking place as austerity intervenes in their lives and relations. The tones and contents of their statements, traversed by different affective dynamics, were central in mapping the intimacy that was formed between them in everyday neighbourhood sociality. On one hand, affect depicted a carriage of potential for the renewal of neighbourly relations and, on the other hand, an affective economy of exclusionary effect.

The affective entanglements of the collective intimacy examined in this ethnographic account revealed the potentialities of relational fields built in the everyday amidst growing social and health inequalities, alongside the affective politics of sharing commonalities of feeling precarious, exploited and exhausted in settings of neoliberal transformation. It also provided an example of the way people are often immersed in affective fields of relations that affirm various forms of exclusion and inequality.

The intimacy between my interlocutors developed from a collective lament into solidarity as they engaged with the affect that emerged in sharing the difficulties and exhaustion they faced in their efforts to help their families during austerity times. They expressed conflicting feelings in the strained self-giving of the body, and contested the precarity and invisibility of social reproduction and the neoliberal rationality of austerity. But, in the same group of neighbours, collective intimacy also took an exclusionary form as it was driven by antagonism brewing in neighbourhood sociality, an affective economy oriented by the conservative ethos of the local institution of the family household, the 'noikokyrio'. In this instance, neighbours interpreted other neighbours' precarious experiences of austerity as personal gender failures. Such evaluations were entirely compatible with the ideological nexus of debt-austerity state-global neoliberal institutions.

What can we draw from this ethnographic case of distinct forms of collective intimacy during austerity coalescing into everyday neighbourliness? Firstly, we see the human and intimate cost of global neoliberal capitalism (Panourgia, 2016). We see how austerity changes peoples' lives and exhausts low-income women. But also, how it is contested and institutionalised at a personal and collective level as it acquires meaning within everyday practices and relations. It appears that experiences of austerity correspond to complex affective realities that lie beyond accepting or rejecting austerity (Hall, 2020). We see, at the same time, how the 'noikokyrio' succeeds in reproducing and maintaining itself not as rationality but as affectivity which operates 'by weaving ways of feeling and acting … into the habitual fabric of everyday life' (Massumi, 2015: 85). Furthermore, we see how the 'noikokyrio' becomes central in people's lives during periods of crisis: as a defence mechanism mobilising patterns of responsibility and support that

burden female members, and as a moral ground on which people interpret other's precarious livelihoods according to gender stereotypes. This
indicates some further consequences: the reinforcement of essentialised
accounts of gender during austerity (Avdela, 2013), and a generalised conservative recoil.

As I finish writing this essay, the outbreak of COVID-19 has generated a
new language of crisis and urgency and a new affective landscape of precarity
exacerbated by a previous period of exhausting austerity. It has divested forms
of collective life and magnified the cultural significance of the 'noikokyrio'
and its heteronormative ethos (Papataxiarchis, 2020), and increased household responsibilities that burden women (Vaiou, 2020). The pandemic situation has recreated imaginaries of the 'noikokyrio' as a realm of safety and a
shield of protection from the virus that once more disavow its cruel dimensions and deeply entrenched gender inequalities. This time though, the patterns of commitment and reciprocity across family and generational ties have
altered under the pressures of confinement. At the same time, the pandemic
has highlighted the urgency of reconsidering the economy of paid and unpaid
care work and the rationality of austerity and its impact on health and health
services. The severe public cuts had left a large part of the population more
vulnerable to the pandemic and exposed to health inequalities.

Notes

1 By social reproduction, I refer, as per Federici (2012: 5), to 'the complex of
   activities and relations by which our life and labour are daily reconstituted',
   which are gendered, devalued and made invisible in capitalist economies.
2 From early ethnographies (Campbell, 1964; Friedl, 1962) on Greece, a central
   topic has been the extra-domestic antagonistic sociality that is opposed to the
   support of familial relations.
3 Contemporary ethnographic accounts of neighbourly intimacy in urban austerity Greece (Kyriazidou, 2019) depict messy zones of care and hostility, which
   are also observed in other neoliberal national contexts of precarity (Han,
   2012).
4 The twenty-first century has also seen recreations of queer histories and con-
   temporaneity in/of Greece and new local queer grassroots movements, which
   are critical towards the 'noikokyrio' (Papanikolaou and Kolocotroni, 2018).
5 I am referring here to the murderous attack in Athens in September 2018 on
   a queer activist and drag performer, Zak Kostopoulos, who was accidentally
   locked in a jewellery store and while trying to get out was beaten to death
   by the shop owner and police in front of a crowd that just stood by. Zak's
   death was linked to the macho culture of the 'noikokyrio' (Athanasiou and
   Papanikolaou, 2020).

References

Ahmed, S. (2014), *The Cultural Politics of Emotion* (Edinburgh: Edinburgh University Press).

Alexandrakis, O. (2016), *Impulse to Act: A New Anthropology of Resistance and Social Justice* (Bloomington, IN: Indiana University Press).

Athanasiou, A. (2006), 'Bloodlines: Performing the Body of the "Demos", Reckoning the Time of the "Ethnos"', *Journal of Modern Greek Studies*, 24:2, 229–56. doi: 10.1353/mgs.2006.0015

Athanasiou, A. (2012), *Η κρίση ως 'κατάσταση έκτακτης ανάγκης'* (*The Crisis as a 'State of Emergency'*) (Athens, Greece: Savalas).

Athanasiou, A., and Alexandrakis, O. (2016), 'Conclusion: On an Emergent Politics and Ethics of Resistance', in *Impulse to Act: A New Anthropology of Resistance and Social Justice*, O. Alexandrakis (ed.) (Bloomington, IN: Indiana University Press), 246–62.

Athanasiou, A., and Papanikolaou, D. (2020), '"Πες το όνομά της": Η κουήρ μνήμη ως κριτική του παρόντος' ('"Say Her Name". The Queer Memory as a Critique of the Present'), in *Κουήρ Πολιτική / Δημόσια Μνήμη. 30 κείμενα για τον Ζακ* (*Queer Politics/Public Memory. 30 Texts for Zak*), A. Athanasiou, G. Gougousis, and D. Papanikolaou (eds) (Athens, Greece: Rosa Luxemburg Stiftung), 9–30.

Avdela, E. (2013), 'Το φύλο στην (σε) κρίση: Ή τι συμβαίνει στις γυναίκες σε χαλεπούς καιρούς' ('The Gender in (the) Crisis or What Happens to Women in Hard Times'), *Σύγχρονα Θέματα*, 115, 17–26.

Avramopoulou, E. (2018), 'Εισαγωγή. Πολιτικές εγγραφές του συν-αισθήματος' ('Introduction. The Political Registers of Affect'), in *Το συν-αίσθημα στο πολιτικό. Υποκειμενικότητες, εξουσίες και ανισότητες στο σύγχρονο κόσμο* (*Affect in the Political. Subjectivities, Power and Inequalitites in the Modern World*), E. Avramopoulou (ed.) (Athens, Greece: Nissos), 11–67.

Bear, L. (2015), *Navigating Austerity: Currents of Debt Along a South Asian River* (Palo Alto, CA: Stanford University Press).

Berlant, L. (2000), 'Intimacy: A Special Issue', in *Intimacy*, L. Berlant (ed.) (Chicago, IL, and London: University of Chicago Press), 1–8.

Berlant, L., and Warner, M. (2000), 'Sex in Public', in *Intimacy*, L. Berlant (ed.) (Chicago, IL, and London: University of Chicago Press), 311–30.

Blyth, M. (2013), *Austerity: The History of a Dangerous Idea* (Oxford: Oxford University Press).

Butler, J. (2004), *Precarious Life: The Powers of Mourning and Violence* (New York, NY: Verso).

Campbell, J. (1964), *Honour, Family and Patronage: A Study of the Institutions and Moral Values in a Greek Mountain Community* (Oxford: Oxford University Press).

Cowan, J. (1990), *Dance and the Body Politic in Northern Greece* (Princeton, NJ: Princeton University Press).

Federici, S. (2012), *Revolution at Point Zero: Housework, Reproduction and Feminist Struggle* (Oakland, CA, and New York, NY: Common Notions).

Feminist Fightback (2011), 'Cuts Are a Feminist Issue', *Soundings*, 49, 73–83. doi: 10.3898/136266211798411165

Friedl, E. (1962), *Vasilika: A Village in Modern Greece* (New York, NY: Rinehart and Winston).

Georgiadi, K (2013), 'Η μητρότητα στην εποχή της "υπογεννητικότητας": Αντιλήψεις και εμπειρίες Αθηναίων γυναικών μεσαίας τάξης στον 21° αιώνα' ('Motherhood in Times of "Low Fertility". Perceptions and Experiences of Athenian Middle Class Women in the 21st Century'), in *Η Μητρότητα στο προσκήνιο. Σύγχρονες έρευνες στην ελληνική εθνογραφία* (*Motherhood in the Forefront. Recent Research in Greek Ethnography*), V. Kantsa (ed.) (Athens, Greece: Alexandria Press), 69–90.

Graeber, D. (2011), *Debt: The First 5000 Years* (Brooklyn, NY: Melville House Publishing).

Hall, S. M. (2020), 'The Personal is Political: Feminist Geographies of/in Austerity', *Geoforum*, 110, 242–51. doi: 10.1016/j.geoforum.2018.04.010

Han, C. (2012), *Life in Debt: Times of Care and Violence in Neoliberal Chile* (Berkeley, CA: University of California Press).

Herzfeld, M. (1985), *The Poetics of Manhood: Contest and Identity in a Cretan Mountain Village* (Princeton, NJ: Princeton University Press).

Herzfeld, M. (2005), *Cultural Intimacy: Social Poetics in the Nation State* (New York, NY: Routledge).

Herzfeld, M. (2016), 'Critical Reactions: The Ethnographic Genealogy of Response', *Social Anthropology*, 24:2, 200–4. doi: 10.1111/1469-8676.12310

Kalantzis, K. (2015), '"Fak Germani": Materialities of Nationhood and Transgression in the Greek Crisis', *Comparative Studies in Society and History*, 57:4, 1037–69. doi: 10.1017/S0010417515000432

Kantsa, V. (2006). 'Οικογενειακές υποθέσεις: Μητρότητα και ομόφυλες ερωτικές σχέσεις' ('Family Matters: Motherhood and Same Sex Relationships'), in *Περιπέτειες της Ετερότητας* (*Adventures of Alterity. The Production of Cultural Difference in Contemporary Greece*), E. Papataxiarchis (ed.) (Athens, Greece: Alexandria Press), 355–82.

Kantsa, V., and Chalkidou, A. (2014), 'Doing Family "in the Space Between the Laws"', *Lambda Nordica*, 19:3–4 (online, 2014), 86–108. Available at: www.lambdanordica.org/index.php/lambdanordica/article/view/428/407 (Accessed: 16 June 2021).

Karamessini, M. (2013), 'Structural Crisis and Adjustment in Greece: Social Regression and the Challenge to Gender Equality', in *Women and Austerity: The Economic Crisis and the Future for Gender Equality*, M. Karamessini and J. Rubery (eds) (New York, NY: Routledge), 165–85.

Kolehmainen, M., and Juvonen, T. (2018), 'Introduction: Thinking With and Through Affective Inequalities', in *Affective Inequalities in Intimate Relationships*, T. Juvonen and M. Kolehmainen (eds) (London: Routledge), 1–15.

Kotouza, D. (2019), *Surplus Citizens: Struggle and Nationalism in the Greek Crisis* (London: Pluto Press).

Kyriakopoulos, L. (2016), 'Establishing Indifference: The Affective Logic of Neoliberalism', in *UniConflicts in Spaces of Crisis: Critical Approaches In, Against and Beyond the University*, K. Athanasiou, E. Vasdeki, E. Kapetanaki, *et al.* (eds) (online, 2016), 88–101. Available at: https://uniconflicts.files.wordpress.com /2016/11/uniconflicts.pdf (Accessed: 16 June 2021).

Kyriazidou, I. (2019), 'Complex Intimacies in a Thessaloniki Refugee Neighbourhood', *Lo Squaderno*, 53, 67–70. Available at: www.losquaderno.net/ wp-content/uploads/2019/09/losquaderno53.pdf (Accessed: 16 June 2021).

Massumi, B. (2015), *Politics of Affect* (Cambridge and Malden: Polity Press).

Muehlebach, A. (2016), 'Anthropologies of Austerity', *History and Anthropology*, 27:3, 359–72. doi: 10.1080/02757206.2016.1167052

Panourgia, N. (2016), 'Surreal Capitalism and the Dialectical Economies of Precarity', in *Impulse to Act: A New Anthropology of Resistance and Social Justice*, O. Alexandrakis (ed.) (Bloomington, IN: Indiana University Press), 112–32.

Papanikolaou, D., and Kolocotroni, V. (2018), 'New Queer Greece: Performance, Politics and Identity in Crisis', *Journal of Greek Media and Culture*, 4:2, 143–50. doi: 10.1386/jgmc.4.2.143_2

Papataxiarchis, E. (2012), 'Shaping Modern Times in the Greek Family: A Comparative View of Gender and Kinship Transformations after 1974', in *State Society and Economy*, A. Dialla and N. Maroniti (eds) (Athens, Greece: Metaichmio Publications), 217–44.

Papataxiarchis, E. (2020), 'Το "Νοικοκυριό", πολιτισμικό αντίδοτο στη πανδημία' ('The Noikokyrio, Cultural Antidote to the Pandemic'), *Σύγχρονα Θέματα*, 149, 63–74.

Paxson, H. (2004), *Making Modern Mothers: Ethics and Family Planning in Urban Greece* (Berkeley and Los Angeles, CA, and London: University of California Press).

Povinelli, E. (2006), *The Empire of Love: Toward a Theory of Intimacy, Genealogy, and Carnality* (Durham, NC, and London: Duke University Press, 2006).

Rakopoulos, T. (2018), *The Global Life of Austerity: Comparing Beyond Europe* (New York, NY, and Oxford: Berghahn).

Rozakou, K. (2006), 'Street-Work: Όρια και αντιφάσεις των συναντήσεων Ελλήνων εθελοντών και προσφύγων' ('Street Work. Limitations and Ambiguities in the Meetings between Greek Volunteers and Refugees'), in *Περιπέτειες της Ετερότητας: Η Παραγωγή της Πολιτισμικής Διαφοράς στη σύχρονη Ελλάδα* (*Adventures of Alterity: The Production of Cultural Difference in Contemporary Greece*), E. Papataxiarchis (ed.) (Athens, Greece: Alexandria Press), 325–54.

Ruddick, S. (2010), 'The Politics of Affect: Spinoza in the Work of Negri and Deleuze', *Theory, Culture and Society*, 27:4, 21–45. doi: 10.1177/0263276410372235

Rushton, L (1998), 'Η μητρότητα και ο συμβολισμός του σώματος' ('Motherhood and the Symbolism of the Body'), in *Ταυτότητες και Φύλο στη Σύγχρονη Ελλάδα* (*Identity and Gender in Modern Greece*), E. Papataxiarchis and T. Paradelis (eds) (Athens, Greece: Alexandria Press), 151–70.

Salamone, S. D., and Stanton, J. B. (1986), 'Introducing the Nikokyra: Ideality and Reality in Social Process', in *Gender and Power in Rural Greece*, J. Dubish (ed.) (Princeton, NJ: Princeton University Press), 97–120.

Shore, C., and Raudon, S. (2018), 'Performing Austerity: Greece's Debt Crisis and European Integration', in *The Global Life of Austerity: Comparing Beyond Europe*, T. Rakopoulos (ed.) (New York, NY: Berghahn Books), 32–47.

Stewart, K. (2007), *Ordinary Affects* (Durham, NC, and London: Duke University Press).

Stoler, A. L. (2002), *Carnal Knowledge and Imperial Power: Race and the Intimate in Colonial Rule* (Berkeley, CA: University of California Press).

Vaiou, D. (2016), 'Tracing Aspects of the Greek Crisis in Athens: Putting Women in the Picture', *European Urban and Regional Studies*, 23:3, 220–30. doi: 10.1177/0969776414523802

Vaiou, D. (2020), '"Μένουμε σπιτι": Συρρίκνωση του χώρου και ψηφίδες μιας δύσκολης πραγματικότητας' ('"Stay Home": Shrinking of Space and Mosaics of a Difficult Reality'), in *Αποτυπώσεις σε στιγμές κινδύνου* (*Depictions in Moments of Danger*), *Τοπικά IΘ*, P. Kapola, G. Kouzelis, and O. Konstantas (eds) (Athens, Greece: Nissos), 516.

Vlahoutsikou, C. (2003), 'Όταν γυναίκες έχουν διαφορές: Αναστολές και ανοίγματα' ('When Women Have Differences: Inhibitions and Exposures'), in *Όταν γυναίκες έχουν διαφορές: Αντιθέσεις και συγκρούσεις γυναικών στη σύγχρονη Ελλάδα* (*When Women Have Differences: Oppositions and Conflicts among Women in Modern Greece*) C. Vlahoutsikou and L. Kain-Hart (eds) (Athens, Greece: Medusa), 14–104.

Vogler, C. (2000), 'Sex and Talk', in *Intimacy*, L. Berlant (ed.) (Chicago, IL, and London: University of Chicago Press), 48–85.

Wilson, A. (2012), 'Intimacy: A Useful Category of Transnational Analysis', in *The Global and the Intimate, Feminism in Our Time*, G. Pratt and V. Rosner (eds) (New York, NY: Columbia University Press), 31–56.

6

Becoming a lesbian at lesbian and gay dance parties: Lesboratories as affective spaces

Tuula Juvonen

Walking through the city of Tampere, Finland, past the Workers' Union House or the Näsinneula sightseeing tower, there are no material traces to indicate that in the 1980s these were areas of great significance to the city's emerging lesbian and gay community.[1] The ephemerality of the lesbian and gay scene has made its history notoriously challenging to study (Reuter, 2008; Forstie, 2014). Whereas historians have successfully used old photographs to study vanishing and mundane material entities and their agency (Männistö-Funk, 2021: 64), in the case of lesbian and gay dance parties in Tampere this cannot be done, as no known photographs exist. Hence, in my research I have relied on an analysis of oral history interviews conducted with people that lived through the time period in question and participated in the communities, hoping that the analysis of their recollections would allow conclusions to be drawn on the lesbian past (Boyd and Ramírez, 2012). I am especially interested in the question of how the venues were also actively participating in the production of meaning and the forming of what was an emerging idea of a lesbian.

The literary scholar Julie Abraham has famously suggested that it takes only a woman and a novel to make a lesbian, since, as a reader, a woman can interpret herself as a lesbian (Abraham, 1996: xvii). Here we may note both the divergence from a notion of an innate lesbian identity and a constructive take that foregrounds the material entanglement of a woman and a book. It is precisely this entanglement that makes possible the materialisation of a specific configuration: a lesbian (cf. Barad, 2007: 140). However, in Abraham's interpretation becoming a lesbian remains a solitary experience, even when acknowledging the involvement of the author and the intertextuality of the written text in that entanglement.

In this chapter, I take the idea of materiality further and also include the role of spaces in the process of making a lesbian. By doing so, I depart from the lesbian, gay and queer scholarship that has mostly theorised LGBTIQ+ lives and identities as based on language, discourses and norms, or focused solely on the social relations between people, thereby considering spaces, if at all, merely as containers for social action (e.g. Forstie, 2014). Here my focus is the premise that spaces and people form affective relations with each other. Amrou Al-Kadhi captures this beautifully in their autobiography *Life as a Unicorn*: 'It was as though the dirt of the surroundings was a mirror to the person I really was, and I sat immobilised, unable to do anything, locked in a limbo of heartache' (Al-Kadhi, 2020).

The interplay of practices, spatial constellations, and emotions in studying lesbian and gay communities has already been scholarly addressed in the history of emotions (e.g. Gammerl, 2016), as well as in lesbian and gay geography. Here researchers have questioned, for example, how queer spaces are perceived, or how queer spaces produce embodied emotions (e.g. Taylor and Falconer, 2015: 45). It is noteworthy that in such approaches we assume a separate body that is in relation with the places it encounters and experiences. I am, however, searching for an avenue that would allow me to consider their relations differently.

Utilising the thinking of Karen Barad, I argue that bodies and spaces cannot be separated, as both arise together in an intra-action in which they are entangled (Barad, 2007: 139–40). Such an intra-action may be approached as an apparatus, which is 'formative of matter and meaning, productive of, and part of, the phenomena produced' (146). The phenomenon I am interested in is the idea of a lesbian, as it emerged in the open-ended practice of lesbian and gay dance parties. Hence, I examine here the dance parties as apparatuses, which I refer to as *lesboratories*. The neologism lesboratories is akin to the term laboratories, or breweries, which are also examples of intra-action; something qualitatively different and new emerges from the material assemblages that form the apparatuses in question.

Additionally, instead of focusing on personalised emotions, I concentrate more on an embodied and collective circulation of affects. Hence, for me, the situationally-emerging intra-active sensations are collective, intercorporeal and transubjective (Kolehmainen and Mäkinen, 2021: 449). As such, affects form and transform those experiencing them. The effects of being affected may of course retrospectively be interpreted as personalised emotions and identities.

In my empirical analysis of lesboratories, I rely especially on Andreas Reckwitz's lucid theorisation on the relationships of materiality and affect, discussed in his article 'Affective Spaces: A Praxeological Outlook' (2012). In the article, Reckwitz participates in the ongoing discussions regarding affective and spatial turns in analysing the past, arguing for the importance of combining the two. Although he, too, analytically separates bodies and spaces, I see that his use of affectivity, whilst also considering materiality's role in social practices, allows me to productively connect his ideas with Barad's notion of entangled intra-actions. This allows me to address affective intimacies of spatially entangled intra-actions that take shape in the collective, participatory social practices of lesboratories.

In this chapter I focus on lesboratories to analyse the collective bonds of affective intimacy through which the affected bodies became-with the materiality of the spaces of lesbian and gay dance parties. I first contextu-alise the 1980s lesbian and gay dance parties in Tampere, and then present my research material and methodological approach. Thereafter I discuss my two case studies, arguing for a conceptualisation of the emerging idea of a lesbian as a collective, embodied and affective formation.

Lesbian and gay life in Finland in the 1970s and 1980s

In contrast to many other countries, in Finland homosexual acts were illegal for both women and men. Homosexual acts were decriminalised in 1971, and demedicalised in 1981. Even when such changes first began to challenge the homogeneous self-understanding of the still rather inward-looking coun-try, a form of heterosexual ignorance regarding sexual diversity was easily maintained due to an anti-propaganda law spanning from 1971 to 1999 that criminalised incitement to homosexual acts. Initially the law resulted in the suppression of most mentions of homosexuality in public service broad-casting. The prescribed silence was disrupted by the AIDS epidemic, but a persistent journalistic habit to not mention or discuss an individual's homo-sexuality in respectable media remained unchallenged until the 1990s, if not the 2000s (Juvonen, 2004).

The first scholarly book in Finnish cowritten by lesbian and gay scholars about homosexuality, *Rakkauden monet kasvot* (*The Many Faces of Love*, edited by Sievers and Stålström) was published in 1984. Prior to that, if one wanted to learn anything about homosexuality, they had to find their way to the original sources: the lesbian and gay associations, their publications and social events. In Helsinki there were two lesbian and gay associations: Psyke (est. 1969), and Seta, from the words 'Seksuaalinen tasavertaisuus' meaning sexual equality (est. 1974). They both published their own periodi-cals, *96* and *SETA* respectively, which were posted in discreet envelopes to their members. Additionally, there were also some local branches of Psyke, such as Vagabondi (est. 1973) in Tampere. In order to finance their social services, such as helplines, and offer possibilities for socialising, the organi-sations also held highly popular dance parties.

In Finnish culture attending dances is a traditional means to get to know prospective intimate partners. As same-sex dancing was rather frowned upon, people engaging in it could easily be thrown out of heterosexual venues. Such a discriminatory practice became illegal in 1995 when an anti-discrimination law concerning service providers was passed. Hence, until the 1990s in particular, dance parties organised by LGBTIQ+ organisations at various venues offered participants the rare possibility to find support and legitimisation from the existence of others 'like that'. It may be argued that the social practice of arranging dance parties produced spaces that were simultaneously material and cultural in nature – and which profoundly affected those that participated in the social experience.

Tampere is a particularly interesting location to study the emerging lesbian and gay community of the time. Even though it was the second-largest Finnish city after the capital, Helsinki, in 1980 it was still rather modest in size with only around 166,000 inhabitants. Since the reputation of Tampere as an industrial city was built around its cotton mills, it was sometimes referred to as the Manchester of Finland. Even though Tampere was one of the major battlegrounds during the 1918 Civil War, the divide between the Reds and the Whites was closing as the city's intellectual and cultural life was blooming. The city received a university in 1960, and its (soon-to-be international) Theatre Festival was founded in 1968, featuring in its first year a Finnish version of the musical *Hair*. As the city had an easy-going leftist feel to it, it also provided fertile ground for sustaining a budding lesbian and gay culture.

Becoming with affective spaces

My research material is drawn from thirty-six oral history interviews I conducted between 2012–2017 with people born between 1940 and 1980 that, in one way or another, participated in the lesbian scene of Tampere between the 1970s and 2000s – as I myself did from 1989 onwards. The interviews were initially gathered for a research project that sought to understand the role of the social and intimate lives of women with same-sex sexual attractions in the constitution of local lesbian communities.[2] The interviews addressed both the social life that took place at various venues and the personal and intimate relations women formed with each other. I approached all of the interviewees in person, based on their participation in the scene. As I also had an interest in the intimate aspects of lesbian relationships, most of the interviews were conducted one-on-one, aside from an interview with a lesbian couple, and a group interview with elderly lesbians reminiscing on scenes of lesbian sociability. All interviewees, barring a heterosexual woman and two gay men, were women that had relationships with other women.

For this chapter I have selected excerpts from ten interviews that refer to two lesboratories in which the local Tampere lesbian and gay association Vagabondi organised its dance parties at the weekends. One of the places of intra-action was fondly nicknamed 'Hinttivintti' (the 'Fag Attic'). It was a club space situated on the fourth floor of the centrally located Workers' Union House at Hämeenpuisto 28, where parties were held from 1977–1986. Another venue was the restaurant Merirosvo (Pirate) owned by a co-op, slightly further away from the city centre and attached to the base of the sightseeing tower Näsinneula in the Särkänniemi Amusement Park at Laiturikatu 1. The dance parties in question took place there between 1987–1988. In addition to the interviews, I also used some printed materials I have been able to recover regarding the venues, such as journal or newspaper articles. However, such material has proven very scarce and hard to locate, due to the ban on incitement.

As someone who has conducted interviews regarding Sydney's drag king scene, Kerryn Drysdale has noted that anecdotes that refer to particular moments or events in a storied form are a preferred way to process experiences within lesbian scenes (Drysdale, 2019: 136–7). This observation also applies to my own interview material, which is punctuated with small anecdotes regarding these particular venues. When listening to these interviews, one gets the feeling that these stories have already been well-rehearsed, sitting with other lesbians around a table in a bar or kitchen (Scicluna, 2017: 158–66). In addition to soliciting these freely told anecdotes, I also asked my interviewees specific questions regarding the materiality of the venues they mentioned in their narrations. I asked, for example, what elements I should bring together if I was to rebuild the venue. However, I failed to ask questions specific to the senses; such as sights, scents and sounds, which Drysdale found particularly productive in her study and which were also crucial for Yvette Taylor and Emily Falconer in their work on class distinctions in queer leisure spaces (Drysdale, 2019: 141; Taylor and Falconer, 2015). Nevertheless, along with tactile and movement-based memories (Reckwitz, 2012: 249), the most detailed descriptions I received often already contained perceptions based on such sensory memories.

Observed through the lens of practice theory fostered by Andreas Reckwitz (2012), the presence of sensory elements in narration is quite reasoned. When people are understood as having sensing bodies, it follows that sensory perceptions would be foregrounded in people's narrations. Bodies are affected by other bodies, as well as by the materiality of the spaces through which they move, the activities that take place in those spaces, and the corresponding artefacts. Even where memory might fail in detail, it may capture the embodied intensity of feeling (Drysdale, 2019: 128). Reckwitz would likely add that this is no wonder, as the states of bodily arousal form the affective relations that link the narrators both with other entities and the world (Reckwitz, 2012: 250). With Barad, one would go even further to argue that in a lesboratory the entangled affective intra-actions bring forth both the embodied narrator and their world in an affected intimacy.

When looking at the artefact-space structuration (Reckwitz, 2012: 251) of these dance parties, I am interested in asking which elements of a lesboratory were crucial for bringing into being the idea of a lesbian. While reading the transliterated interviews I am observing both the spatial and social practices of entangled intra-actions. Moreover, in my analysis I pay attention to the descriptions concerning the materiality of the venues, following Reckwitz's (2012: 250) reminder: 'Every analysis of practices … necessarily involves an analysis of the artefacts which are assembled to constitute these practices'. Consequently, reading his work through Barad, I especially examine the sensory-perceptive connections the interviewees collectively formed when intra-acting with the materiality of the venues while participating in various social practices. Furthermore, I am interested in the affective intimacies and bodily arousals that the participation in and the becoming with these artefact-space assemblages induced, often perceived as the atmosphere of these venues.

As people form affective relationships with their environments, the environments take part in shaping both people and their understanding of themselves. Thus, it makes sense to argue that different artefact-space assemblages induce different sets of affective structuration. This assumption can be substantiated in studies that trace how the change of a venue transforms and rearranges the affective relations of the patrons (Reckwitz, 2012: 256). In the following I demonstrate how that change took place in the lesboratories of Tampere in the 1980s, as the lesbian and gay dance parties moved from a clubroom on the fourth floor of the Workers' Union House to a proper restaurant, Merirosvo, thus offering novel possibilities for the collective, embodied and affective becoming of lesbians.

The closeted space of the Fag Attic

The location and architecture of the venues in which the dance parties were held provide particular spatial frameworks and induce affective relations that cannot easily be circumvented by their users (Reckwitz, 2012: 250). In the case of the Fag Attic, one should consider the impressive nature of the Workers' Union House; completed in 1900 and located on the city's main boulevard, it added to the power and prestige of the city's workers. In addition to a theatre, on its third floor the building housed a purpose-built event venue, where people attended large and highly popular heterosexual dance parties. Vagabondi's dance parties were organised in the same building, yet those parties – as if demoted – took place in a much smaller space on the fourth floor that could at best cater to no more than 120 people.

Since Vagabondi's dance parties were the only ones considered safe for lesbians and gays in the city, all of those who were somehow able to discover its existence came and participated.

> Most of the patrons were men, slightly older men, but younger ones too, and some women, but not that many. It varied over the years. Most eye-catching were the biological men that were allowed to dress as women. At that time, they may have been transvestites. It was only later on that transgender people became involved with the group.[3]

The ages of the patrons ranged from barely eighteen, the legal age for alcohol consumption, through to seventy. The parties were also mixed by gender, class and social standing. Although there are also women that have very fond memories of the exciting and fun parties on the fourth floor, the events were heavily male-dominated, especially in the early years. While even married men were able to learn about the existence of these parties through the grapevine when cruising for other men in city parks; women, especially those with children, lacked similar information networks. Thus, some nights there may have been only two women, later on perhaps ten, and even at its best maybe only a quarter of the guests were female. The scarcity of women was detrimental to lesbian bonding, and it led women to seek out the company of their gay male best friends.

The heterosexual dance parties taking place in the same building on the same evenings posed a challenge to the lesbian and gay visitors: how could they reach the fourth floor without being recognised, when they nevertheless had to use the same entrance and staircase? Those who were mindful that they had to protect their queer identities, not to mention their livelihoods, chose to use the lift; which would – if they were lucky – allow them to arrive on the fourth floor unnoticed. Yet others, such as this lesbian with her girlfriend, were determined to use the stairs, withstanding the curious glances from the party guests on the third floor:

> However, going there was always a little … dubious. Kind of 'oh, that's where you're going'. But see, me and Anne, we always just strode in with our skirts swirling and heels clicking, heads held high.

Arriving on the fourth floor, guests would register a set of bodies and artefacts that marked the entrance to the party. The first of them was a sign reading 'Closed Circle Only' at the door of the clubroom. For many of the interviewees, the Fag Attic was the first lesbian and gay party venue they ever dared to enter. 'I remember that Workers' Union place, the fourth floor, I think it was kind of like, it was straight up like the gates of hell [laughing]. When you opened the door, everything was so terribly red'. That hellish impression was created not only by the accumulated anxiety regarding the impending meeting of other gay people, but also by the long and heavy red velvet curtains that covered tall windows, adding to the intimate atmosphere of the space.

A gay man recalls the venue in further detail:

> When you entered the area, there was a rather narrow corridor which led to the toilets. There was [the] ticket sales [counter], and straight after was the dance floor, which you walked through to the larger side. There you had tables, heavy weight tables, heavy chairs, and then on some beer crates, or some folding tables, the bar was set up, where they sold ... was it bottles of beer and long drink[s], that sort of thing, I don't recall them having any modern beer taps.

Becoming with the space began when walking into the clubroom through a small intimate hallway. There was a ticket counter at which volunteers greeted arriving guests and sold tickets to members and visitors. From here on the ensuing acts of collective participation in the event amounted to practical knowledge of how to become, at least for an evening, a legitimate member of that community (Drysdale, 2019: 78; Kolehmainen and Mäkinen, 2021: 457–9). Here the act of selling and buying a ticket to a lesbian and gay party helped to sustain the community by financially supporting its helpline and fostering its aspirations to buy an office space of its own for group meetings.

Crossing the dance floor brought one to a larger room, where sturdy tables and chairs awaited guests. Around many of the tables, one would find a mixed group of lesbian and gay friends, their evening having begun a couple of drinks earlier at their local bar. Sitting at heavy tables and chairs gave one the sensation of being firmly grounded in the space that hosted people 'like that'. Moreover, the activists of the lesbian and gay organisation would invite newcomers to dance, helping them feel included, and the regulars would make room for them at their tables. A woman who came there as a young lesbian remembers the intimacy of the place fondly: 'It was such a small and safe place, and you knew the people. And got to know older people, and many others you think back fondly on now, some of whom have already passed away'. One soon acquired a sense of belonging in the collective community of the Fag Attic.

Same-sex dancing was obviously one of the main attractions of the parties. The music alternated between disco and music for social dancing, reflecting the varying tastes of the patrons. On the dance floor one could spot – perhaps for the first time in one's life – two men immersed in social dancing that allowed bodily contact. This exciting and intimate sight of same-sex couples tuned one into the permissive atmosphere of the venue.

Initially the music was played on a portable cassette player. Especially proud was the lesbian 'disc jane' with the hottest new disco, which she had been able to obtain from a Danish disc jockey that had recorded bootleg copies for her: 'The Vagabondi folks heard that music about a year before it sort of came to Finnish discos'.

Whereas the orderly rules of social dancing created a predictable structure for proper social interaction and behaviour, dancing to disco music broke free from all of that (Gammerl, 2016: 60–2). Dancing to disco also allowed for a different form of self-expression, as an author of the lesbian and gay magazine *96* explained: 'In dance [the current young generation] expresses its happiness and sorrow, desire and pain, fear and aggression. Dance titillates and liberates, it is endless joy of movement for its own sake, it is intoxicating without drugs, it is wriggling and orgasmic jerking with screams and shouts' (Haapala, 1983: 22). The Fag Attic was felt to be a safe space for patrons to try these things out. A lesbian recalls her experience:

> On that tiny stamp-sized dancefloor I learned to loosen my feet from the floor. I had never been anywhere, dancing, so in my first fumbling disco moves I had both feet flat on the floor, just wiggling myself a little. At some point I dared to dance with my heels off the floor a little. And eventually, my feet were coming off the floor entirely.

Hence the intra-action of her dancing to disco music together with other lesbian and gay bodies – with the aid of alcohol not to be forgotten – provided her with the necessary encouragement to experience different bodily capacities and reach a different kind of self-understanding; that of a more daring person.

The alcohol served at the parties further eased communication and helped create a joyous atmosphere (Tan, 2013). However, as the keen gay observer noted, the party venue did not have a proper bar, just beer crates and bottled long drinks stacked on folding tables. The cheap, lightweight arrangement of the bar with its lack of proper beer taps highlighted the make-do character of the lesbian and gay parties. On the one hand, the existence of a beer-selling table in a space that was not intended to be a bar in the first place was a testimony to the success of the collective work poured into organising the parties. Yet on the other hand, it was also a reminder of the temporary nature of the arrangement. One could let their hair down only for an evening, and come next Monday morning, all traces of that party would have been stacked away and hidden – quite as one had to hide one's homosexuality and pretend to be straight again.

Yet the possibility of escaping the need to conceal one's same-sex sexual orientation, even if for only one night, was highly valued. The people, women and men alike, abundantly enjoyed the rare freedom to affectively entangle in looking, flirting, dancing and drinking with friends and former, current or prospective partners without the need to hide their desires which would have been pathologised elsewhere (Tan, 2013: 720, 728).

> It was terribly fun. I can't remember there ever even being any fights, and we all loved the music. There was all kinds of music, and we really danced a lot, and frankly speaking, we were all pretty drunk. Almost everybody was always there to the end.

The reluctance to let go of that stolen freedom is also apparent in an anecdote regarding the activities that would take place after a party (Drysdale, 2019: 79). A raffle was a reoccurring event at the parties, and a further way to raise funds to support the ambitious plans of Vagabondi.

> There was always a raffle, and of course the prizes were always alcohol. And it was always someone we knew who won. So off we went, when the party was over, we went to the Hämeenpuisto boulevard, drank, and puked. But we had to drink it cos we won it [laughter]. It was the same thing every night.

Yet it is evident that the same venue was not perceived in a similar manner by everyone. In the early 1980s it was highly exceptional that people would have outed themselves outside of the Vagabondi events, something the organisers understood very well. This awareness was epitomised by the long and heavy velvet curtains of the Fag Attic: 'The curtains were closed, which indicated that this was not a public space'. When the dance parties were in their seventh year, the generational conflict that was previously suggested through differing tastes in music materialised into a controversy over the red velvet curtains. Two female journalists who had dared to come to the party observed the following incident:

> A very cute looking, yet very intoxicated young man heads toward our table from across the floor [...]. The youngster only wants to open the curtains behind us. 'Why must all the windows be covered? Why are we enclosed in here like in a cage? Are we animals?' he slurs. [...]
>
> Soon after the youngster has stumbled away from our table an anxious-looking middle-aged man arrives.
>
> 'I think the curtains need to be closed. I don't trust that guy. I saw him leave the bar once with someone that's ... not one of us', he says quietly. [...] 'Perhaps I'm just paranoid, but we're always treated in such a nasty way', he says apologetically and closes the curtains. (Hassinen, 1984)

The intimate and closeted space of the Fag Attic accommodated the needs of those that had a lot to lose. Whereas closeted gay identities are often associated with shame (Gammerl, 2016: 58), they can also adequately be linked with a reasonable fear of being found out. As being outed would most likely have shattered any parallel heterosexual family lives, or jeopardised one's social standing, employment and financial survival; the fear of being found out, sometimes amounting to paranoia, becomes quite understandable. However, in the mid-1980s a new generation of young lesbians and gay men emerged who were no longer content with hiding away.

One may observe how the recurring social practice of attending dance parties in the secluded space of the Fag Attic, with its old-fashioned social dancing, offered predictability and security for the older generation and sustained its affective habitus of incorporated schemes (Reckwitz, 2012: 255) around closeted homosexuality. Yet at the same time, new and liberating disco music signified a disruption of this stability. Additionally, the recurrent organising of these parties helped to create a group of capable activists who took pride in their sustained efforts and achievements in keeping the party going. Yet this venue's capacity to function as a lesboratory was limited, due to the heavily male-dominated makeup of its collective body. However, things were about to change both abruptly and permanently when Vagabondi lost its lease on the venue and had to move on at the end of 1986.

Merirosvo as a lesboratory

Fortunately, in 1987 Vagabondi's efforts resulted in a new venue being found. In the somewhat outlying location of the Särkänniemi Amusement Park, a co-op restaurant called Merirosvo decided to lease its premises to the association over the weekends. However, the co-op did not wish to have its name mentioned in connection with a lesbian and gay party, so the advertisements were only run with the name Gay Disco Zip. At the same time, the local conservative newspaper persistently refused to publish advertisements containing the word 'gay'. This catch-22 led Vagabondi to set up an answering machine on which taped messages would reveal the necessary details of the venue's whereabouts.

These difficulties aside, the place itself was a major improvement to the former clubroom, as Merirosvo was a 1971 purpose-built restaurant and bar. The reactions of a younger patron demonstrate how the space was perceived in the light of anticipation, recollection and comparison: 'It was an astronomical improvement, since it was a normal space, and not such a cave of concealment'. The fact that Merirosvo was a purpose-built restaurant with a proper bar made the guests feel instantly better – and also more normal.

Additionally, here the entanglement of the guests with the spatial architecture created a particular affective intimacy, one very different from the Fag Attic. When one walks into the building and through a spacious glass hall, the open staircase leading to the next floor is immediately visible on the right-hand side. When climbing the staircase, one feels almost elevated by the panoramic views offered by the wall of windows that await at the top.

The previously mentioned perceptive gay man also gave his recollections on the interiors of this venue:

> Merirosvo was a curved restaurant at the base of the Särkänniemi sightseeing tower. When you enter from outside, you walk up the stairs and then there are tables along the way, the bar and dance floor are at the back, at the end of the curve. I think the space was really functional, more modern, furnished as a restaurant. Nice windows that open up to lake Näsijärvi. Sort of atmospheric in the summer for example, [when] you can see the lake. The place was pretty nice.

The wide-open view from the wall-to-wall windows over the nearby lake was a welcome novelty, especially in comparison with the firmly covered windows of the Fag Attic. The uninterrupted openness of the space also suggested that the patrons themselves had more leeway and less to hide than before.

The venue's new location also contained a few obstacles for some of the older guests. The decrease in accessibility from both the entryway staircase and from the parties no longer taking place in the city centre made the venue itself less inclusive. Additionally, the differing generational tastes in music continued to cause friction. Even as some social dancing prevailed to accommodate the needs of the older patrons, at the Gay Disco Zip the music skewed noticeably toward disco tunes. The culmination of these factors resulted in a generational break in the local lesbian community.

With the founding of Vagabondi's Youth and Student Group in 1985, and their Women's Group with its decidedly feminist agenda a year later, the participation of younger women in the events increased. When Vagabondi dedicated the first Friday of every month to a lesbian party called Zippina, it paved the way to additional intra-actions. The women who knew each other from the Women's Group always went to the party together: 'We met somewhere first and ate, or ate at somebody's place, and then went to the party. That was really fun'. Sharing a meal together was a further lesbian social practice that both built up anticipation and added to the atmosphere of the party itself (cf. Bille, Bjerregaard and Sørensen, 2015: 34).

Consequently, and contrary to the Fag Attic, at Merirosvo there were plenty of young women. They also preferred to spend time with each other, though they did not fully abandon their gay friends either. Meeting and talking not only in the Women's Group but also at the parties meant that individualised reflections and disparate social experiences of lesbians were rendered through the retrospective reminiscing into a collective social consciousness (Drysdale, 2019: 128). Attending Vagabondi's dance parties offered a safe environment for young women to become lesbians by participating in this collective social practice. Hence, the possibility of sharing both spaces and stories turned out to be a further vital aspect of a lesboratory.

The parallel existence of a Women's Group also led to other inventive social practices that aimed to cultivate lesbian collectivity at the parties:

> We had just been discussing at the Women's Group how awful it is to come to the party alone [...]. And then together with another girl we – we were still girls back then – decided that in our group we'll look out for if someone is alone, and we'll go and ask her to dance or something, and bring her back to our table. Then at the bar there was a woman all alone, so I went over and asked her to dance, and she said, 'I'm waitressing here' [laughter]. After that I lost the nerve to ask anyone else to dance.

Dancing was obviously an important attraction for the women. Merirosvo also had a proper sound system and, together with disco lights, it created an immersive sensory experience of music, vibration and losing oneself in the crowd (Gammerl, 2016: 61–2). In addition to dancing, the interviewees also specified a novel feature of the emerging lesbian culture present at Merirosvo: 'We always sang "Aikuinen nainen", always.'

'Aikuinen nainen' ('Mature Woman') is a song that has become the unofficial anthem for Finnish lesbians, and was covered from the Italian original 'Maledetta primavera' by gay icon Paula Koivuniemi in 1982. The Finnish lyrics contain many empowering lines, including the following which lesbians would sing along to with dedication:

> I will not turn my back
> I fight for my love, I'm not afraid
> Taking care of each other
> We'll hold back adversity
> The waves won't bring us down,
> I'll shelter you from the winds
> If you'll let me

The song resonated affectively not only with the women on the dance floor, but also with those who, in various states of intoxication, were singing along to the tune and group hugging. Being entangled with the music, bodies and singing not only added affect and intimacy to the atmosphere on the dance floor, but the musical intra-action also made the women bond more tightly with each other across the venue as lesbians.

The adversity referred to in the song was also a reality, apparent in the challenge to even arrive at Merirosvo. The local youth had a habit of cruising in their cars in the nearby parking lot, and many of the patrons were concerned that the gay crowds walking down the road from the closest bus stop to the rather remotely located bar would invite violent attacks. Hence several women chose to come to the bar by taxi rather than walk. However, when the elated women left the party together in the night, such worries evaporated. The group of drunken lesbians dared each other to do things few would have risked doing alone – such as celebrating a birthday with an adventurous skinny dip at the lake shore sauna of the nearby Sara Hildén Art Museum.

> We went to Sara Hildén and went for a swim from the sauna at the lake shore at like two in the morning, like after the party, and it was really fun, it was a really fun party. I remember we had a big group of women, many different kinds of women.

The same lesbians were now more eager to also take up space in the city: 'We always walked down there, by the fast-food stand, always laughing, walking side-by-side, singing like there was no tomorrow'.

After a great night out at the party, it no longer seemed dangerous for the women to leave Merirosvo on foot. The pack of hungry and drunken lesbians headed towards a fast-food stand in the city, taking up its space walking side-by-side on the boardwalk and singing out loud to hilarious and spontaneously invented lyrics. The affective resonance emerging in that group of young women was one of intimate togetherness and an entitlement to be a lesbian. Hence Merirosvo can be seen as one of the first real lesbo-ratories in Tampere, a place where the intra-acting women could and would collectively become lesbians.

It may be argued that the new normality of becoming a lesbian was reflected in Merirosvo, a conventional bar in a free-flowing space. There 'new possibilities or new actualizations of matter – new utterances and pleasures and ways of moving, as well as alternative attunements to bodies and desires – are invented by the collision of multiple material trajectories coming into arrangement in relation to another' (Ewalt, 2016: 138). The increase in openness of that curtainless space suggested boundless possibili-ties and open-ended potential. It also influenced the collectivity of women who had developed a novel form of entitlement in being a lesbian.

Conclusion

In this chapter I have examined the development of the idea of a lesbian in Tampere by utilising accounts from oral history interviews regarding les-bian and gay party venues run by the local lesbian and gay organisation Vagabondi from 1977 to 1988. I maintain that women were affected not only by the gender composition of the events, but, quite importantly, also by the material entanglements and affective intimacies that became possible within the social practices of these particular places. When considered collectively, these apparatuses, which I refer to as lesboratories, had consequent effects on the ways in which these women were able to become lesbians and create communities of their own.

Reckwitz (2012: 256) proposed that a change of space provides incalculable incentives for the rearrangement of affective relations, and my findings show that this was also the case for the lesbian and gay dance parties in shifting locations. The rampantly gay atmosphere of the Workers' Union House parties from 1977 to 1986 was partly due to the fact that the parties were rather extraordinary events in an everyday life that was otherwise, for most of the guests, highly closeted and restricted. Even the intimate party venue itself resembled a protective cocoon. As not very many gay women had been able to find their way there yet, the women mostly partied happily with their fellow gay male friends, without ever even calling themselves lesbians.

Moving the parties to Merirosvo in 1987 meant not only a marked shift in the party concept, but also a considerable change in female attendance. The more youthful disco music, and especially the Zippina parties, attracted more young women to the events. Taking cues from the open and ordinary space of the bar venue, the young women were also able to take a more open and relaxed attitude toward lesbianism. The intimate and affective intra-actions with a collective of other women, together with the airy nature of the venue, made them better equipped to conquer new spaces for themselves as lesbians in the wider world as well.

Whereas Drysdale (2019: 139) urges us to look at the localised politics of lesbian identity, Clare Forstie (2014: 196) argues for connecting the meanings of lesbian identity further to particular spaces. My analysis suggests that we can go even further; to consider the formative power of the materiality of the entangled intra-actions that take place within these spaces. Coining the apparatus of entangled material and social intra-actions as a *lesboratory* draws attention to the productive and affective role it has in producing the idea of a lesbian. As I have demonstrated, the materiality of these two different party venues provided not only the pre-conditions for bodily encounters, but they also significantly co-constituted and informed the self-understanding of the participating guests. Each place with its own forms of affective intimacy had consequences for the emerging idea of being a lesbian that the women collectively welcomed.

Whereas the secluded space of the Fag Attic provided predictability and security, Merirosvo in contrast offered a novel sense of freedom and possibility for lesbians – and not only for them alone. When they lost the lease for Merirosvo in 1988, Vagabondi was no longer happy to be vagabonding around in different low-key rented spaces. Realising now that it was worth it, Vagabondi decided to buy a restaurant of its own in the city centre of Tampere. In 1990 the country's second lesbian and gay night club Mixei opened its doors at Otavalankatu 3, where once again the materiality of the venue gave impetus to a new kind of lesboratory.

Notes

1 For a nuanced and critical discussion on the use of the concept of community in lesbian and gay scholarship, see Formby (2017).

2 *Queer narratives: Intimate and social lives of women with same-sex sexual attractions in Tampere 1971–2011*, funded by the Academy of Finland (project number 249652).

3 As my study of this very small community also addresses intimate aspects of my interviewees' relationships, I protect their identities by using pseudonyms and by keeping the interview excerpts anonymous. The audio and transliterated interview data is available for scholarly use at the Finnish Labour Museum Werstas, Tampere.

References

Abraham, J. (1996), *Are Girls Necessary? Lesbian Writing and Modern Histories* (Ann Arbor, MN: University of Minnesota Press).

Al-Kadhi, A. (2020), *Life as a Unicorn: A Journey From Shame to Pride and Everything in Between* (Glasgow: Fourth Estate).

Barad, K. (2007), *Meeting the Universe Halfway: Quantum Physics and the Entanglement of Matter and Meaning* (Durham, NC: Duke University Press).

Bille, M., Bjerregaard, P., and Sørensen, T. F. (2015), 'Staging Atmospheres: Materiality, Culture, and the Texture of the In-Between', *Emotion, Space and Society*, 15, 31–8. https://doi.org/10.1016/j.emospa.2014.11.002

Boyd, N. A., and Ramírez, H. N. R. (eds) (2012), *Bodies of Evidence: The Practice of Queer Oral History* (Oxford: Oxford University Press).

Drysdale, K. (2019), *Intimate Investments in Drag King Culture: The Rise and Fall of a Lesbian Social Scene* (London: Palgrave Macmillan Cham).

Ewalt, J. P. (2016), 'The Agency of the Spatial', *Women's Studies in Communication*, 39:2, 137–40. https://doi.org/10.1080/07491409.2016.1176788

Formby, E. (2017), *Exploring LGBT Spaces and Communities: Contrasting Identities, Belongings and Wellbeing* (London: Routledge).

Forstie, C. (2014), '"Bittersweet" Emotions, Identities, and Sexualities: Insights from a Lesbian Community Space', in *Selves, Symbols and Sexualities: An Interactionist Anthology*, S. Newmahr and T. Weinberg (eds) (Thousand Oaks, CA: Sage Publications), 183–200.

Gammerl, B. (2016), 'Curtains Up! Shifting Emotional Styles in Gay Men's Venues Since the 1950s', *SQS – Journal of Queer Studies in Finland*, 10:1–2, 57–64. https://doi.org/10.23980/sqs.63667

Haapala, E. (1983), Skitsofreeninen kulttuuri, *96* 1/1983, 21–23.

Hassinen, T. (1984), Kuka olikaan poikkeava? *Karjalan Maa*; cited in *Bondi*, 6/1984, 12–13.

Juvonen, T. (2004), 'Nyt se näkyy, nyt taas ei. Heteronormatiivisuus ja homoseksuaalisuuden esillepano *Helsingin Sanomissa*' ('Now You See It, Now You Don't. Heteronormativity and the Display of Homosexuality in Helsingin Sanomat'), *Tiedotustutkimus*, 27:2, 34–55. Available at: https://journal.fi/mediaviestinta/article/view/62442 (Accessed: 21 June 2021).

Kolehmainen, M., and Mäkinen, K. (2021), 'Affective Labour of Creating Atmospheres', *European Journal of Cultural Studies*, 24:2, 448–63. https://doi.org/10.1177/1367549419886021

Männistö-Funk, T. (2021), 'What Kerbstones Do: A Century of Street Space from the Perspective of One Material Actor', *Cultural History*, 10:1, 61–90.

Reckwitz, A. (2012), 'Affective Spaces: A Praxeological Outlook', *Rethinking History*, 16:2, 241–58. https://doi.org/10.1080/07491409.2016.1176788

Reuter, D. F. (2008), *Greetings from the Gayborhood: A Nostalgic Look at Gay Neighborhoods* (New York, NY: Abrams).

Scicluna, R. M. (2017), *Home and Sexuality: The 'Other' Side of the Kitchen* (Palgrave Macmillan Studies in Family and Intimate Life) (London: Palgrave Macmillan).

Sievers, K., and Stålström, O. (eds) (1984), *Rakkauden monet kasvot: Homoseksuaalisesta rakkaudesta, ihmisoikeuksista ja vapautumisesta* (*Many Faces of Love: About Homosexual Love, Human Rights and Liberation*) (Espoo, Finland: Weilin+Göös).

Tan, Q. H. (2013), 'Flirtatious Geographies: Clubs as Spaces for the Performance of Affective Heterosexualities', *Gender, Place & Culture*, 20:6, 718–36. https://doi.org/10.1080/0966369X.2012.716403

Taylor, Y., and Falconer, E. (2015), '"Seedy Bars and Grotty Pints": Close Encounters in Queer Leisure Spaces', *Social and Cultural Geography*, 16:1, 43–57. https://doi.org/10.1080/14649365.2014.939708

Part III

Queering intimacies: Affective un/becomings

7

'Lack' of languages: Affective experiences of female same-sex intimacies in contemporary China

Yiran Wang

Introduction

In our everyday lives, we deal with, talk about, long for and/or run away from intimacies; however, intimacy is differently understood and embodied in different times, groups of people and circumstances, since intimacies are always entanglements of specific notions, emotions, bodies and environments (Sanger and Taylor, 2013). Due to the Euro-American-centrism in the (re)production of most normative knowledge, the uneven globalisation of information and the personal and national pursuits of 'modernity' in developing countries, Western-rooted experiences and interpretations of intimacy, especially those about sexuality and romantic love, have often been taken for universal 'truths' in many societies (Chao, 2000; Reddy, 2012; Weeks, 2003; Sang, 2003). Of course, people's everyday practices, languages and feelings about intimacy in the contemporary world are not 'Westernised' homogeneously. Rather, an increasing number of studies have mapped the hybridised and contested configurations and understandings of intimacy across the world (e.g. Martin *et al.*, 2008; Padilla *et al.*, 2008; Sanger and Taylor, 2013), which, despite embodying unequal power relations, are ever-multiplying and ever-transforming.

Among the sites where diverse ideas about intimacy dynamically encounter one another is China, a society renowned for its unique cultural traditions and well-developed philosophies since ancient times. Chinese histories of sexual eroticism, kinship relationships and understandings about the self and the other have provided inspiring materials for Euro-American scholars to write about intimacies and subjectivities (e.g. Butler, 2004: 103; Deleuze and Guattari, 1987; Foucault, 1978: 57; Van Gulik, 1961). Since the beginning of the twentieth century, China has witnessed waves of introductions of transnationally and transregionally circulating concepts, theories and ideals related to intimacy, including the terms of 'sexuality' and 'gender', the categorisation of sexual orientations, and the normalisation of heterosexual, monogamous marriage based on 'free choices' (Evans, 1997; Rocha, 2010; Sang, 2003). In the twenty-first century, scenes of intimacies in China, as vibrant 'non-Western' but globalising experiences, have become highly contested and are rapidly changing (Ho *et al.*, 2018). These scenes have inspired a boom in empirical studies conducted in China that reflect on Euro-American theorisations of both heteronormative and 'queer' desires and practices (e.g. Engebretsen, 2014; Kam, 2013; Kong, 2011; Zheng, 2015).

This chapter, developed from an anthropological study on Chinese women-loving women's subjectivities and everyday lives, investigates the affective experiences of female same-sex love and sex in the 2010s in mainland China. Scholars have noticed that, compared with the ways that sexuality is routinely discussed in Euro-American societies, finding a language to openly talk about sexuality is not an easy task for East Asian researchers and their researched subjects, especially when they are women (Jackson *et al.*, 2008). On the other side, in studies on Chinese women-loving-women intimacies, the 'love' between women functions more as a pre-existing, fixed fact, which is rather left unexplored compared with other research questions such as 'coming out of the closet' and LGBTQ[1] activism (see Engebretsen, 2014; Kam, 2013). This situation can also be a result of the tradition of queer theory: compared with sexuality, love often seems too normative to play a critical role in queer inquiries (Halperin, 2019). Thus, processes of the 'becoming' of female same-sex love and the embodiment of love in the lived experiences of Chinese same-sex attracted women have seldom been depicted in detail. In my own study, however, I tried to talk, write and feel female same-sex love and sex. Interestingly, I found that – whether in my fieldwork or in the everyday lives of the participants and myself – there were unspoken or ineffable feelings, 'misused' words, and lessons learned by bodily practices. This 'lack' of languages was beyond fluent, precise and rational verbal expressions but still powerfully presented how love and sex could make sense in processes of becoming intimate and becoming a women-loving woman.

Across the Euro-American humanities and social sciences, an 'affective turn' from the dominance of linguistic, semiotic and discursive practices has been fuelled, which instead pays attention to the affective capacities of bodies, emotions and materials (Clough, 2010). These emerging theorisations about affects are embedded in the genealogies of Western philosophy and other disciplines, while making innovative reflections on them (Seigworth and Gregg, 2010). Although it is hard to find a single Chinese word to precisely translate the English term of 'affect', affect theories to a large extent echo Taoist and Buddhist thoughts that nourish Chinese classical philosophy (Braidotti *et al.*, 2018). Additionally, affect theories criticise dualistic thinking about the individual and society, body and mind, culture and nature, self and other, inside and outside, material and immaterial, human and non-human (Blackman and Venn, 2010; Clough, 2010), and 'the West' and 'the Rest' of course. Since such dualistic thoughts have also dominated Chinese modern and contemporary languages, texts and ideologies, analysing my data through the lens of 'affect' will produce new knowledge about the intimacies experienced by female, non-heteronormative, global South, post-traditional and post-colonial subjects beyond the limitation of the standard usage of authoritative languages.

Of course, this chapter does not render the sexual histories and politics of the global South as mere 'footnotes' in English-written academic texts, 'providing the empirical material upon which Northern academics build their theories' (criticised by Wieringa and Sívori, 2013: 6). Rather, I create a space that allows Chinese intimate experiences and the ever-growing body of work focusing on affects to encounter each other. My analysis in this chapter is inspired by and aims to enrich feminist new-materialism, especially the 'nomadic subjectivity' theorised by Rosi Braidotti (1994, 2002, 2011a, 2011b, 2014), as well as the approaches to the body with more embodied perspectives, rather than linguistic ones (see Blackman, 2008). In this chapter, I am interested in the question of what kinds of embodied emotions and memories, affected and affecting bodies, and assembled and relational subjectivities are emerging from Chinese same-sex attracted women's love and sexual experiences, especially when these love and sexual experiences grapple with and/or grow beyond verbal expressions and discourses. My chapter contributes to rethinking intimacies by recognising the trans-subjective, inter-corporeal experiences that constitute affective experiences.

Focusing on love and sexual experiences, this chapter by no means agrees that intimacy should be reduced to individual privacy and the private sphere; rather, 'intimacy is shaped by, and helps shape, a variety of spatial scales – from the domestic, the local, the urban and the national, to the global' (Sanger and Taylor, 2013: 2). Scholars who combine affect theories and feminist and queer studies have even pushed the discussions of intimacies towards a post-humanist frontier, breaking the traditionally supposed boundaries that separate human subjects (especially white, male subjects) from 'other' statuses of being and becoming (e.g. Braidotti, 2013; Haraway, 2008; Lykke, 2018). In this chapter, although my analysis of intimacies revolves around human experiences, I bear in mind that love and sexual relationships are not vacuums built by (normatively two) individuals and bounded bodies. Instead, I view intimacies as affective 'intra-actions', rather than interactions, which defy boundaries between subjects, bodies, materials and discourses (see discussion about 'intra-action' in Barad, 2007). Of course, not all affects experienced by 'others' can easily be observed and understood by social science research, and the difficulty of 'offering an empirical portrait of a world filled with holes' has not been completely solved by affect theories (Rutherford, 2016: 295). As an anthropologist, while in my studies I explored the affective experiences that had 'failed' to be represented by unambiguous, rational verbal language, I had to rely on understandable communications and palpable empathy to collect data in my fieldwork. Not despite but because of this, I believe that my approach in this chapter enables the observations and analyses of affective intimacies to avoid the dualism of mind/body.

Chinese lesbianism and the participants of the study

Same-sex eroticism and practices, especially those between men, were richly documented and fictionalised in pre-modern Chinese texts, yet this does not mean that same-sex sexualities were unconditionally tolerated in Chinese traditions (Kang, 2009). Female same-sex relationships that tried to refuse heterosexual married life and escape patriarchal kinship were unthinkable according to traditional Chinese familial and social norms, even though some women did manage such non-normative lives (Sang, 2003; Wieringa, 2007). During China's Republican era (1912–1949), Chinese (male) intellectuals selectively introduced European sexologist and eugenic thoughts in order to develop a modernised nation-state, and the pathologised notion of 'homosexuality' ('tongxinglian', or 'tongxing'ai') entered modern Chinese vocabularies (Sang, 2003).

After the founding of the People's Republic of China, during the Maoist decades the topics of sexuality were rarely discussed openly, and private lives were regulated in support of national development and collective benefits (Evans, 1997). Accordingly, in this period female same-sex practices were largely silenced in public discourse and personal narratives (Ruan and Bullough, 1992). Later, in post-Mao China under the policy of 'economic reform and opening up' (gaige kaifang), sexuality, gender and feminism re-emerged from academic and popular discourses (Zhong, 2007). Male same-sex behaviours were decriminalised in 1997, and homosexuality was officially de-pathologised in 2001 (Kang, 2012). After the twenty-first century started, owing to the development of the internet and accelerated global mobilities, same-sex attracted women in mainland China have communicated with one another, and with their counterparts in Taiwan, Hong Kong and overseas; online and offline communities of lesbians, or 'lalas',[2] have emerged (Engebretsen, 2014; Kam, 2013). However, since women are usually not recognised as autonomous sexual subjects and are not encouraged to be 'leftover women' (shengnü) on the heterosexual marriage market, issues related to female same-sex intimacies have not received adequate attention within and without China's 'tongzhi'[3] communities (Engebretsen, 2014; Kam, 2013).

Methodologically, the data analysed in this chapter were collected in the ethnographic fieldwork of my PhD project, which was intensively conducted between 2013 and 2014 in Shanghai, a cosmopolitan city in the contemporary world, and Yunnan, a province located in southwestern China which is often considered to be economically less developed. Scattered follow-up investigations were carried out until 2019. Thirty-nine self-reported same-sex attracted women (seventeen living in Shanghai and twenty-two in Yunnan Province), aged between their early twenties and mid-forties at the time, participated in my study through in-depth interviews, focus groups, participatory observations and casual conversations. In order to find these participants, I mixed different sampling methods, including purposive sampling, snowball sampling and convenience sampling (see Bernard, 2011). I posted invitations on popular Chinese-based social network websites and apps such as Sina Weibo, WeChat, Douban.com and QQ chat groups. I contacted organisers of grassroots 'lala' groups in my fieldwork locations and asked them to introduce potential participants, who then introduced more.

Although my study originally focused on collecting and analysing narratives, in this chapter I re-examine the data from a perspective that is more sensitive to the affective aspects of female same-sex love and sex, and of an anthropological study. According to the scholars who have sought inventive research methods for collecting/producing embodied-affective data (e.g. Kinnunen and Kolehmainen, 2019; Knudsen and Stage, 2015; Walkerdine and Jimenez, 2012), affective forces can be traced in forms and styles of verbal expressions, in gestures and non-verbal languages, as well as in trans-subjective flows co-constructed by the researcher and the researched, even if the data of a study mainly consists of narratives and texts. During the process of revisiting my data and writing this chapter, I have recognised myself as a 'vulnerable observer' (Behar, 1996), who was easily affected by – and actively affecting – my own study.

In the following two sections, I respectively discuss 'love', especially 'first love', and 'sexual intimacies', two topics about which both the participants and myself yearned to express ourselves and discuss, but often found a 'lack' of language. Pseudonyms are given to the participants. Instead of piling up similar cases in the two analysis sections, I select typical experiences shared by many participants and special experiences that can 'jar our ideas' and 'make us question what we think we know' (Becker, 1998: 8).

(First) love without articulation

In my fieldwork there was a particularly welcomed icebreaking question for initiating a conversation: 'Could you say something about your "first love"?'

(chulian). This question was always followed by rich, spontaneous narrative flows. Ironically, while the participants had much to say, retrospectively, about their earlier feelings of love for other women or teenage girls, many of them had never explicitly expressed these feelings to those beloved persons under the name of 'love'; and those beloved persons also reacted in ambiguous or ambivalent ways. In this section, I discuss cases of such affective experiences without or beyond precise verbal definitions and confirmations, what I call 'love without articulation'. By combining these cases with the concept of 'nomadic subjectivity' developed by Braidotti (1994, 2002, 2011a, 2011b; a feminist new-materialist philosopher who has critically elaborated the Deleuzian affective theorisation of 'becoming'), I argue that becoming a women-loving woman in contemporary China defies the verbal language that confines 'love/aiqing'[4] within a heteronormative framework, confines subjectivity within a consistent (self-)identification, and confines the understanding of intimacy within the present relationship between a couple of individuals.

According to the official guide on the subject, *The Theories of Ideology and Politics* (Sixiang Zhengzhi Lilun), a compulsory subject in China's national post-graduate entrance exam, the nature of 'aiqing' (love) is:

> a strong, pure, and single-minded affection, between a man and a woman who have gained certain social relations and material supports and share the same ideal of life, entailing mutual admiration and yearning for building a life-long partnership.[5]

Obviously excluding same-sex intimacies, these lines count as the standard definition of 'love/aiqing' given by the Ministry of Education of China, representing the authoritative knowledge and the government-advocated ideal of romantic love in contemporary China. Chinese women who are attracted to women are ignored or even stigmatised by this heteronormative discourse. They also live under the familial and social pressure of 'compulsory marriage' (Kam, 2013: 6), which means that (hetero)marriage is considered to be the only normal and desirable lifestyle for all adults. Thus, for many participants of my study, being an openly identified homosexual (tongxinglian) and maintaining their same-sex intimacies – especially their early explorations of same-sex love – are often incompatible with each other.

The first-love story told by the participant 'Shore' is typical. Shore, born in the early 1990s and grown up in Kunming, the provincial capital of Yunnan Province, had cherished her continuous special attachment to a young woman named 'Seagull' since primary school. For more than thirteen years, neither Shore nor Seagull had touched on the word 'love/aiqing' when they expressed the special feelings they had for each other, even though they had celebrated 'Qixi Festival'[6] and 'May Twentieth'[7] together several times – the counterparts of Valentine's Day in Chinese popular culture. Seagull usually defined their relationship as 'friendship' (youqing), and she had dated several boys alongside. However, she tried her best to trivialise these dates in front of Shore. Shore recalled: 'She [Seagull] once said that if I was against her dating that boy, she could absolutely give him up.' On the other side, Shore had never told Seagull that she actually saw the young men who courted Seagull as 'love rivals' (qingdi). Thus, only under a name other than 'love/aiqing', such as 'friendship', did the love between the two women survive.

Here, I phrase 'love without articulation' as a pun, since the word 'articulation' means either the action of giving utterance or the action of inter-relating. For many Chinese women (once) involved in same-sex love, it is unbearable to explicitly name the intimate connection between women as 'love' – until it is no longer possible to maintain this connection, for example when they can tell their (first-)love stories retrospectively (see also, Martin, 2010). However, silenced verbal expressions of love and emotional detachments from the experiences of love do not mean that these women have passively compromised on a heteronormative life script and social pressure. Rather, embodied intimacies without verbal definitions sometimes allow these women to eschew social stigmas such as sexual and/or gender 'deviant'.

'Tea', a working-class participant in her early forties who was born in a small town in Yunnan Province, spent hours in the interview reminiscing on her three ex-girlfriends, to whom she had never uttered the word 'love/aiqing'. Despite the frustration and sadness brought about by the break-ups, Tea expressed that she was quite satisfied with holding on to the memories of these three women – 'the three good dreams' in her own words – for the rest of her life. For twenty years, Tea had a close bond with her second ex-girlfriend, although at the time of the interview she preferred to name this bond as 'sisterhood' or 'family', rather than 'lovers'. Tea was this ex-girlfriend's bridesmaid and her son's 'nanny'; and this woman in return supported Tea financially and emotionally when she faced difficulties. This ex-girlfriend's husband, who had never known of the same-sex intimacy between the two women, had a mutual appreciation and respect for Tea. In other words, without verbally self-identifying as a 'lesbian' or 'lala', Tea had maintained a life filled with exclusive women-loving-women attachments, regardless of the past tense she applied to describe her same-sex love relationships.

Knudsen and Stage (2015) have analysed the complicated relations between affect and language, based on two groups of scholars who research and theorise affect. On one hand, affect is beyond language categorisation, and semantics and semiotics can turn out to be distorted traces of affect; on the other hand, language has a sensitive capability of expressing affective experiences (4). In the case of 'love without articulation', affective intimacies between Chinese women show both abovementioned characteristics. Through embodying emotions, sensations, longings and belongings that travel between bodies, and through expressing subjective feelings, memories and understandings about such embodiments, these women and their subjectivities are not insulative, static and consistent 'selves', but are 'ever-becoming journeys' able to be affected and to affect.

As Braidotti points out, the subject is non-unitary, which means that it is 'split, knotted, and complex' (Braidotti, 2011a: 37), and the subjectivity is 'becoming nomad', which 'marks the process of positive transformation of the pain of loss into the active production of multiple forms of belonging and complex allegiances' (Braidotti, 2011a: 80). Entangled with memories, 'the present' that is being lived and visions about the future are affirmed through 'nomadic remembering', which, in Braidotti's words, is 'not indexed on the authority of the past' but 'occurs in relation to creative imagination in the future anterior' (Braidotti, 2011b: 34). If we do not see time, life and the formation of subjectivity as linear, consistent continuums, the seeming ruptures between the so-called 'past' and 'present', such as Tea's 'three dreams', can also be ways to create an endurable future.

For 'nomads', or for female (post-)colonial, sexual-minority subjects, whose bodies and emotions are usually otherised by white, male, middle-class, heteronormative languages and knowledges as 'site[s] of animality, primitivism and irrationality' (see Blackman, 2008: 48), 'loving without articulation' does not mean a 'lack' of language, but means a proliferation of embodied intimacies. The dominant discourse about romantic love in contemporary China only recognises heteronormative relationships and only values life-long monogamy – a narrow definition of 'loyalty'. Facing these types of discourse, Chinese same-sex attracted women understand their intimate experiences without fully depending on one version of 'common-sense' logic, but through acknowledging complex affective feelings and experimenting with multiple affective expressions.

In Chinese, the word 'chulian' refers to both 'first love' the experience and 'first lover' the person. This overlapping usage has created not only trouble, but also inspiration in my own same-sex intimate relationship.[8] Although both my current partner and I agree that our relationship brings us ever-renewed knowledge about love, as if this relationship is always a 'first love', we still have a habit of calling our first lovers, with whom we no longer keep contact, our 'chulian' in the chronological sense. Besides the predictable jealousy, dispute, awkwardness or sulky atmospheres, embodied memories – many of which are bitter and painful – revisit us unexpectedly when we touch on the word 'chulian'. These 'inharmonious' moments, however, keep reminding us that '"others" are the integral element of one's successive becomings' (Braidotti, 2011b: 153), no matter whether an articulation still exists between us and our former lovers. In contemporary China, where same-sex love is not recognised as respectable 'love/aiqing' and where women outside the hetero-marriage are not believed to deserve a fulfilled life, becoming a women-loving woman is rather a collective, trans-subjective process. One's first love/r without articulation can become an organic and affective part of one's current and future intimate experiences.

The gaps between verbal languages, and affective understandings through embodied thinking and feeling, show that 'love without articulation' is an intimacy that grows beyond the exclusively categorised, committed and sanctioned relationship between two self-contained individuals – the 'love/aiqing' defined by the Ministry of Education of China. Neither can such intimacies be reduced to being one's 'better half' (the Chinese translation of which is 'ling yiban', literally 'the other half'), as heteronormative romantic discourses often say. Female same-sex love in a heteronormative, homophobic, patriarchal, misogynous context seeks inventive languages for describing the affective intimacies that travel between bodies and make them both incomplete and simultaneously assembled. During my fieldwork, I was impressed by the query expressed by 'Brook', a participant born in the late 1980s in northeastern China and working in Shanghai at the time. Not satisfied with the existing Chinese vocabulary that names romantic intimacies, Brook said:

> [Rather than] the existing definition of 'aiqing', perhaps [there is] a word we haven't created yet, a feeling we haven't put into words. [...] I think love should have an inclusiveness [that is more inclusive than 'aiqing'].

Although Brook did not give an answer herself, her query is a good starting point to search for more nuanced affective languages that can better depict relational subjectivities, non-normative connections and affective intimacies.

Sexual intimacies as 'penetrations'

In traditional social scientific methodologies, language has played a central role in constructing human understanding; expressions of self are often explored through paying disproportionate attention to statements and accounts, which tend to submerge the body as merely a silent, physical presence (Blackman, 2008). During my fieldwork, when I tried to collect information about the participants' sexual experiences, which were related more to embodied and affective experiences, I faced a multi-fold lack of language. After I asked the participants about their sex lives, many of them responded with stammering sentences and shy smiles. Since openly talking about sexuality is still more or less a taboo for women in China, discussing same-sex sexual practices outside of private spaces, such as in the cafés, restaurants and karaoke lounges where I conducted interviews and observations, was even more challenging. Neither was I sure about what follow-up questions could sound appropriate and professional. As an anthropologist and a self-identified lesbian/lala woman, I grappled with the taboo of talking and writing about my own sexuality and erotic subjectivity in social science research (see discussions in Kulick and Willson, 1995). As a result, although both the participants and I appreciated the opportunities to discuss topics about sexuality (see also Chan, 2008), we found it less easy to communicate in direct and efficient language.

At the beginning of my fieldwork, I was surprised and even a bit disappointed when I received the participants' answers to my question: 'How do you define "having sex" [fasheng xing guanxi] with women?' Their answers shared key words of 'penetration' (charu) or 'enter' (jinru), which seemed no different from the normative knowledge about heterosexual, penis-vagina penetrative sex. I am of course not saying that female same-sex practices are imitations of heterosexuality, but I could not avoid getting an impression that many participants did believe that bodily intimacies involving vagina penetration were more qualified as 'real' sex, including the sex between women.

However, as I went on conducting my fieldwork, I gradually realised that there was a gap between how the participants talked about 'having sex' and how they embodied it. Scholars who study the body through more embodied perspectives point out that the body thinks and feels rather than simply being an inert mass; they conceptualise the body through notions of connectedness and mixing rather than of singularity and separation, and they do not separate mind from the body (e.g. Blackman, 2008; Brennan, 2004; Despret, 2004; Tamborinino, 2002). In this section, I apply such perspectives, which recognise the body's capacity to affect and be affected and recognise both the materiality and immateriality of the body (see Blackman, 2012) to analyse the sexual experiences of Chinese same-sex attracted women. I argue that the heteronormative discourses of penetrative sex have affected the bodies and emotions of these women in their intimate relationships and everyday lives. However, if we re-appropriate the idea and the term of 'penetration' through lenses that are sensitive to affective and embodied entanglements, 'penetration' can be a concept which helps us observe, understand and contour the body, the self and intimacies that are often unspeakable or unspoken. Moreover, the multi-fold lack of language I mentioned earlier actually sharpens a researcher's own affective knowing, thinking and feeling, rather than limits her study.

In contemporary China, while sex education provided by schools or families for adolescents and young adults is seriously lacking, information about sexuality has been rapidly (re)produced and circulated via the internet and emerging new media (Wang and Wang, 2012). Alongside these processes, ideas about sexual violence, gender stereotypes, gender inequality, heteronormativity and LGBT phobia have also been reinforced through images and language. Although the formal term describing physical sexual contact, 'xingjiao' (sexual intercourse), is hardly used in people's everyday language, the commonly heard, sex-related slang terms in Chinese usually portray sexual behaviour as heterosexual, penis-vagina penetration, which is initiated and dominated by the male body.

Such discourses even permeate among people with same-sex desires. As I have mentioned earlier, many of the participants of my study narrowly defined the sex between women as vagina penetration without thinking twice. However, I also noticed that some other parts of our interactions revealed the contradictory and complicated role that the notion of 'penetration' played in their everyday sexual encounters. For example, 'Kite', a participant and a lesbian/lala friend of mine in her mid-twenties, who had grown up in a city on China's southeast coast and was living in Shanghai, mentioned her best sex experience:

> Usually, we [Kite and her girlfriends] fucked [shang][9] each other, which means we entered each other's body. But in my best [sex] experience, which happened between my second girlfriend and me, she didn't even enter me at all. That experience was really amazing.

Obviously, while Kite used a term that normalised vagina penetration as more naturally occurring and more qualified sex behaviour, she could not deny the particularly impressive pleasure her body had felt in an intimate experience without penetration. Of course, not all the participants had managed to live comfortably with the gaps between heteronormative discourse and non-normative practices and 'abnormal' feelings. For example, 'Scarlet', a participant who was born in the southwestern part of Yunnan Province and attended college in the city of Kunming, reported how the normative idea of penetrative sex had created emotional and physical pain in her sex life with her ex-girlfriend:

> My ex-girlfriend and I did have sex. But I didn't have much [pleasurable] feeling. ... I was in a lot of pain, and she dared not enter [my vagina with her fingers] deeper. ... We were both frustrated. She asked me: 'Why? Do you have sexual apathy [xing lengdan]?' I answered: 'I don't know. Maybe I do.' ... A friend of her[s], who is also a T,[10] told her: 'The deepest point of pain is the greatest feeling. Pain is fine.' These words made me sick.

Under the surface of Scarlet's accounts, which viewed vagina penetration as the taken-for-granted definition of 'having sex', we can find how Scarlet struggled with the discourse that objectifies and disciplines female bodies in the name of 'sexual pleasure'. On one hand, many popular sex-related concepts, such as 'sexual apathy', essentialise and standardise women's 'normal' reaction when having sex, and meanwhile stigmatise the women who 'fail' to meet this standard. Such concepts have been popularised in Chinese everyday vocabularies alongside the emergence of pro-sex medical and consumerist discourses among urban, middle-class, well-educated people in contemporary China. On the other hand, the physical and mental pains felt by female subjects/bodies during penetrative sex are often silenced and trivialised by a symbolic idea of 'sex pleasure' built on phallocentric and heteronormative logics, which have even been embodied in same-sex practices between women.

Sexual intimacies are not only related to pleasure but also to oppression. 'Hermit', a native-born Shanghainese participant in her early thirties, mentioned a traumatic experience. Once in a group excursion, Hermit shared a room with a female acquaintance, 'Firefly'. A male friend of Firefly who had just found out that Hermit was a T and expressed curiosity about her insisted on staying overnight in their room. They did not refuse him. In the middle of the night, after giving Firefly a large amount of alcohol, the man had sex with her without her full consent. Hermit recalled in the interview with sobs:

> I thought they [Firefly and the man] had some mutual fondness, [so] when he said that he would stay overnight, I didn't mind so much. ... [When he tried to have sex with Firefly], I was lying there [in another bed] and could not help but say: 'Don't force her.' [But he did not stop.] ... I don't know if this counted as rape. ... The [next] morning, Firefly said to me [nothing about this incident except] one sentence: 'Did that [incident last night] disgust you?' I felt so uncomfortable. I said to her: 'I didn't leave, ... because I thought you might cry for help. [If you had done so,] I would have pushed him away and rescued you.' [But she didn't do so.] I felt I was mentally raped [jingshen bei qiangjian]. ... This man knew my homosexual [tongxinglian] identity and my T identity, and this made him even more excited [when he had sex with Firefly]. ... I shared the room with Firefly only because she said that staying with me made her feel safer. ... I bet that she wasn't willing to [have sex with that man]. ... I regret that I joined that excursion. ... Sometimes, I want to become a man, because I don't have a sense of security [anquangan]. Many lesbians, especially Ts, want to become masculine. I think this is because we want ... the rights to have a sense of security.

While Hermit managed to use language to review an incident that had brought her sexually traumatic feelings, she could only say three words ('Don't force her') when the incident was happening. Being forced to take part in a scene of heterosexual coercive sex, Hermit, a female but masculine homosexual, found that, under a homophobic male gaze, she was both a sexual and gender deviant, who could provide exotic sexual excitement, but also less qualified than men to pursue sexual pleasure with women. This feeling of discomfort and insecurity made Hermit feel a sensation of being 'raped' by the male power while at the same time a desire to gain this power.

Firefly, according to Hermit's understanding, experienced sexual coercion but could say nothing on the spot to reject the unwanted sex. Although it was the male friend who disappointed her fondness for him, it was Hermit who made her feel safer but could not save her. What Firefly could verbally express was only a concern about whether her acquiescence to an imposed sexual contact was 'disgusting'. Neither was she able to say aloud that she was (or was not) raped. In other words, sometimes, one's body feels and thinks that one has been 'penetrated' in a forced, unwanted, uncomfortable, oppressive way, for example rape, but one just cannot find the language to name, describe, refuse and protest it. Here, I want to re-appropriate the notion of and the term 'penetration' from the literal answers given by many participants when I asked them to define 'having sex', to help us understand, contour or even speak about, the often-unspeakable embodied experiences of intimacy, many of which may be related to pain, shame, trauma and violence.

Of course, I am not saying that 'penetration' only implies the restrictive, institutionalised, normative power; rather, it also implies an active and creative power (see Braidotti's discussion on 'potestas' and 'pontentia', 2014). When doing anthropological research and (also) living a lesbian life, 'penetration' is my understanding about every 'intra-action', rather than 'inter-action', that is to say, every 'embodied cut delineating the object from the agencies of observation' (Barad, 2007: 115) but never taking distinction for granted. After my fieldwork, I started a long-distance relationship with one of the participants, who I later moved in with and she and I are now life partners. When we were still unable to touch each other since we lived in different hemispheres, time zones and seasons,[11] we desperately relied on high-tech communication tools to channel our emotions. It was via assemblages of images, sounds and other embodied virtual and actual means that we created feelings of love and desire. As affective entanglements without connected bodies, those moments penetrated through the gaps of time and space, the limits of particular senses, and the boundaries that are conventionally set between a researcher and the researched subjects or objects. In this process, I personally experienced and defined 'penetration' as affective energies that always broke through (seemingly) physical barriers and brought me 'home' – the good feelings of intimacy.

Conclusion

This chapter, developed from an anthropological study, analysed the affective experiences of female same-sex intimacies, especially love and sex, in contemporary China. Although Chinese same-sex-attracted women, myself included, often find a lack of 'proper' language for expressing love and describing sexual practices in/about different contexts, I argue that it is through this lack that we can observe, think and feel how bodies, emotions and subjectivities are 'becoming' in our intimate practices. In re-examining the data originally collected for narrative analysis, I have applied concepts and ideas that are sensitive to affects, including the 'nomadic subjectivity' developed by feminist new-materialist Rosi Braidotti (1994, 2002, 2011a, 2011b, 2014), and the embodied – rather than linguistic – perspectives for studying the body (e.g. Blackman, 2008, 2012).

In this chapter, I have found that Chinese same-sex attracted women understand and practise love through non-consistent, non-linear, trans-subjective journeys of 'becoming', rather than by naming 'love' explicitly in verbal language. Their refusal of the normative discourses about 'aiqing/love' and their embodied emotions and memories are re-definitions – although not in terms of language – of what love is and what love can be. I have also found that, in China, female same-sex relationships are strongly affected by the heteronormative idea(l) that vagina penetration marks a more qualified sexual (f)act, although many women with same-sex desires are exploring affective intimacies beyond this norm. Meanwhile, Chinese women, regardless of their sexual orientations, also embody the shame, anxiety, trauma and violence caused by such a phallocentric, misogynous, homophobic sexual culture, yet they can hardly find the language to voice these painful affective experiences.

Furthermore, I have theorised the concepts of '(first) love without articulation' and 'penetration', deriving from the abovementioned findings. 'Articulation' – a pun with parallel meanings of 'speaking out' and 'being jointed' – captures the affective complications of intimacy that consist of material and immaterial happenings while growing beyond conventional rules of verbal expression. On the other side, re-appropriating the notion and term of 'penetration' for portraying the inter-corporeal, trans-subjective entanglements and 'becomings' in sexual – and love – experiences is to sense and express the diverse affective forces that shape and reshape feelings about intimacy.

Notes

1 I choose the acronym of 'LGBTQ', rather than 'LGBTIQ+', to describe gender and sexual minorities in China, because the concept of intersex and other emerging identities that are represented by the plus sign in some societies have not been widely known and discussed within Chinese gender and sexual minority communities. For ordinary Chinese people, however, while 'LGBT' as a single (imported) word has become more and more commonly seen in mass

media, the concept of 'queer' is still less familiar. Therefore, when mentioning the 'LGBT phobia' in China, I do not include 'Q' in the acronym.

2 'Lala' is a local Chinese term used by same-sex-attracted women for self-identification.

3 'Tongzhi', literally 'comrade', is a local Chinese term referring to LGBTQ people.

4 In modern Chinese, the term 'ai' refers to the general love, while 'aiqing' is narrower, only referring to the romantic love accompanied by sexual desires and passionate and erotic feelings. In this chapter, my discussions about love focus on the latter.

5 This paragraph is an excerpt from Chapter 5, under the rubric of 'Family Virtue' (Jiating Meide), in *Ideological and Moral Cultivation and Basic Law Education* (Sixiang Daode Xiuyang Yu Falü Jichu) (the 2015 edition), published by the Higher Education Press in China.

6 Qixi Festival is on the seventh of July in the Chinese Lunar calendar. According to Chinese folklore, the fairy Zhinü and the cowherd Niulang are a loving couple separated by the Milky Way, who can only meet other once a year on the date of Qixi Festival via a bridge built by magpies in the heavens. Qixi Festival is viewed as a traditional festival for lovers and has become highly commercialised in the twenty-first century.

7 May Twentieth, '5.20', the three numbers of which have a homophonic pronunciation of 'I love you' in Chinese, 'wo ai ni'. Similar to the Qixi Festival, this day has also been celebrated by couples and commercialised as a festival for lovers.

8 My partner has been informed and consented that her personal experiences would be portrayed in this chapter.

9 Here, 'shang' is a sex-related slang term in Chinese. Literally meaning 'being top', this slang term indicates a more active party, often a man or a masculine person, initiating a sexual intercourse with a more passive party, often a woman.

10 'T', short for the English word 'tomboy', is a local Chinese term referring to a masculine woman who usually prefers to date feminine women. In this particular case, Scarlet said that she herself was more feminine while her ex-girlfriend was more masculine.

11 When I did fieldwork between 2013 and 2014, I interviewed my future partner, a Chinese woman residing in Australia but on a temporary stay in Shanghai. After my fieldwork ended, she went back to Melbourne while I went back to Amsterdam, the Netherlands, where I was doing my PhD.

References

Barad, K. (2007), *Meeting the Universe Halfway: Quantum Physics and the Entanglement of Matter and Meaning* (Durham, NC: Duke University Press).

Becker, H. S. (1998), *Tricks of the Trade: How to Think About Your Research While You're Doing It* (Chicago, IL: University of Chicago Press).

Behar, R. (1996), *The Vulnerable Observer: Anthropology That Breaks Your Heart* (Boston, MA: Beacon Press).

Bernard, H. R. (2011), *Research Methods in Anthropology: Qualitative and Quantitative Approaches*, 5th edition (Lanham, MD: AltaMira Press).

Blackman, L. (2008), *The Body: The Key Concepts* (New York, NY: Berg).

Blackman, L. (2012), *Immaterial Bodies: Affect, Embodiment, Mediation* (London: Sage).

Blackman, L., and Venn, C. (2010), 'Affect', *Body & Society*, 16:1, 7–28. doi: https://doi.org/10.1177/1357034X09354769

Braidotti, R. (1994), 'Toward a New Nomadism: Feminist Deleuzian Tracks; or, Metaphysics and Metabolism', in *Gilles Deleuze and the Theater of Philosophy*, C. V. Boundas and D. Olkowski (eds) (New York, NY: Routledge), 157–86.

Braidotti, R. (2002), *Metamorphoses: Towards a Materialist Theory of Becoming* (Cambridge: Polity).

Braidotti, R. (2011a), *Nomadic Subjects: Embodiment and Sexual Difference in Contemporary Feminist Theory*, 2nd edition (New York, NY: Columbia University Press).

Braidotti, R. (2011b), *Nomadic Theory: The Portable Rosi Braidotti* (New York, NY: Columbia University Press).

Braidotti, R. (2013), *The Posthuman* (Cambridge: Polity).

Braidotti, R. (2014), 'Writing as a Nomadic Subject', *Comparative Critical Studies*, 11:2–3, 163–84.

Braidotti, R., Wong, K. Y., and Chan, A. K.-S. (eds) (2018), *Deleuze and the Humanities: East and West* (New York, NY: Rowman & Littlefield International).

Brennan, T. (2004), *The Transmission of Affect* (Ithaca, NY: Cornell University Press).

Butler, J. (2004), *Undoing Gender* (New York, NY: Routledge).

Chan, A. H. (2008), 'Talking About "Good Sex": Hong Kong Women's Sexuality in the Twenty-First Century', in *East Asian Sexualities: Modernity, Gender and New Sexual Cultures*, S. Jackson, J. Liu, and J. Woo (eds) (London: Zed Books), 195–215.

Chao, A. (2000), 'Global Metaphors and Local Strategies in the Construction of Taiwan's Lesbian Identities', *Culture, Health & Sexuality*, 2:4 (2000), 377–90. doi: http://dx.doi.org/10.1080/13691050050174404

Clough, P. T. (2010), 'The Affective Turn: Political Economy, Biomedia, and Bodies', in *The Affect Theory Reader*, M. Gregg and G. J. Seigworth (eds) (Durham, NC: Duke University Press), 206–25.

Deleuze, G., and Guattari, F. (1987), *A Thousand Plateaus: Capitalism and Schizophrenia*, translated by B. Massumi (Minneapolis, MN: University of Minnesota Press).

Despret, V. (2004), 'The Body we Care For: Figures of Anthropo-Zoo-Genesis', *Body and Society*, 10:2–3, 111–34.

Engebretsen, E. L. (2014), *Queer Women in Urban China: An Ethnography* (New York, NY: Routledge).

Evans, H. (1997), *Women and Sexuality in China: Dominant Discourses of Female Sexuality and Gender Since 1949* (Cambridge: Polity).

Foucault, M. (1978), *The History of Sexuality, Volume 1: An Introduction*, translated by R. Hurley (New York, NY: Pantheon Books).

Halperin, D. M. (2019), 'Queer Love', *Critical Inquiry*, 45:Winter, 396–419. Available at: www.sas.upenn.edu/~cavitch/pdf-library/Halperin_QueerLove.pdf (Accessed: 21 June 2021).

Haraway, D. J. (2008), *When Species Meet* (Minneapolis, MN: University of Minnesota Press).

Ho, P. S. Y., Jackson, S., Cao, S., and Kwok, C. (2018), 'Sex With Chinese Characteristics: Sexuality Research in/on 21st-Century China', *The Journal of Sex Research*, 55:4–5, 486–521. doi: https://doi.org/10.1080/00224499.2018.1437593

Jackson, S., Liu, J., and Woo, J. (2008), 'Introduction: Reflections on Gender, Modernity and East Asian Sexualities', in *East Asian Sexualities: Modernity, Gender and New Sexual Cultures*, S. Jackson, J. Liu, and J. Woo (eds) (London: Zed Books), 1–30.

Kam, L. Y. L. (2013), *Shanghai Lalas: Female Tongzhi Communities and Politics in Urban China* (Hong Kong: Hong Kong University Press).

Kang, W. (2009), *Obsession: Male Same-Sex Relations in China, 1900–1950* (Hong Kong: Hong Kong University Press).

Kang, W. (2012), 'Decriminalization and Depathologization of Homosexuality in China', in *China in and Beyond the Headlines*, T. B. Weston and L. M. Jensen (eds) (Lanham, MD: Rowman & Littlefield), 231–48.

Kinnunen, T., and Kolehmainen, M. (2019), 'Touch and Affect: Analysing the Archive of Touch Biographies', *Body & Society*, 25:1, 29–56. doi: https://doi.org/10.1177/1357034X18817607

Knudsen, B. T., and Stage, C. (eds) (2015), *Affective Methodologies: Developing Cultural Research Strategies for the Study of Affect* (New York, NY: Palgrave Macmillan).

Kong, T. S. K. (2011), *Chinese Male Homosexualities: Memba, Tongzhi and Golden Boy* (London: Routledge).

Kulick, D., and Willson, M. (eds) (1995), *Taboo: Sex, Identity, and Erotic Subjectivity in Anthropological Fieldwork* (London: Routledge).

Lykke, N. (2018), 'When Death Cuts Apart: On Affective Difference, Compassionate Companionship and Lesbian Widowhood', in *Affective Inequalities in Intimate Relationships*, T. Juvonen and M. Kolehmainen (eds) (London: Routledge), 109–25.

Martin, F. (2010), *Backward Glances: Contemporary Chinese Cultures and the Female Homoerotic Imaginary* (Durham, NC: Duke University Press).

Martin, F., Jackson, P. A., McLelland, M., and Yue, A. (eds) (2008), *AsiaPacifiQueer: Rethinking Genders and Sexualities* (Urbana, IL: University of Illinois Press).

Padilla, M. B., Hirsch, J. S., Muñoz-Laboy, M., Sember, R. E., and Parker, G. (eds) (2008), *Love and Globalization: Transformations of Intimacy in the Contemporary World* (Nashville, TN: Vanderbilt University Press).

Reddy, W. M. (2012), *The Making of Romantic Love: Longing and Sexuality in Europe, South Asia, and Japan, 900–1200 CE* (Chicago, IL: The University of Chicago Press).

Rocha, L. A. (2010), '*Xing*: The Discourse of Sex and Human Nature in Modern China', *Gender & Society*, 22:3, 603–28. doi: https://doi.org/10.1111/j.1468 -0424.2010.01609.x

Ruan, F., and Bullough, V. L. (1992), 'Lesbianism in China', *Archives of Sexual Behavior*, 21:3, 217–26.

Rutherford, D. (2016), 'Affect Theory and the Empirical', *Annual Review of Anthropology*, 45:October, 285–300. doi: https://doi.org/10.1146/annurev -anthro-102215-095843

Sang, T. D. (2003), *The Emerging Lesbian: Female Same-Sex Desire in Modern China* (Chicago, IL: University of Chicago Press).

Sanger, T., and Taylor, Y. (eds) (2013), *Mapping Intimacies: Relations, Exchanges, Affects* (New York, NY: Palgrave Macmillan).

Seigworth, G. J., and Gregg, M. (2010), 'An Inventory of Shimmers', in *The Affect Theory Reader*, M. Gregg and G. J. Seigworth (eds) (Durham, NC: Duke University Press), 1–25.

Tamborinino, J. (2002), *The Corporeal Turn: Passion, Necessity, Politics* (New York, NY: Rowman & Littlefield).

Van Gulik, R. H. (1961), *Sexual Life in Ancient China: A Preliminary Survey of Chinese Sex and Society from ca. 1500 B.C. Till 1644 A.D.* (Leiden, Netherlands: Brill).

Walkerdine, V., and Jimenez, L. (2012), *Gender, Work and Community After De-Industrialisation: A Psychosocial Approach to Affect* (New York, NY: Palgrave Macmillan).

Wang, X., and Wang, Y. (2012), 'A Critical Review on Sex Education for Chinese Adolescents in the New Millennium' (in Chinese), *Qingnian Yanjiu (Youth Studies)*, 2, 48–57.

Weeks, J. (2003), *Sexuality*, 2nd edition (London: Routledge).

Wieringa, S. E. (2007), *The Admonishment of Vegetarian Great Aunt: Reflections on Sexual and Gender Multiplicity and Culture* (Amsterdam, Netherlands: Vossiuspers UvA).

Wieringa, S., and Sívori, H. (2013), 'Sexual Politics in the Global South: Framing the Discourse', in *The Sexual History of the Global South: Sexual Politics in Africa, Asia, and Latin America*, S. Wieringa and H. Sívori (eds) (London: Zed Books), 1–21.

Zheng, T. (2015), *Tongzhi Living: Men Attracted to Men in Postsocialist China* (Minneapolis, MN: University of Minnesota Press).

Zhong, X. (2007), 'Who is a Feminist? Understanding the Ambivalence Towards *Shanghai Baby*, "Body Writing", and Feminism in Post-Women's Liberation China', *Gender & History*, 18:3, 635–60. doi: https://doi.org/10.1111/j.1468 -0424.2006.00459.x

8

Affective obligations and obliged affections: Non-binary youth and affective (re)orientations to family

Nina Perger

Introduction

In this chapter, I analyse the experiences of gender non-binary individuals using the web of affects and obligations experienced within the family. I seek to show how the ordinariness of family intimacy is transformed when it encounters transgender non-binary lives. Building on research on the everyday lives of gender and/or sexual non-binary people conducted from 2015 to 2019, I present case studies of four gender non-binary individuals and their stories of 'journeying away from' – and sometimes back to – family intimacy that failed to deliver on its promises. By analysing four case studies of non-binary individuals and their stories of negative family reactions to the disclosure of their gender identity, I attempt to capture the messiness of family intimacy as it unfolds through the affective orientations of family members.

I approach the family and its relations with gender non-binary youth through the conceptual framework offered by Sara Ahmed's work on emotions and affective orientations and Pierre Bourdieu's work on affective obligations and obliged affections. Ahmed (2014a; see also Ahmed, 2010; Schmitz and Ahmed, 2014) calls for an intellectual horizon within which emotions and affects are 'not taken as choices that lead us down separate paths', as if working on one means neglecting the other (Ahmed, 2014a: 230; see also 2006a: 32). According to Ahmed (2010), bodily sensations, emotions and thoughts are not distinct realms of experience, but rather constitute complex, and sometimes, if not often, ambivalent processes and practices of moving and being moved. Moreover, emotions,[1] as movements that encompass bodily sensations and thoughts, also orient and attach agents to particular objects, other agents and collective entities (Schmitz and Ahmed, 2014). According to Ahmed (2004, 2010), these movements are not completely random or autonomous but are preceded by histories and experiences (Ahmed, 2004: 120). Sociality, including the historicity of affect and its orienting, directive power, is evident in the case of the family, which is socially constituted as a 'happy object' not because it brings happiness but because it promises happiness 'in return for loyalty' (Ahmed, 2006a: 35). It is this socially driven and taken-for-granted assumption and expectation that family is 'good' because it promises and brings happiness that precedes agents and orients them towards the family. In this sense, emotions and affective orientations are not only about movements but also about attachment and holding in place. More than that, they are also directive: that which is constituted as a 'happy object' is at the same time constituted as something one *should* orient oneself to (Schmitz and Ahmed, 2014).

In telling their stories of family responses to their gender non-binary identities – of silencing, rejection and neglect – these individuals also tell the story of subtle and more forceful affective mechanisms of shame, guilt and responsibility for upholding the fiction of family as an unconditional, intimate, affectionate and a haven-like relationship, even at the cost of undoing their transgender identities. The forcefulness of these mechanisms stems from the sociality of affective orientations, and to gain insight into this I will draw on the conceptions of Ahmed and Bourdieu, which enable a deeper insight into the ways in which affective orientations towards family as a happy object are maintained, even as the promise of unconditional support and happiness is being undone. In the next section, I discuss Ahmed's thoughts on the sociality of emotions as they circulate within familial intimacy and act as a straightening device and Bourdieu's approach to family and habitualised affective obligations and obliged affections. In the third section, I focus on the case studies, which demonstrate not only the conditionality of the promise of happiness but also how affective intimacies are (also) 'bound up with the securing of social hierarchy' (Ahmed, 2014a: 4).

On 'family feelings' and failing to live up to the promise

Intimacy, which implies close connections, close familiarity (Seymour, 1999), affect, mutual knowledge, actions and norms, is socially shaped (Berlant and Warner, 1998; Forstie, 2017). It is, as Forstie (2017) points out, a socially, politically, historically and even geographically specific idea. Although socially embedded, intimacy is not just about the social and its tendency to create intimacies in its own image. It also involves reflexive practices, active constructions, negotiations and compromises, and an active present and 'future building' of intimate worlds (Holmes, Jamieson and Natalier, 2021; see also Berlant and Warner, 1998; Seymour, 1999; Jurva and Lahti, 2019). It is constituted through relational practices that build and make up the feelings and experiences of close relationships and a specific affective atmosphere based on feelings of mutual love and of being special to one another (Jamieson, 2011).

In relation to the family, there exists a 'love plot of intimacy and familialism' (Berlant and Warner, 1998: 554), or, in Bourdieu's (2001: 110) words, the promise of an almost 'miraculous truce', 'loving dispositions' and 'family feelings', of unconditional love, support and loyalty (Bourdieu, 2000: 144–5). However, precisely because it is socially embedded, family intimacy can be disrupted when it encounters transgender lives. As Ahmed (2010: 46) notes, the family can become a 'pressure point', a point of encouragement and nudging towards certain (cisgender) lines that are inherited and expected to be reproduced. This encouragement can take on the subtle language of 'love, happiness, and care' (Ahmed, 2006b: 90). As the family is the space of an agent's initial investment and immersion in the social game (Bourdieu, 2000), the straight lines – of heterosexuality and cisnormativity – that are inherited and expected to be followed are difficult to transcend (Ahmed, 2010), as parental verdicts and judgements, including their affective dimensions (Ahmed, 2014a), are buried at the 'deepest level [of the child's] body' and are moved by the child's desire to be recognised by those who should count the most' (Bourdieu, 2000: 167).

As numerous studies demonstrate, relational family dynamics can be altered and reconfigured, at least temporarily, by the range of reactions to the transgender child's coming out (see, e.g., Catalpa and McGuire, 2018; Fuller and Riggs, 2018; Robinson, 2018; von Doussa, Power and Riggs, 2020; McDermott *et al.*, 2021). Feelings of hopelessness, helplessness, grief, sadness and ambiguous loss (Catalpa and McGuire, 2018) can circulate within the family, making way for affective reorientation among family members, not only towards each other but also towards the future temporality of the family, as roles, boundaries and meaning must be reconceptualised within family relationships (Alegría, 2018; Kelley, 2020). When the child's gender non-normativity is experienced as a deviation from the line and when this deviation is experienced as a threat to the family's 'idealisation of domestic privacy' (Ahmed, 2010: 90), the gender non-normative agent can become an affect alien, killing the 'joy of the family' and, by extension, 'killing the family by killing the association with joy' (49). Alienation can lead to a particular uncertainty about being in or out of the family (Catalpa and McGuire, 2018).

The family tends to function as a mechanism of social reproduction (Bourdieu, 2000) or, as Ahmed (2010: 91) puts it, as a 'straightening device' that attempts to line the agents up with the lines that are already given. Despite familial intimacy carrying the promise of recognition, generosity, reciprocity and loyalty, it sometimes ends up as a 'terrible spectacle' of disrespect, violence and negation (Berlant, 1998: 281). Even if the promise remains at least partially unfulfilled, its hold over agents can persist, if only for a time, in an almost 'cruelly optimistic way' (Berlant, 2011: 24). This 'stickiness' of affective orientation towards the family as a happy object can be difficult to overcome, and as such, it can hold agents in place, even discourage them from straying away from the given gendered lines one is expected to follow: 'emotions are "sticky", and even when we challenge our investments, we might get stuck' (Ahmed, 2014a: 16).

To gain insight into what makes this particular affective orientation stick and an agent get stuck, even when the family disregards transgender identity, I turn to Bourdieu's approach to the family. According to Bourdieu (1996), the family is grounded in particular affective principles embodied in agents. Family intimacy is constituted and sustained by the immense amount of social and symbolic work that almost magically transforms obligations (e.g. caring for a child) into affects (parental love) and affects into obligations (e.g. feeling a certain way towards family members; filial love), giving rise to affective obligations and obliged affections (Bourdieu, 1996; 2000). This web of affects and obligations should be approached specifically as a web rather than as clearly delineated and separate domains, and it is this web that acts as a force of family fusion – especially an affective one (Bourdieu, 1996) – for 'getting along' (Ahmed, 2006a: 36) and aiming to overcome the family's forces of fission (Bourdieu, 1996). Furthermore, and in line with Ahmed's (2004; Schmitz and Ahmed, 2014) conception of the sociality and historicity of affective orientations, the familial web of affects and obligations covers its traces: it is naturalised (Bourdieu, 1996), and roles within the family, such as 'sibling' and 'child', along with the practical dimensions of enacting them, are experienced as 'private, personal and natural identities' (Freeman, 2007: 298). Because affective orientation to family is naturalised and habitualised – being a matter of the unconscious and routine, of 'second nature', as Ahmed (2006b: 129) summarises Bourdieu's concept of habitus – it is hard to stray from well-trodden paths (Ahmed, 2019), including from the lost promise of familial intimacy (Sanger and Taylor, 2013; Ahmed, 2006b). If familial intimacy typically plays a large role in 'shaping habitus' (Jamieson, 2011: 5), such a failure of the family to maintain intimacy when confronted with transgender lives may necessitate the formation and re-formation of the transgender self as tensions between self-identity and its maintenance, on one hand, and, on the other, the relationships with emotionally close others intensify (Seymour, 1999; Sanger and Taylor, 2013).

I am interested in the subtle and powerful affective mechanisms – the one-way stickiness of guilt, shame and responsibility – that circulate within the family and call the familial affective obligations and obliged affections into action in an attempt to overcome the forces of fission. These forces are mistakenly attributed to transgender life rather than to a failure of familial intimacy to deliver what was promised by disregarding, neglecting or rejecting transgender existence (Bourdieu, 1996, 2000; Ahmed, 2004, 2006a, 2010). Affective obligations and obliged affections (Bourdieu, 1996) can sustain a particular affective orientation towards the family as an object to attach to – alive and sticky, despite its now-revealed 'conditionality of happiness' (Ahmed, 2010: 56) – and it is these dynamics I turn to in the next section.

On monsters, murderers, betrayals and 'no matter whats'

As mentioned earlier, in this section I present four narratives told by gender non-binary youth. The generic term 'non-binary' is used here to capture the plurality of gender identities beyond the socially dominant genders (men, women). Those who identified as non-binary (23), were over eighteen years old at the time of the interviews, and resided in Slovenia were eligible to participate in the research. The research method used was in-depth interviews, as this allowed participants to dictate the pathways of the narrative and gave us deeper insights into the experiences that are most relevant to non-binary people. I used snowball sampling, where new participants are sampled through the existing ones, which is most useful when researching marginalised, hard-to-reach social groups (Emmel *et al.*, 2007; Ritchie and Lewis, 2003). The average age of all participants was 27.2 years, and the majority of participants (fifteen) were between twenty-three and twenty-eight years old. Interviews were transcribed and analysed (Berg, 2001; Braun and Clarke, 2013), using the MAXQDA program tool for analysing qualitative data (VERBI Software, 2017). Transcripts were read several times to make a set of initial observations and identify core themes across the data. This was followed by code assignments and the formation of a set of higher-level categories based on the thematic similarity of codes (Braun and Clarke, 2013; Saldaña, 2009; Kuckartz and Rädiker, 2019).[2]

The research focused on various themes, including identity meanings, identity trajectories, experiences of misrecognition of transgender identities and strategies for coping with socially prevalent misrecognition. The latter theme was particularly highlighted in the case of gender non-binary individuals, as at the time of writing there is no legislation that specifically addresses transgender people in Slovenia. Medical and social gender confirmation procedures are possible if an individual receives a diagnosis of a mental health condition, but formal protocols are lacking, and trans health care is considered a low priority (Perger, 2021). In short, trans legal citizenship 'appears to be emerging in a fragmented and contested way' and includes many shortcomings, including rights for gender non-binary people, who lack the possibility of achieving legal recognition (Kuhar, Monro and Takács, 2017: 107). The transgender community is increasingly encountering organised resistance from the so-called 'anti-gender movements' (Kuhar, Monro and Takács, 2017; Kuhar and Patternote, 2017; Rener, 2018), which further exposes transgender individuals to practices aimed at devaluing their gender identities (Perger, 2020). Furthermore, Slovenia is considered to be a 'family-oriented society' (Rener, 2006a), with families strongly characterised by what Rener (2006b) calls 'generational peace' with strong vertical (intergenerational) and horizontal (extended kinship) instrumental and emotional support. Thus, family values are strong in Slovenia. According to the 2020 Slovenian Public Opinion Survey (Hafner-Fink *et al.*, 2020), 81.2 per cent of participants considered family as something that is extremely important in their lives (receiving ten out of ten points).

In this section, I focus on selected narratives of gender non-binary individuals who experienced negative responses from their families when disclosing their gender identity. I focus on these stories in order to gain insight into the mechanisms of affective obligations and obliged affections that help to sustain affective orientations towards the family. To achieve this, I draw on four narratives by Izak (demiboy, twenty-three), Djuro (non-binary, twenty-two), Metka (trans woman, agender; twenty-three) and Alex (queer, non-binary, twenty-four).

Undoing the social fiction of familial intimacy

Despite negative and often violent reactions, it can prove difficult for non-binary agents to distance themselves from familial relationships precisely because bodily emotions hold them in their place. They find themselves in an ambivalent situation because they are invested in the family according to the social fiction surrounding it – love, loyalty, care, support – but do not find this in practice. A large body of research shows that parents' negative or ambivalent reactions ('tolerating but not accepting') are the main modalities of initial reactions to their child's disclosure of transgender identity (Grossman *et al.*, 2005; Nuttbrock *et al.*, 2009; Fiani and Han, 2019; Bennett and Donatone, 2020; Johnson *et al.*, 2020). Additionally, non-binary individuals are exposed to 'contradictory processes of inclusion and exclusion' (Vijlbrief, Saharso and Ghorashi, 2020: 101) and invalidation practices, giving rise to 'negative affective and cognitive processes' (confusion, self-doubt, shame, frustration) (Johnson *et al.*, 2020: 222). However, the affective responses of transgender individuals to such reactions are usually overlooked (Catalpa and McGuire, 2018), and this chapter aims to fill this gap.

By silencing and disregarding transgender identity, the social fiction of the family begins to come apart and is at least temporarily exposed as conditional. The ambivalence of affective obligations and obliged affections, as amplified in the case of transgender identity, is made visible in the following story told by Alex about 'sibling love':

> [My brother] was very verbally abusive, emotionally abusive. He threatened me a lot, he yelled at me and he was very manipulative ... but at the same time, he had this traditionalist, conservative view – that we're still a family, that I'm his brother, that he would kill for me because he loves me. And there was a lot of aggression, a lot of humiliation that ended with, 'But no, you're my brother, and I would kill for you. You're everything.' Such an intense conflict between the obligation that we're brothers and what that's supposed to mean, and on the other side, he disrespected the only thing about me; he rejected it and wanted it to change. On one side, 'I love you and I would kill for you', but on the other side, 'You have to change because if you don't, our family is [expletive] up.' (Alex)

Even though the family is socially endowed with the idea of being a 'world of non-violence', grounded in full reciprocity and 'mutual recognition', which enables family members to feel justified in existing as they are (Bourdieu, 2001: 110), sibling love, as Alex experiences it, is full of (gendered) conditions. By being conditional, familial intimacy proves fragile because it is vulnerable to affective circulations in all directions, from aggression to declarations of love. Because of Alex's transgender identity, the family's existence is perceived to be threatened, and demands for 'remedies' are made that run counter to the social fiction of the family: 'You have to change, because otherwise ...' It is this demand for the family to be reproduced that reveals the 'vulnerability of its form' (Ahmed, 2010: 49, fn. 40). Rather than recognising the lack of acceptance as a threat to the family, the source of the 'injury' to the family is misplaced to transgender life (Ahmed, 2006a). From the above quote, it is clear that Alex's sibling is himself stuck in the complex interplay and ambivalence of affective obligations and obligated affects (unconditional love for his sibling) (Bourdieu, 1996) on one hand, and the sociality and conditionality of happiness and family as a 'happy object' that contains the demand to reproduce straight (cisnormative) lines (Ahmed, 2010) on the other. Izak's narrative of the violence they experienced from parents due to their transgender status further shows how complex the web of affective obligations and obliged affections is. In the same gesture in which Izak is rejected by their parents, the parents attempt to emotionally compel Izak to 'be who they are' – that is, to live in a gender assigned to them at birth – by appealing to Izak's affections for their siblings. In other words, affective obligations and obliged affections – Izak's love for their siblings – are turned against Izak and their transgender identity, rather than enacted for Izak:

[My parents asked me] why I have to make such drastic changes, whether I couldn't accept myself as I am … that I should think of my brothers and sisters and how they will suffer. I don't know, [my parents said] that the fact that I am who I am is worse than dying. That I'm a freak. … Who's going to love me anyway? Because when I get hormones, I'll be, like, I don't know, the biggest freak in the world. (Izak)

To secure its fiction of stability and unity, the family can use the force of affective obligations and obliged affections against those who supposedly threaten to dissolve the family by their gender non-normativity. Izak's story shows that affects move and circulate between agents in ways that are not entirely random (Ahmed, 2004). They can (predominantly) stick to those who transgress boundaries (e.g. the boundaries of gender normativity). In this case, the 'calls for affection' – towards siblings, towards family – while one is denied the same because of being transgender, act as 'calls to order' (Bourdieu, 1991: 124), aiming to discourage straying away from the well-trodden path of cisnormativity in the name of family and to maintain the signs of 'getting along' (Ahmed, 2006a: 36).

Loosening the grip of affective obligations and obliged affections: 'Journeying away' from (and sometimes back to) the family

Despite the suspension of the aforementioned 'miraculous truce' of familial intimacy, the weight of affective obligations and obliged affections on non-binary individuals remains, even though their transgender identity is disregarded. This shows the affective dimensions of the difficulties of walking 'the wrong way', as it is the collective feeling of a crowd, including a collective affective orientation towards the family as a happy object, that keeps pushing and shoving the non-binary individual towards the 'straight line' (Schmitz and Ahmed, 2014: 106). These difficulties attest to a deeply embodied principle of affectivity, inclining individuals to feel a certain way towards the family, regardless of its practices, and these inclinations are not easily overcome by will and choice alone; they may demand attempts, failures and fighting against what is embodied in the agents themselves (Bourdieu and Wacquant, 1992; Bourdieu, 2000, 2020):

Every weekend, they [expletive] me up, and then it would take me the whole workweek to get myself back into shape so they could [expletive] me up all over again. … I had to go through some processes because I was brought up to believe that family is an environment that suits you best, is the coolest and is kind of a safe haven … and then the pure physical distance – that I wasn't going home every week – helped. … It helped me to see that I'm cool without them, that they're the real problem that's been gnawing at me, that I've always gone into some kind of fight mode when I've been home because of them so I could survive the fact of being home. (Izak)

As Izak's story shows, the weight of affective obligations and obliged affections attempts to hold them in 'the most appropriate' place, despite the family 'gnawing' at Izak's existence. The story shows how Izak is affected by the promise of the family as a happy object, and how a refusal to reproduce straight lines gives rise to attempts to affectively reorient themself (Ahmed, 2006a). Nevertheless, the weight of affective obligations and obliged affections is not fully determining; a gap remains in the determination of feeling (Bourdieu, 1996; Ahmed, 2006a). Alternative affective intimacies of 'other worlds', such as friendship and LGBTIQ+ communities (Hines, 2007; Sanger, 2010; Perger, 2020), and physical and temporal distance can encourage affective reorientations towards and attachment to the family by allowing the grip of affective obligations and obligated affects to loosen its hold. This may suffice to strengthen the steps taken on the less-trodden gender-non-normative paths enough to make them resistant to affective 'calls to order' by family (Bourdieu, 2000: 176). At the same time, it is a child's distancing from familial intimacy that can push the family to acknowledge its initially failed promises and attempt to fulfil them after all. The following story shows the possibilities of (re)building affective practices in such a way that non-binary gender existence becomes (more) possible without sacrificing either transgender identity or familial intimacy:

> I went back [to the family] and [the brother] is still in those stories, but I managed to set the boundaries and tell him that things are not black and white. [...] Now it's really good because even though our relationship is not optimal yet, he doesn't overwhelm me or my parents. [...] I also told my parents that, yeah, my gender identity is confused, and they were like ... we talked explicitly for the first time about my orientation, my identity, and it was like, 'Look, Alex, whatever happens, happens. We're in this together.' [...] It's important for me [...] that there are no outright rejections now like there were in the beginning. (Alex)

For others, loosening the grip of the web of affective obligations and obligated affects and affectively reorienting away from the promise of a happy object is not so much a temporal step as it is a prolonged, if not a final, step. Metka's story below demonstrates the weight of affects as obligations that make it difficult for her to distance herself from the family that silences her transgender identity in order to secure the seemingly threatened existence of the family. The web of affective obligations and obliged affections remains embodied and is carried around in a more or less heavy 'bag' of guilt, shame and feelings of betrayal: of betraying the family by becoming transgender and of betraying herself by allowing her gender identity to be misrecognised and devalued by remaining in contact with the family and maintaining the idea and image of its intimacy:

> Guilt? Yes. Absolutely. I still have it. Still, because I would prefer not to have any interaction with [family] at all. This supposed relationship that I have with them – that we call each other, that I visit them at Christmas … while my life as such is completely disregarded, that's terrible. I don't want to have that. Nevertheless, I still do that; I'd feel guilty if I said, 'Hey, I never want to hear from you again because you have a bad influence on me.' I don't know. Would that make me responsible for my parents' heartbreak? I would feel totally guilty. I already felt guilty when I told them I had a boyfriend because there was such a negative reaction that I thought I'd killed people, like I was a [expletive] murderer, like I literally destroyed their lives, like they told me. And I was like – am I really that person? So, yeah, you can … maybe guilt is a very mild word. I don't even know how to describe it. (Metka)

Furthermore, and as shown in the next excerpt, despite intimacy being lost due to a disregard of Metka's transgender identity, family still 'binds and is binding' (Ahmed, 2010: 45). In other words, affective obligations and obliged affections – especially guilt and the feeling of responsibility – hold Metka in place in terms of her orientation towards the family:

> You know, I think I've lost respect. I've lost so much of this … sharing of intimacy, sharing of, you know, things that matter. I don't care about it anymore. I think … I feel bad because it's obvious that, I don't know, my mother wants to have some kind of relationship with me. […] But look, honey, it can't be good as long as you refuse to see me as a person. […] Yeah, we can talk about the weather once a week. We can tell each other what we're going to make for lunch on Sundays, but that's it. What kind of relationship is that? None at all. It's the dregs of a relationship. (Metka)

In other words, despite losing the 'things that matter', the signs of 'getting along' (Ahmed, 2006a: 36) are maintained. The pretence is kept up because the price of not doing it – feeling responsible for the heartbreak of one's parents, for destroying their lives, for 'murdering' one's family, in other words, of feeling responsible for family fission because of one's transgender identity – is felt to be too high. It is the feelings of responsibility and guilt that circulate within the family and one-sidedly stick to Metka that holds her in place despite becoming affectively alienated (Ahmed, 2006a) by familial relationships becoming 'none at all'. Deeply embodied affective obligations and obliged affections (Bourdieu, 1996) set the price for her supposed 'betrayal' of the family, stemming from her straying away from the inherited lines of cisnormativity. The family, stripped of its intimacy, persists but at the expense of Metka's transgender identity, which remains unrecognised and silenced. Despite maintaining family relations, affective intimacy is lacking precisely because of the demands to silence transgender identity 'in the name of family'.

While a family's chipping away at transgender existence ('we don't accept you as you are') serves as a 'pressure point' for directing one towards the straight lines of cisnormativity, it may also become a 'breaking point' that unbinds one from the family and the embodied affective orientation towards it that stems from the promise of happiness attached to an image of family (Ahmed, 2006b: 90). Nevertheless, even though it is now reduced, the weight of affective obligations and obliged affections remains, as the promise of a happy object leaves its traces in the form of a feeling of loss:

> In the end, [family] are the people you know all your life. 'Knowing' is now something relative, but you live with them, coexist with them, and it's not easy to lose that. That sense of belonging and the sacredness of [family] that presumably stays when everyone else leaves you – I've never experienced that. [...] At the same time, they don't give you that actual sense of belonging – 'We don't accept you as you are. We are bothered by you, but you are still one of us.' And I presumably belong. [...] But it's terrible to miss people who are toxic to you. Once, I wrote down a phrase – wait, I need to remember it – 'Trying hard to heal my wounded heart by loving its poison.' ... That's one of the worst things because you love that poison, like a drug, even though you know it's killing you, but you can't do without it until you make a decision, but you'll always need it. Because this addiction doesn't stop! (Djuro)

To avoid a deterministic reading of the affective orientation towards particular objects, that is, of being disposed to feel in certain ways, it is important to keep in mind that the above stories are a snapshot in time. They provide a snapshot of a dynamic rather than once-and-for-all affective (re)orientations towards familial intimacy. Although Djuro's narrative was fatalistic at the time ('because this addiction doesn't stop!'), affects do move and re/make worlds (Ahmed, 2004), and affective orientations towards the family can be reconfigured based on heterogeneous experiences throughout life (Bourdieu, 2000; see also McNay, 2000). Nonetheless, Djuro's narrative offers significant insight into the ways in which affective obligations and obliged affections can be experienced and felt. The perceived and experienced *fatum*, a fatalistic verdict of never being able to renounce that which 'kills you', of what is tearing away one's transgender existence in order to secure the existence of family – ironically as united and mutually loving – shows how the sociality and historicity of an affective orientation towards the family, embodied as affective obligations and obliged affections, tend to hold people in place.

Discussion

Experiences of family rejection due to one's transgender status are not the only possible outcome, although they are common, given cisnormativity (see, e.g., Fuller and Riggs, 2018; Riggs, von Doussa and Power, 2016; Weinhardt *et al.*, 2019). Moreover, Bourdieu (2001: 83) notes that the family is one of the most important mechanisms contributing to the 'maintenance' of social permanencies, including gender divisions. An agent who deviates from what the family unwittingly and sometimes unwillingly reproduces, namely, gender normativity, is perceived as becoming 'unsupportive' of the forces of family fusion. As Ahmed (2014b: 113) notes in her discussion of wilful subjects, such a child is perceived as refusing to become 'a support- ive limb' to 'give a hand' in the social reproduction that (also) takes place through and with the help of the family. In other words, an agent becomes a 'non-reproductive agent', an agent who does not follow the (gendered) 'footsteps of those who have gone before' (Ahmed, 2019: 212).

By being perceived as a force of fission (Bourdieu, 1996) – of division rather than fusion – the agent is held responsible for disturbing the prom- ises of family as the happy object (Ahmed, 2010). Through these cracks seeps a story of naturalised rather than natural affective orientation towards the family, of socially shaped affective obligations and obliged affections. It exposes the social dimension of affects, involving an orientation towards the particular objects. What is more, the story exposes the normative and evalu- ative dimension of the affects, to which the affective intimacy of family is not exempt despite the myths surrounding it: 'The process of deciding what is bad or wrong involves affects' (Ahmed, 2014a: 203), which makes emo- tions, understood as moving and being moved, bound up 'with the securing of social hierarchy' (4). Through these stories, the affective intimacy of fam- ily is exposed as being full of 'subtle affective mechanisms' directing agents towards the inherited lines that one is supposed to follow. What is more, these affective mechanisms of familial intimacy are powered by affective obli- gations and obliged affections (Bourdieu, 1996, 2000; see also Threadgold, 2020) that one should feel towards the family and its members, and it is these affective obligations and obliged affections that make the stakes high. Namely, straying away from the inherited paths, refusal to inherit them, means being perceived as responsible and, what is more, feeling responsible for others' unhappiness: 'To follow a different path would be to not only compromise your own happiness but the happiness of others' (Schmitz and Ahmed, 2014: 103). In this way, Metka fears becoming a 'murderer' of her family, 'as if her life would amount to the killing of the body of which she is a part' (Ahmed, 2014b: 113). What is more, this web of affective obliga- tions and obliged affections keeps an affective orientation towards the fam- ily – as an object one should be oriented and attached to – alive, because it *promises* happiness, even when it fails to deliver on the promise. However, it is also affects, including affective obligations and obliged affections, that can reorient parents towards a child's transgender status, as is evident from Alex's narrative, where family fusion ('no matter what') was reaffirmed after an initial rejection of Alex's transgender identity.

Thus, the stories of gender non-binary individuals tell as much about habitualised affective orientation to family as they do about dynamic reorientations that are not contained by sociality and historicity (see, e.g., Blackman and Venn, 2010; Seigworth and Gregg, 2010; Slaby, Mühlhoff and Wüschner, 2019). These are also the stories of affective dimensions – of anger, frustration, disappointments, sadness and pain – that can act as a breaking point for distancing oneself from these relations. Those who 'journey away' from affective intimacy may do so only for a time – the time necessary to build up resilience to the family's negative judgements. Yet, for others, affective reorientation to the family – as something that chips away at their existence by giving rise to feelings of humiliation, disrespect and guilt – is a more final step. However, even in these cases, where affective obligations and obliged affections have been transcended despite the difficulties of doing so, subjective historicity in the shape of memories remains to 'haunt' gender non-binary individuals, if only in the form of feelings of loss that give rise to an awareness of a lack of familial affective intimacy in a space where one is socially expected to find it. These stories reveal the messiness of affective orientations and reorientations, of an entangled web of affects and obligations, and, as Ahmed puts it (2006a: 33), 'how we are touched by what comes near' and, what is more, by what goes away.

Conclusion

In this chapter, I have attempted to sketch out the dynamics of an affective orientation towards familial intimacy as a happy object and towards the promise of happiness that is disrupted when met with the transgender lives of family members. Using Ahmed's approach to emotions as encompassing 'bodily processes of affecting and being affected' (2014a: 208; see also 2004, 2006a; Schmitz and Ahmed, 2014) and Bourdieu's concept of affective obligations and obliged affections (1996, 2000), I have attempted to show how gender non-binary individuals are affected by the promise of family as a happy object. Their stories show that family produces not only a 'happy immersion' (Bourdieu, 2000: 166) – pleasures, well-being, joys – as the myths surrounding it promise, but also the ambivalences of belonging and alienation. As the stories of gender non-binary individuals demonstrate, it is (also) the deep embodiment of affective obligations and obliged affections that makes distancing oneself from these intimacies difficult and hardly amenable, according to the agent's 'controls of the will' (Bourdieu, 2000: 171).

I argue that this very point of acknowledging the embodiment of affective obligations and obliged affections – affects in their habitualised form – and their social dimensions are one of the most productive intersections of Bourdieu's and Ahmed's approaches, on one hand, and affective intimacies on the other. As the data show, affective intimacies are not only about closeness and proximity, but also about exposures, vulnerabilities, and orientations. The narratives reveal an often neglected side of affective intimacies – not only in terms of vulnerabilities and exposures – but also in terms of the social weight they might carry. More than that, they expose the web of affects – obligations that persist within the family even as its intimate character diminishes due to the disregard for, and rejection of, transgender lives.

Although the chapter addresses the phenomenon of affective intimacies from a particular perspective that is in no way capable of fully encompassing their complexities, it nonetheless enables us to gain an insight into socially shaped, habitualised and embodied affective orientations towards family intimacy, where emotions, including their entanglement with bodily sensations and thought categories, move agents towards and away from certain objects as well as render them stuck in an ambivalent experiential mess, containing bags of guilt, shame and responsibility. These bags are hard to put down, precisely because – as gender non-binary individuals' stories show us – they are carried alongside experiential dimensions of care, pleasure, joys and affections, even if those persist only in the form of memories.

Notes

1 Sara Ahmed uses the concept of 'emotions' in a way that encompasses bodily/ corporeal reactions, values, ideas and judgements, thus including the level of thoughts (Schmitz and Ahmed, 2014). I will use emotions and affects in the broader sense of *emovere* (Ahmed, 2014a: 11) – to move and be moved – while acknowledging that in everyday life, affecting and being affected, as well as moving and being moved are inseparable domains. Put differently, I follow Ahmed and her understanding of *emotions* as well as her understanding of *affective* orientation and *affective* economies.

2 The research titled 'Everyday life of individuals with non-binary gender and sexual identities' was co-financed by the Slovenian Research Agency through its Young Researcher Programme (2015–2019). Additional research work on the empirical data was financed by the Slovenian Research Agency (research core funding No. P5-0183). The funder played no role in study design, collection, analysis and interpretation of data, and they accept no responsibility for contents.

References

Ahmed, S. (2004), 'Affective Economies', *Social Text*, 22:2, 117–39. doi: https://doi.org/10.1215/01642472-22-2_79-117

Ahmed, S. (2006a), 'Creating Disturbance: Feminism, Happiness and Affective Differences', in *Working with Affect in Feminist Readings: Disturbing Differences*, M. Liljeström and S. Paasonen (eds) (Abingdon and New York, NY: Routledge), 31–44.

Ahmed, S. (2006b), *Queer Phenomenology: Orientations, Objects, Others* (Durham, NC, and London: Duke University Press).

Ahmed, S. (2010), *The Promise of Happiness* (Durham, NC, and London: Duke University Press).

Ahmed, S. (2014a), *The Cultural Politics of Emotions*, 2nd edition (Edinburgh: Edinburgh University Press).

Ahmed, S. (2014b), *Willful Subjects* (Durham, NC, and London: Duke University Press).

Ahmed, S. (2019), *What's the Use? On the Uses of Use* (Durham, NC, and London: Duke University Press).

Alegría, C. A. (2018), 'Supporting Families of Transgender Children/Youth: Parents Speak on Their Experiences, Identity, and Views', *International Journal of Transgenderism*, 19:2, 132–43. doi: https://doi.org/10.1080/15532739.2018.1450798

Bennett, K., and Donatone, B. (2020), 'When "Coming Out" is (Even More) Complicated: Considerations for Therapists Helping TGNB Emerging Adults Navigate Conversations About Gender With Family', *Journal of College Student Psychotherapy*, published as Online First Article on 29 July 2020. doi: https://doi.org/10.1080/87568225.2020.1791776

Berg, B. L. (2001), *Qualitative Research Methods for the Social Sciences* (Needham Heights, MA: Pearson Education).

Berlant, L. (1998), 'Intimacy: A Special Issue', *Critical Inquiry*, 24:2, 281–8. Available at: www.jstor.org/stable/1344169 (Accessed: 15 June 2020).

Berlant, L. (2011), *Cruel Optimism* (Durham, NC, and London: Duke University Press).

Berlant, L., and Warner, M. (1998), 'Sex in Public', *Critical Inquiry*, 24:2, 547–66. Available at: www.jstor.org/stable/1344178 (Accessed: 5 March 2021).

Blackman, L., and Venn, C. (2010), 'Affect', *Body and Society*, 16:1, 7–28. doi: https://doi.org/10.1177/1357034X09354769

Bourdieu, P. (1991), *Language and Symbolic Power* (Cambridge: Polity Press).

Bourdieu, P. (1996), 'On the Family as a Realized Category', *Theory, Culture and Society*, 3:13, 19–26. doi: https://doi.org/10.1177/026327696013003002

Bourdieu, P. (2000), *Pascalian Meditations* (Palo Alto, CA: Stanford University Press).

Bourdieu, P. (2001), *Masculine Domination* (Cambridge: Polity Press).

Bourdieu, P. (2020), *Habitus and Field: General Sociology, Volume 2, Lectures at the Collège de France, 1982–1983* (Cambridge: Polity Press).

Bourdieu, P., and Wacquant, L. (1992), *An Invitation to Reflexive Sociology* (Cambridge: Polity Press).

Braun, V., and Clarke, V. (2013), *Successful Qualitative Research: A Practical Guide for Beginners* (London: SAGE Publications).

Catalpa, J. M., and McGuire, J. K. (2018), 'Family Boundary Ambiguity Among Transgender Youth', *Family Relations – Interdisciplinary Journal of Applied Family Science*, 67, 88–103. doi: https://doi.org/10.1111/fare.12304

Emmel, N., Hughes, K., Greenhalgh, J., and Sales, A. (2007), 'Accessing Socially Excluded People: Trust and the Gatekeeper in the Researcher-Participant Relationship', *Sociological Research Online*, 12:2, 1–13. doi: https://doi.org/10.5153/sro.1512

Fiani, C. N., and Han, H. J. (2019), 'Navigating Identity: Experiences of Binary and Non-Binary Transgender and Gender Non-Conforming (TGNC) Adults', *International Journal of Transgenderism*, 20:2–3, 181–94. doi: https://doi.org/10.1080/15532739.2018.1426074

Forstie, C. (2017), 'A New Framing for an Old Sociology of Intimacy', *Sociology Compass*, 11, 1–14. doi: https://doi.org/10.1111/soc4.12467

Freeman, E. (2007), 'Queer Belongings: Kinship Theory and Queer Theory', in *A Companion to Lesbian, Gay, Bisexual, Transgender, and Queer Studies*, G. E. Haggerty and M. McGarry (eds) (Malden, MA, Oxford and Carlton, Australia: Blackwell Publishing), 293–314.

Fuller, K. A., and Riggs, D. W. (2018), 'Family Support and Discrimination and Their Relationship to Psychological Distress and Resilience Amongst Transgender People', *International Journal of Transgenderism*, 19:4, 379–88. doi: https://doi.org/10.1080/15532739.2018.1500966

Grossman, A. H., D'Augelli, A. R., Jarrett Howell, T., and Hubbard, S. (2005), 'Parents' Reactions to Transgender Youth, Gender Nonconforming Expression and Identity', *Journal of Gay and Lesbian Social Services*, 18:1, 3–16. doi: https://doi.org/10.1300/J041v18n01_02

Hafner-Fink, M., *et al.* (2020), *Slovensko javno mnenje 2020/1: Ogledalo javnega mnenja, življenje in stališča v času epidemije COVID-19* (*Slovenian Public Opinion 2020/1: Mirror of Public Opinion, Life and Attitudes During the COVID-19 Epidemic*) (Ljubljana, Slovenia: Fakulteta za družbene vede).

Hines, S. (2007), *TransForming Gender: Transgender Practices of Identity, Intimacy and Care* (Bristol: Policy Press).

Holmes, M., Jamieson, L., and Natalier, K. (2021), 'Future Building and Emotional Reflexivity: Gendered or Queered Navigations of Agency in Non-Normative Relationships?', *Sociology* (online first, 2021). doi: https://doi.org/10.1177/0038038520981841

Jamieson, L. (2011), 'Intimacy as a Concept: Explaining Social Change in the Context of Globalisation or Another Form of Ethnocentrism?', *Sociological Research Online*, 16:4, 151–63. doi: https://doi.org/10.5153/sro.2497

Johnson, K. C., LeBlanc, A. J., Deardorff, J., and Bockting, W. O. (2020), 'Invalidation Experiences Among Non-Binary Adolescents', *The Journal of Sex Research*, 57:2, 222–33. doi: https://doi.org/10.1080/00224499.2019.1608422

Jurva, R., and Lahti, A. (2019), 'Challenging Unequal Gendered Conventions in Heterosexual Relationship Contexts Through Affective Dissonance', *NORA – Nordic Journal of Feminist and Gender Research*, 27:4, 218–30. doi: https://doi.org/10.1080/08038740.2019.1682662

Kelley, A. D. (2020), 'Cisnormative Empathy: A Critical Examination of Love, Support, and Compassion for Transgender People by Their Loved Ones', *Sociological Inquiry* (online first, 2020). doi: https://doi.org/10.1111/soin.12390

Kinnunen, T., and Kolehmainen, M. (2019), 'Touch and Affect: Analysing the Archive of Touch Biographies', *Body & Society*, 25:1, 29–56. doi: 10.1177/1357034X18817607

Kuckartz, U., and Rädiker, S. (2019), *Analyzing Qualitative Data with MAXQDA: Text, Audio, and Video* (Cham, Switzerland: Springer).

Kuhar, R., Monro, S., and Takács, J. (2017), 'Trans* Citizenship in Post-Socialist Societies', *Critical Social Policy*, 38:1, 99–120. doi: https://doi.org/10.1177/0261018317732463

Kuhar, R., and Patternote, D. (eds) (2017), *Anti-Gender Campaigns in Europe: Mobilizing Against Equality* (London: Rowman & Littlefield).

McDermott, E., Gabb, J., Eastham, R., and Hanbury, A. (2021), 'Family Trouble: Heteronormativity, Emotion Work and Queer Youth Mental Health', *Health*, 23:2, 177–95. doi: https://doi.org/10.1177/1363459319860572

McNay, L. (2000), *Gender and Agency: Reconfiguring the Subject in Feminist and Social Theory* (Cambridge: Polity Press).

Nuttbrock, L. A., Bockting, W. O., Hwahng, S., *et al.* (2009), 'Gender Identity Affirmation Among Male-to-Female Transgender Persons: A Life Course Analysis Across Types of Relationships and Cultural/Lifestyles Factors', *Sexual and Relationship Therapy*, 24:2, 108–25. doi: https://doi.org/10.1080/14681990902926764

Perger, N. (2020), *Razpiranje horizontov možnega: O nebinarnih spolnih in seksualnih identitetah v Sloveniji* (*Widening the Horizons of the Possible: On Non-Binary Sexual and Gender Identities in Slovenia*) (Ljubljana, Slovenia: Fakulteta za družbene vede, Založba FDV).

Perger, N. (2021), *Transspolne osebe v obdobju epidemije COVID-19: Dostop do zdravstvenih storitev. Končno poročilo o rezultatih raziskave* (*Transgender People During the COVID-19 Epidemic: Access to Health Services. Final Report on the Research Results*) (Ljubljana, Slovenia: DIC Legebitra). Available at: https://legebitra.si/wp-content/uploads/2019/08/TransBuddy-POROCILO_slo_splet.pdf (Accessed: 3 May 2021).

Rener, T. (2006a), 'Družina in njene nove podobe' (The Family and its New Images), in *Socialni razgledi 2006* (*Social Outlooks 2006*), J. Javornik (ed.) (Ljubljana, Slovenia: Urad RS za makroekonomske analize in razvoj), 72–85. Available at: www.umar.gov.si/fileadmin/user_upload/publikacije/socrazgledi/SR2006.pdf (Accessed: 3 May 2021).

Rener, T. (2006b), 'Odraščati v družinah' (Growing Up in Families), in *Družine in družinsko življenje v Sloveniji (Families and Family Life in Slovenia)*, T. Rener, M. Sedmak, A. Švab, and M. Urek (eds) (Koper, Slovenia: Univerza na Primorskem,

Znanstveno-raziskovalno središče, Založba Annales, Zgodovinsko društvo za južno Primorsko), 89–125.

Rener, T. (2018), '"Seveda gre za otroke": družine v primežu (slovenskih) ideoloških bojev' ('Of Course It's About Children': Families in the Grip of (Slovenian) Ideological Struggles), in *Zasebno je politično: kritične teorije vsakdanjega življenja* (*The Private is Political: Critical Theories of Everyday Life*), M. Ule, T. Kamin, and A. Švab (eds) (Ljubljana, Slovenia: Fakulteta za družbene vede, Založba FDV), 199–206.

Riggs, D. W., von Doussa, H., and Power, J. (2016), 'The Family and Romantic Relationships of Trans and Gender Diverse Australians: An Exploratory Survey', *Sexual and Relationship Therapy*, 30:2, 243–55. doi: https://doi.org/10.1080/14681994.2014.992409

Ritchie, J., and Lewis, J. (eds) (2003), *Qualitative Research Practice: A Guide for Social Science Students and Researchers* (London and Thousand Oaks, CA, and New Delhi, India: SAGE Publications).

Robinson, B. A. (2018), 'Conditional Families and Lesbian, Gay, Bisexual, Transgender, and Queer Youth Homelessness: Gender, Sexuality, Family Instability, and Rejection', *Journal of Marriage and Family*, 80:2, 383–96. doi: https://doi.org/10.1111/jomf.12466

Saldaña, J. (2009), *The Coding Manual for Qualitative Researchers* (London: SAGE Publications).

Sanger, T. (2010), *Trans People's Partnerships: Towards an Ethics of Intimacy* (London: Palgrave Macmillan).

Sanger, T., and Taylor, Y. (2013), 'Introduction', in *Mapping Intimacies: Relations, Exchanges, Affects*, T. Sanger and Y. Taylor (eds) (Basingstoke: Palgrave Macmillan), 1–14.

Schmitz, S., and Ahmed, S. (2014), 'Affect/Emotion: Orientation Matters. A Conversation Between Sigrid Schmitz and Sara Ahmed', *Freiburger Zeitschrift für GeschlechterStudien*, 20:2, 97–108. doi: https://doi.org/10.3224/09489975214

Seigworth, G. J., and Gregg, M. (2010), 'An Inventory of Shimmers', in *The Affect Theory Reader*, M. Gregg, and G. J. Seigworth (eds) (Durham, NC, and London: Duke University Press), 1–25.

Seymour, J. (1999), 'Relating Intimacies: Power and Resistance', in *Relating Intimacies: Explorations in Sociology*. British Sociological Association Conference Volume Series (London: Palgrave Macmillan).

Slaby, J., Mühlhoff, R., and Wüschner, P. (2019), 'Affective Arrangements', *Emotion Review*, 11:1, 3–12. doi: https://doi.org/10.1177/1754073917722214

Threadgold, S. (2020), *Bourdieu and Affect: Towards a Theory of Affective Affinities* (Bristol: Bristol University Press).

von Doussa, H., Power, J., and Riggs, D. W. (2020), 'Family Matters: Transgender and Gender Diverse People's Experiences With Family When They Transition', *Journal of Family Studies*, 26:2, 272–85. doi: https://doi.org/10.1080/13229400.2017.1375965

Vijlbrief, A., Saharso, S., and Ghorashi, H. (2020), 'Transcending the Gender Binary: Gender Non-Binary Young Adults in Amsterdam', *Journal of LGBT Youth*, 17:1, 89–106. doi: https://doi.org/10.1080/19361653.2019.1660295

VERBI Software, MAXQDA 2018 (2017). Available at: www.maxqda.com (Accessed: 22 July 2018).

Weinhardt, L. S., Xie, H., Wesp, L. M., *et al.* (2019), 'The Role of Family, Friend, and Significant Other Support in Well-Being Among Transgender and Non-Binary Youth', *Journal of GLBT Family Studies*, 15:4, 311–25. doi: https://doi.org/10.1080/1550428X.2018.1522606

9

Affective intimacies of gender assemblages: Closeness and distance in LGBTQ+ women's relationships

Annukka Lahti

> I think that sharing everyday life with a woman is somehow very easy going and smooth, being together and separate, it intertwines much more easily [than with a man]. Communicating is easier and it is easier to stay on board [with] what the other person is going to do, wants and wishes, the communication is somehow open. (Interview with a bisexual woman, 2014)

When women[1] (including cis, trans and genderqueer women) who I have interviewed talk about their past or current relationships with women, there is often closeness and intimacy – a kind of easiness – present in the female relationships. In the extract above, Jenny, who was married to a man at the time of the interview, talked about her past female relationship in longing terms. Minna, a lesbian woman, whose relationship with her female partner had ended recently due to the partners' conflicting childbearing intentions, described the relationship: 'Our relationship was in every way very good and balanced.' This kind of easiness did not exclude LGBTQ+ women from depicting problems and difficulties in their relationships, and often they did, particularly when I interviewed them about relationships that had ended.[2] Yet, those women who had been in relationships with men often contrasted relationships with women with their past or current relationships with men, wherein they spoke of a certain kind of distance between themselves and their male (ex-)partners and 'being in different worlds'. Women and non-binary interviewees who had mainly had relationships with women saw more variation between relationships. These observations evoke many questions and thoughts about the significance of gender in relationships between women.

Another theme that raised questions of how gender matters in LGBTQ+ women's relationships was how they built families, took care of their children and shared childcare and domestic responsibilities with their women partners before and after their separations. Often when a child was born to a couple or one of the partners yearned for a child, it could either enhance the closeness and proximity between the partners or create distance between them. Sometimes the arrival of a child also meant the arrival of unequal ways of sharing childcare and domestic responsibilities in a relationship. While previous studies have demonstrated that in general same-sex couples, especially female couples, share household chores, childcare and emotion work more equally than mixed-sex couples (e.g. Brewster, 2016; Gotta *et al.*, 2011; Umberson *et al.*, 2015), this does not happen automatically in all LGBTIQ+ relationships (Kelly and Hauck, 2015). This might concern particularly those LGBTIQ+ people's relationships that have ended, as is the case in this study. Often sharing of housework and childcare are analysed from the point of view of how LGBTIQ+ people challenge or reproduce unequal gendered conventions of heterosexual relationships (Jurva and Lahti, 2019; Kelly and Hauck, 2015). However, I argue that the framework of gendered conventions is limited. Unequal gendered practices in female couples do not necessarily mean that one of the partners would carry a greater responsibility of every domestic sphere: e.g. childcare, household chores and supporting one's partner emotionally. Rather there are practices that resemble hierarchical gendered conventions of heterosexual relationships, but they are mixed and matched between partners in various ways. In this chapter I utilise the Deleuzian concept of 'assemblage', which enables me to develop the line of inquiry of gendered conventions, as I seek to account for variety and change in how gender matters in female relationships (Coleman and Ringrose, 2013).

Assemblage theory initiates a consideration of multiplicity, not just in terms of multiple gender identities, but in opening up thinking of gender as a radically open and unpredictable process (Linstead and Pullen, 2006; Kolehmainen, 2020; Schuller, 2020). Instead of seeing gender as an identity residing within an individual, gender is thought of as emerging out of the dynamic encounters of multiple elements and relations that come together in an assemblage (Kolehmainen, 2020; Schuller, 2020). This kind of conceptualisation challenges the human-centred paradigm of conceptualising gender and shifts the focus to processes, entanglements and encounters between human and non-human elements (Bennet, 2010; Blackman, 2012; Kolehmainen and Juvonen, 2018; Lahti and Kolehmainen, 2020; Ringrose and Renold, 2014). Gender is seen as process of becoming across social, material, discursive, human and more-than-human worlds: it entangles different elements and relationships from partners and relationship dynamics to other involved people (friends, children, relatives etc.), from societal power relations and ideals (gendered conventions, relationship norms, heteronormativity, homo- and transphobia etc.) to non-human elements (gendered spaces, events, living/housing arrangements etc.). However, it is not only the elements that make up the multiplicity, but rather the relations between elements, which are essential for analysing assemblages (Coleman and Ringrose, 2013; Lahti and Kolehmainen, 2020).

Thinking of gender as a flexible assemblage illuminates the multiple affective intimacies that emerge when bodies meet in these complex configurations. Intimacy is not only seen as a feature of human relations, but rather affective intimacies are emergent qualities of the web of relations and interactions of many bodies and forces in the gender assemblages (Latimer and Gómez, 2019). My analysis will highlight how the closeness and distance between partners, as well the unjust ways of sharing childcare and housework, is an effect of multiple elements in a gender assemblage, which connects bodies, matter, affects, ideas and societal processes in various ways. In this chapter, I will pay special attention to the ways gendered bodies become intimate or are pushed away from one another as an effect of diverse elements coming together in dynamic gender assemblages.

Gender in LGBTIQ+ relationships: From lesbian psychology to gender as an assemblage

In the 2010s–2020s, gendered dynamics has not been a very popular topic in the research on LGBTIQ+ relationships. As a means to fight the stigmatisation of LGBTIQ+ relationships, the studies have often compared LGBTIQ+ relationships and mixed-sex relationships with an emphasis on how 'similar' LGBTIQ+ couples are to mixed-sex couples (e.g. Balsam *et al.*, 2008; Goldberg and Garcia, 2015). Any differences between LGBTIQ+ and mixed-sex couples are usually explained by the minority stress and discrimination faced by LGBTIQ+ couples (Balsam *et al.*, 2017; Frost and LeBlank, 2019). In Finland, which can be thought of as part of the LGBTIQ+-friendly, progressive Nordic countries (Ilmonen *et al.*, 2017: 96), several legislative changes have been made since the year 2000 in order to improve the legal position of LGBTIQ+ people and their families, although at the time of writing (2021) it has been only four years since the Finnish Marriage Act became gender neutral (Act 234/1929). During the long and complex LGBTIQ+ struggle for recognition, appearing 'just like heterosexuals' has been a central means through which non-heterosexual desires and relational lives have been made intelligible (Warner, 2000; Lahti, 2015). While stressing the sameness to heterosexual couples' norms, it has been difficult to articulate any difference from heterosexual relationships (Lahti, 2015). My previous study suggested that female couples sometimes downplay the positive aspects of their relationships, for example their very positive experiences of intimacy, sex, sharing housework and taking care of children, to appear as similar as possible to mixed-sex couples (Lahti, 2015).

In contrast, in lesbian psychology – a lesbian affirmative psychological research from the late 1970s onwards, which did not assume homosexual pathology and strived to counter discrimination and prejudice against lesbians (Ellis, 2015) – of the 1990s and the beginning of the 2000s, the partners' gender was used to explain both intimacy and conflict in lesbian relationships. It was thought that female couples were prone to be overly close and lack personal boundaries – which was referred to as 'fusion' – because the partners have been socialised as women (Laird, 2000; Causby, Lockhart, White and Greene, 1995). The notion of fusion in lesbian relationships was first problematised and later proved to be a false assumption (Ellis, 2015). It was pointed out that viewing lesbian relationships as fused revealed that these relationships were being evaluated through the gender stereotypes and standards of heterosexual relationships (Ellis, 2015; Laird, 2000; Frost and Eliason, 2014). Also, Frost and Eliason's (2014) comparative study showed that lesbian couples are not more 'fused' than other couples. This shows that the characteristics that are culturally linked to a good relationship – spending time together, closeness and making decisions together – were seen as negative and pathological when they appeared in a female relationship (Greene, Causby and Miller, 1999).

Several studies show that female couples are often very satisfied with their relationships compared to mixed-sex couples, as found by a study in Finland for example (Aarnio *et al.*, 2018; Gottman, Levenson, Gross *et al.*, 2003; Gottman, Levenson, Swanson *et al.*, 2003; Kurdek, 2008). This is often explained by the female couple's assumed equality in sharing household chores, finances and childcare. Some studies also indicate that female couples' communication and fighting skills might be better than those of mixed-sex couples (Gottman, Levenson, Gross *et al.*, 2003; Gottman, Levenson, Swanson *et al.*, 2003). Studies also show that women in heterosexual relationships do more emotion work than men, for example, work of taking care of others' emotional needs, improving others' well-being and maintaining harmonious relationships (Duncombe and Marsden, 1993; Strazdins and Broom, 2004). Umberson *et al.*'s study (2015), which included lesbian, gay and heterosexual couples, paid attention to emotion work in long-term relationships. The study found that emotion work – sharing feelings and supporting each other emotionally – was important to all women in the study regardless of their relationship form. In heterosexual relationships, men justified not doing emotion work by saying, for example, that they did not know what to do about the feelings that bothered their wives. On the contrary, in female couples both partners engaged in emotion work, by sharing and discussing emotions and supporting each other emotionally.

However, in the following I will explore how gender matters in LGBTQ+ women's relationships with women, arguing that it is not only a matter of (hierarchical) gendered conventions – e.g. how the housework and child-care are shared between partners. Neither can it be reduced to assumptions of women's good communication skills or ability to do emotion work in their relationships. My aim is to move beyond frameworks that mobilise the binary category of gender as a framework for understanding these relationships. Firstly, since the beginning of the 2000s there has been a multiplication of non-binary gender and trans* identities, and a diversification of sexualities beyond the binary categories of sex, gender and sexuality. Thinking of the diversified possibilities to identify with various gender identifies, it is not very simple to say who is 'of the same gender' and who is 'of a different gender', and is it only a narrow group of people that one can refer to with a notion, for example, of 'same-sex female relationships' or 'lesbian relationships'. In this chapter, I will show that gender matters in LGBTIQ+ relationships in various ways that go beyond binary notions of gender and stereotypical ideas about female relationships. In order to map this idea, there is a need to depart from frameworks that reduce gender into individual human subjects, individual characteristics or as an identity that 'belongs to a person'. Further, the lens of relational affect theories (Seyfert, 2012) complicates the analysis of gender, shedding light on the forms of constituting gender that might hide in the affective flow of 'happening' of everyday life – relationship events, scenes and experiences – where gender comes to matter (Stewart, 2007).

As Stephen Linstead and Alison Pullen (2006) note, any undertaking that strives to move beyond the binary thinking of gender initiates a consideration of multiplicity, and the way in which multiplicity is conceptualised has consequences for what kinds of possibilities of thinking about gender are opened up. I argue that the question is not only about the multiplication of gender identities, but rather that Deleuzo-Guattarian thinking opens up new ways of thinking about gender beyond identities. In the Deleuzo-Guattarian framework, gender is not seen as an identity that can be 'possessed' by an individual subject or something that resides in a particular gendered body (Linstead and Pullen, 2006; Kolehmainen, 2020; Schuller, 2020). Rather, gender is conceptualised as becoming in and through affective assemblages (Kolehmainen, 2020; Schuller, 2020; Ringrose and Renold, 2014). In this framework, gender can be re-imagined as a non-personal 'capacity' assembled through the various elements that temporally come together in the dynamics of everyday life (see also Coffey, 2020; Fox and Alldred, 2021). Capacities are not inherent but emerge relationally as bodies interact with other bodies, things and ideas in an assemblage (Deleuze and Guattari, 2004; Fox and Alldred, 2021). The unique assembling of bodies increases or diminishes the affective capabilities of the bodies involved in a particular assemblage (Malins, 2004; Buchanan, 2015; Fox and Alldred, 2021).

In this chapter, I am particularly interested in how proximity and distance between partners emerge as an effect of multiple elements and relations of gender assemblages, often in temporally shifting ways (De Landa, 2006; Ringrose and Renold, 2014). Affective intimacies are emergent qualities of the webs of relations and connections in gender assemblages, which can entangle and disentangle elements that do good and give pleasure, but also elements that are problematic and can expose us to harm and pain (Kinnunen and Kolehmainen, 2019; Latimer and Gómez, 2019; Lahti, 2018, 2020). Although assemblages are dynamic and multiple, often there are the processes and elements assembled in certain ways, such as in gendered power dynamics, as well as in the harmonious and/ or painful relationship dynamics that come together in relationships. By approaching gender as an assemblage, I explore the multiplying effects of various gender assemblages, and highlight their ongoing relational processes and shifting power dynamics.

Data and methodology

For the purposes of this chapter, I analyse two data sets: 1) thirty interviews with LGBTIQ+ people who have experienced a recent relationship break-up. Of the thirty interviewees, sixteen identified as women, one as a trans woman, and six said that their official gender was female. Yet those six who referred to this 'official gender' reflected their gender in various ways: for example, one of them identified as non-binary and had gone through a trans process, one identified as 'gender-neutral', one said that they didn't see their gender as '100% female' and one referred to expressing gender in varying ways. In this chapter, I mainly analyse these twenty-three interviewees and I refer to the interviewees as LGBTQ+ women. The four accounts of non-binary gendered interviewees and the interviews with three men are not excluded on the basis of their gender identities, but rather because the themes analysed in this chapter did not come up in their interviews. 2) The other data set is a longitudinal set of interviews, which consists of five (originally seven) couple interviews with bisexual women and their variously gendered partners, conducted in 2005, and eleven follow-up interviews conducted some ten years later in 2014–2015. Participants were aged twenty-two to forty-two at the time of the first interview, and thirty-two to fifty-two at the follow-up interview. By the time of the follow-up interviews, the majority of the couples interviewed in 2005 had separated, and most of them had new partners. Both sets of interviews were in-depth and conducted in Finnish cities and towns. Because of COVID-19 in 2020–2021, the last twenty-one separation interviews were conducted via Zoom. All interviews lasted between one and four hours. They were audio-recorded and transcribed.

Despite the data deriving largely from a separation study, it must be noted that in this particular study I'm not interested in finding the reasons for LGBTIQ+ people's separations. Yet, one should be cautious when drawing conclusions about relationships based on portrayals of relationships that have ended. The stories might have been told from a specific affective register of a separated person – often angry, sad and disappointed, especially if the separation happened only a short time ago. As one bisexual interviewee said: 'Maybe after ten years I can give a good synthesis about our relationship, what was good and what was bad in it. What one remembers depends a lot [on] the situation at hand, from which one remembers it. And here I am reminiscing [on] it as [a] quite recently separated [person].' Yet, it must be noted that bisexual women, in this study in particular, portrayed their past relationships with women in a very positive light, even if those relationships had ended.

Instead of representing all of the themes present in the data, I focus on two themes in my analysis. These two themes show how proximity, distance and gender are entangled in various ways in LGBTQ+ women's relationships: 1) the closeness and easiness of LGBTQ+ women's relationships and 2) how the interviewees built families, took care of their children, shared childcare and domestic responsibilities before and after their separation. Inspired by Taina Kinnunen and Marjo Kolehmainen (2019), I analyse the two sets of interview data as an archive of material-semiotic experiences related to gender assembled in a certain way (see also Schuller, 2020). My analysis is detached from ideas that gender could be located in a certain gendered body, or that it would be 'just a social construction' (Kolehmainen, 2020; Schuller, 2020). Rather, I analyse it as a dynamic and changing assemblage, which conjoins various elements, multiple power relations and affective intimacies (Kolehmainen, 2020; Schuller, 2020). From a Deleuzian viewpoint, the methodological task is to identify these various elements and relations within an assemblage (Fox and Alldred, 2015). My aim is to shift the focus from the human-centred paradigm that would approach gender as pre-defined individual property, to a more nuanced approach wherein the multiple elements and affective effects of a gender assemblage can be identified. My analysis will show how the entangled elements and affective intimacies of gender assemblages can create proximity and distance between partners in temporally shifting ways. Instead of analysing only one element or dimension as determinant over others – for example, thinking that relationships are determined by partners' genders – I pay attention to the

multiple elements that come together in gender assemblages, shaping emerging affective intimacies, as well as equalities and inequalities in LGBTQ+
women's relationships.

Accumulating affective intimacies in LGBTQ+ women's gender assemblages

In this section I analyse gender assemblages of LGBTQ+ women, which
emerge as a co-constitution of human and non-human elements such as
sexual desire, past and current relationship experiences, gendered spaces,
cultural ideas regarding masculinity and femininity and (shared) values and
interests. I further analyse the multiple affective intimacies that emerge as an
effect of the different elements and relations coming together in these gender
assemblages.

Desire was an important element that brought women closer to other
women as partners. Thinking with the Deleuzian notion of desire as productive and seeking (see Mazzei, 2013) it is possible to analyse the forces of
desire that are acting through and with the research participants, producing changes within the complex configurations of their gender assemblages
(Ringrose and Renold, 2014). For Malvina, it was her child's birth that gave
a push to her intensifying desires for women, which affected the entanglements of her relational assemblage:

> I have always had sexual relationships with both men and women ... but
> ... I come from ... a very conservative background and family... When my
> child was born, things started to pour over me like an avalanche ... In that
> wrestling I started to tear down walls around me and in the long run the long
> relationship, the marriage was left behind and then men completely. I am not
> in contact with my parents any more ... after ... I've got [the] freedom to live
> the kind of life I want to have for myself.

In this gender assemblage, Malvina's parents and conservative upbringing had
blocked the becoming of her desires for women from developing into a couple
relationship. It was the desire for women that was a productive, propulsive
force working across the assemblage – producing changes in her relational
entanglements as she left her marriage and cut the ties to her conservative and
abusive parents. Although these changes were powerful and led to a divorce
from her heterosexual marriage, they were gradual and the sum of many elements rather than being a sudden discovery of one's LGBTQ+ identity. One of
the women, Sara, who had experienced changes in her sexuality in her fifties,
referred to sexuality as a continuous becoming: 'I cannot know what I am
going to desire when I am sixty or seventy. I cannot say if this is some kind of
stage ... I give myself permission to enjoy it now, at the stage [that] is going

on at the moment.' Yet, sex here also refers to elements beyond individual and isolated processes, as becoming sexual also means becoming with societal values, different spaces and experiences. Emma relates that she has struggled with sexuality in her female relationship: 'There [have] been difficulties with sexuality, maybe with my own inhibitions. It has always been easiest for [us] to make love when we have been travelling abroad, [there we have] really been able to escape this normative society.'

For Malvina, Sara and other women who referred to themselves as 'late bloomers' there was often an exhilarating feel when they talked about sexuality with women. Sara experienced her desire and her body's openness when having sex with a woman:

> it is somehow almost shocking how a person can be in their lusts when one gets to romp with a woman [laughs]. It just feels so dif – , it is on a completely different level, and it is [a] very good place for me to be, I enjoy it enormously. – and also how [my] body reacts.

Yet, the desire for women was not only experienced as an exhilarating feeling when bodies become open to another when having sex, but entangled with social and material processes. Becoming an LGBTQ+ woman is a collective, intersubjective process, rather than an individual and isolated matter, as Yiran Wang notes in this volume (Chapter 7). The next excerpt points to Emma's becoming with a gender assemblage that extends itself beyond the two female partner's bodies, working across spaces, events and interests, vibrating with affective intimacies:

> When I think about the beginning of me and Marja's relationship, it was ... going in the same direction, doing things together and going about, we travelled a lot. All the Pride events and gay bars you can find in Europe and all over the world, they were really nice trips – also, cultural life and that kind of thing [interests] we shared ... I remember after a scientist-heterosexual [Emma's male ex-partner was a scientist] relationship, how important it was for me to get to be with a person who shared the same interest[s] and values. It brought us together very much and was important to me.

The affective intimacies of this gender assemblage emerge as a co-constitution of many entangled elements: travelling together with one's female partner to 'gay destinations', collectively becoming with pride events and spaces of gay bars, sharing interests and values and attending cultural events with one's partner. These complexly entangled elements and affective intimacies thereof also brought the partners closer to each other. Emma contrasts this becoming to her previous relationship with a man, who was a scientist, implying that the assembled elements, interests and values of a 'scientist-heterosexual' gender assemblage were of a different kind, possibly creating distance between the partners.

Affective intimacies in LGBTQ+ women's gender assemblages often extend beyond the intimate couple in other ways. Gender assemblages are not just about desire or intimacy between two partners. The intimacies of Emma and Marja's gender assemblage extended to the collective of their friends as they organised an event for them to celebrate their fifteenth anniversary.

> When we had been together for fifteen years, we arranged this event for our friends on the International Women's Day and celebrated our time together by inviting our friends, raised a toast there. We didn't make a point about it, that this was our fifteenth anniversary, rather like 'you are most welcome and we offer drinks and something to eat' for our friends.

In contrast, the next excerpt shows how the binary ideas of gender and segregation of gender in many fields of society affect the assembling of gendered bodies and spaces in ways that can have distancing effects between partners in mixed-sex relationships.

> When the partner is of [the] same gender, there is not that certain kind of living in different worlds, which forms, starting from all kinds of [men's] sauna nights and other things. [In a relationship with a woman] it's not that I would hang out with completely different bunch of people [than my partner]. ... that kind of segregation can be found in Finland quite a lot. The vocations are very gendered, and there is other stuff, in men's and women's socialising and talk, male bonding and all that ... That is something that I find quite hostile – there is [a] certain kind of hostility that I haven't found in female relationships. – It is strange that even there where you are in a very close love relationship, in a heterosexual relationship, even inside of that I have experienced that kind of cultural hostility, it is there.

In this gender assemblage, gender segregation affects how gendered bodies are brought together and distanced from one another in different spaces. Here 'being in different worlds' extends itself beyond the two partners, as Sanna's male partners are becoming with a gender assemblage that extends to men's sauna nights and bonding between other male bodies. Working life is strongly segregated in Finland to 'men's and women's' occupations (Kauhanen and Riukula, 2019). Segregation and gendered inequalities are reproduced in everyday activities, practices and processes, from which men's sauna night is one example (Bolin and Olofsdotter, 2018). Gender segregation has an accumulative effect of a certain kind of affective intimacies, as Sanna feels that there was hostility present even between the mixed-sex intimate partners. This kind of effect of gender segregation is demonstrative of the ways that bodies are conditioned and condition themselves to one another in a set of unequal and uneven relations of power (also Ahmed, 2000; Zengin, 2016). This does not mean that all LGBTQ+ women would have experienced close relationships with men as hostile, but many spoke of a certain kind of distance from their male (ex-)partners.

The accumulation of affective intimacies of a positive tone in LGBTQ+ women's relationships with women does not mean that all female relationships would have necessarily been 'easy'. Some harmonious and close couples also ended up separating for various reasons. In Deleuzo-Guattarian terms, assemblages are rhizomatic in that they connect embodied, affective and psychic elements in many different ways. The compositions of these assemblages are varying and unique, as the next excerpt shows:

> A relationship with a woman is somehow, it goes mentally on a deeper level and it can be both straining and also kind of more giving, it feels deeper … With those men that I have dated, it has been more straightforward somehow easier. Men don't have that many expectations of me or the relationship.

The effects of gender assemblages are multiple, as Helena experienced the accumulating affective intensities of a female relationship to be both rewarding and straining, and felt that relationships with men could be easier. Malvina's first relationship with a woman, in turn, had been tumultuous and ended in separation. Yet she looked forward to her future relationships with women:

> Maybe I can best describe it in that I already eagerly look forward [to the time] that I am older, in granny's age. How wonderful it will be when the two grannies go about out there, do nice things together … I like to take part in all kinds of cultural events, and go to museums. I like to hang around in cafés and libraries … In my relationships with men, the interests haven't been quite the same. We have done all that [together], but I've had this feeling that the other person is not so excited about that kind of thing, and does not get as much out of it, and then it also flattens one's own enthusiasm about it.

In Malvina's imagining of a future relationship with a woman with shared interests, attending cultural events and spaces has an effect of enhancing intimacies in the gender assemblage. Gender here again extends to spaces and events like museums, libraries, cafés and becoming with them together with one's partner vitalises Malvina as the whole gender assemblage is vibrating with energy and affective intimacies. These complexly entangled elements and affective intimacies also have the capacity to bring the partners closer together and energise their bodies as they are becoming with the gender assemblage.

Shifting equalities and inequalities in affective gender assemblages with a child

Having a child or desire for a child was often a very important element in a gender assemblage of LGBTQ+ women. Often when a child or a desire for a child was brought into a gender assemblage it could both enhance the closeness and proximity between the partners and create distance between them, as an effect of various elements in the assemblage. First, it must be noted that whereas it can be normatively expected in a gender assemblage of a heterosexual woman that (hetero)sexuality, partnership (or marriage) and motherhood are tightly entangled (Rich, 1976; Sevon, 2009), in the gender assemblages of LGBTQ+ women, love, partnership, desire for a child and building family were not entangled in any straightforward way, but rather in many different ways. In many women's gender assemblages the desire for a child was a strong cohesive force, stronger than their wish for a partner. Malla, a woman in her fifties, said: 'Then I met my future partner and we got together. It was tinted by the fact that I had already decided that I want to have children. – For my partner it was like OK, but she wasn't the pushing force in it.'

Often the partners experienced changes in their relationship when the first baby came. Katja and Laura are ex-partners who both reminisced on the beginning of their relationship as romantic falling-in-love and a time of closeness – in both an emotional and practical sense as they spent a lot of time together at the beginning of their relationship. Katja reminisces: 'The first phase [of the relationship] was before I got pregnant with our first child. We were "head over heels in love" and it was always the two of us ... even when we were in the company of other people.' In turn, Laura says: 'The first years were such a wonderful time, we had such a great time together, we laughed a lot.' However, both of them imply that their relationship changed when the baby came. Laura relates: 'But then Jaakko was born and the life changed a little and then she [Katja] had her teaching job and positions at the university and that kind of thing [on] her mind. Then it was more like this ordinary day-to-day life, which made it [the relationship] more difficult. Jaakko was a colicky baby and he cried ... for the first six months.'

In the couple interview between Katja and Laura, when their first child had just been born, Katja described the relationship in terms of the equality ideals of a female relationship (see Lahti, 2015). She said to Laura: 'Well, there isn't such an [expectation] that if you were a guy it would be a big thing if you do laundry or ... that kind of expectation like my heterosexual female friends talk about how nice it is that the guy also cleans at home, etc. I think it would be burdensome if the roles would differ by default.' Yet, after more than ten years and two children, the situation was different – yet, very complex. Katja describes in retrospect, after their separation, how the housework and child care was divided in their family:

> Well it has been a two-sided thing ... I am the biological mother of the children and I stayed at home with both of them for about a year after they were born ... and yet I was the most career-oriented of us, so after that year I did very long working days and she [Laura] was the one who took care of our home. So how we shared housework: I think she did 70 percent and I did 30 percent,

because I did longer working hours ... and then again I have taken care of everything related to children's hobbies, taking the children to their friend's birthdays, taking the children to day care ... once I almost fainted when I was sick and had to fetch a child from the day care ... that was not part of what she did with the children.

I have noted in my field diary that these parts of Katja's follow-up interview are affectively very intense, she has tears in her eyes many times. I also remember that at that time, in 2014, I had not heard very many similar stories of unjust distributions of housework and childcare in LGBTQ+ relationships. Since then, when doing the separation interviews for my postdoctoral study, I heard more stories of this kind. For example, Malla described: 'My partner took the role, which is the other role than that of the role of biological mother. During the ten years [they were together] it moulded into a shape, where I carried the main responsibility of the home and the kids.'

I have demonstrated elsewhere with Marjo Kolehmainen (Lahti and Kolehmainen, 2020) that when a child is brought into a relationship assemblage, the focus often shifts from a dyadic couple relationship and gender-neutral ideas into the heteronormative ideas of a family with a mother and a father. Following Gilles Deleuze and Félix Guattari's (2004) notion of the rhizomatic organisation of assemblages, a part of an assemblage can always be plugged into another assemblage, where it can grow along its old line or along a new line. It seems that heteronormative ways of 'doing' gender can also be plugged into LGBTQ+ women's gender assemblages, affecting their lines of becoming.

Yet, as this could be the case, the situation was often much more complex than simply following the unequal gendered conventions of heterosexual relationships (Jurva and Lahti, 2019). The unjust ways of sharing childcare and housework were often an effect of multiple elements in an assemblage. The biological mother carrying the baby in her womb for nine months affected how the bodies were conditioned and conditioned themselves to one another in female couples' families as well (also Ahmed, 2000; Zengin, 2016). Emma depicts:

> When the child was born, the everyday life became easier ... when the child was there concretely and she [her partner] could help concretely, the baby was a real human being. During the pregnancy she [her partner] couldn't empathise ... like what often happens in a heterosexual relationship. The stomach gets bigger ... you live through all the phases of the child's development. I felt that after the baby was born our relationship got better and we got closer to one another all the time, but it just wasn't enough.

While Emma was pregnant, Emma felt that Marja could not relate to the embodied experience that Emma went through when the baby grew and developed in her womb. Things got better when the baby was born, and Marja could engage with the physical act of taking care of the baby. Yet, for

Katja and Laura's family, gender was assembled in a different way, as the cultural idea that the biological mother also assumes the main responsibility of taking care of the baby when it is born was plugged in. Katja describes Laura's relationship to the baby: 'She didn't want to take care of a small child – like we had very traditional gender roles in that sense ... the man goes to work and the woman takes care of the children.' Yet, the gender assemblage was assembled in more complex ways than just reproducing heterosexual gendered conventions. While Katja carried the main responsibility of taking care of the baby, the sharing of household chores was unequally distributed as well, but there the heaviest burden was on Laura's shoulders. Katja notes, 'The ... difference [to the traditional gender roles] was that my ex-spouse took care of the laundry and cooked the food.' In this gender assemblage, parts of unequal heterosexual relationship dynamics were plugged into the female couple's gender assemblage, but they were assembled in ways that put both partners in unjust, difficult situations.

Gender assemblages were thus complex, and although heterosexual gendered ways could partly be guiding the ways in which the division of care and housework was done, the situation was also affected by other elements such as the partners being of different LGBTQ+ women's generations. At the time of their first interview, when Katja was in her twenties, a heated public debate on same-sex couples' right to infertility treatments was going on in Finland. Although disputed, the emerging ideas of LGBTQ+ families might have especially affected Katja's becoming as a bisexual woman, whereas Laura had also lived her life as part of an earlier generation of lesbians and queer women who had often embraced and accepted lifestyles without normative families or children (Kuosmanen, 2007; Weston, 1995). This resonates with what Emma told about her partner, 'She never thought [of] herself as a parent, and didn't want to define herself as [a] parent ... well she defines herself as a lesbian, but she is Marja, an independent person.' Yet, in this family the everyday living was smooth, and the housework and childcare nevertheless were shared equally, as depicted by Emma. This highlights how gender assemblages are multiple and varied, affecting the division of housework and childcare in various ways. It depends on the multiple elements and relations that come together in a particular assemblage.

After a relationship break-up, the assembled (unjust) ways of caring for the children often continued in various ways. Often the specific gender assemblage of unjust ways of taking care of the children could extend itself beyond the individual body to material spaces; for example, after the breakup one of the women moved into a small flat, where there was no space for the children to stay the night. Another woman said that her ex-partner had moved twenty kilometres away from her and the children, which made it very difficult for the teenage children to visit her as they had various intensive hobbies near their other mother's home.

The gender assemblage thus extended to material spaces and living arrangements, which made it impossible for the parent to take full responsibility for the children after the break-up. An example of another kind comes from Kerttu and Sinikka, whose relationship soon went off rails after their child was born. The child had been the cohesive force in their relationship, and it continued that way after the break-up. Here the gender assemblage of fair sharing of childcare duties extended to the other partner's flat: 'There was one time, like Sinikka had almost always put him to sleep when he was small, and then one time he was ill and somehow he couldn't sleep in my place and instead of saying "bring him here", she just came here, put him to sleep and went away.'

Coming back to Katja and Laura, in the gender assemblage of this female couple closeness and distance between the partners was strongly entangled with the disputes about housework and childcare, but also entangled with disputes about the time the couple should spend together and apart. Katja said:

> The reason for the break-up was in the end … the fact that we had such a different view on how much time we should spend together just the two of us … she didn't need other people so much, for her our relationship and our family was enough and that we would do things together. But for me after a year it started to bother me more that I spend too little time with my friends.

Laura on her part wished that they had had more time together as a family and she also felt the burden of the housework: 'There was too little time we spent together. And I was there at home doing housework, taking care of that [so that] everything works at least somehow.' Yet, again, the matter is complex and might have to do with the generational gap between the two women. When Katja had wished Laura would take a bigger part in their public life as a family and socialising with Katja's friends, Laura missed the lesbian community she had been an active member of in another town before she had met Katja. She had to leave the community behind when they moved to a smaller town with their family. It seemed that Katja was more open to socialising as an LGBTQ+ family with the 'wider world'; whereas in Laura's depictions of these encounters, homophobia and antipathy towards their family was present. The generational gap between the two women might have also affected how they viewed their possible social circles as a female couple and an LGBTQ+ family.

Conclusion

This chapter makes a novel contribution to the study of affective intimacies and affective inequalities by exploring the significance of gender in LGBTQ+ women's relationships from an assemblage point of view. The chapter shifts the focus from the human-centred paradigm that would approach gender as an identity that 'belongs to a person', to exploring gender as an assemblage. Gender is seen as a multiplicity emerging out of various elements, relations and affects that come together in an assemblage (Coleman and Ringrose, 2013; Kolehmainen, 2020; Schuller, 2020). This makes it possible to attune to the accumulating affective intimacies as an effect of the interactions of many bodies and forces in gender assemblages, enabling proximities between certain gendered bodies and creating distance between others, in temporally shifting ways (De Landa, 2006; Ringrose and Renold, 2014).

The chapter began with an observation of the closeness and easiness of certain LGBTQ+ women's relationships, while others struggle with unequal ways of sharing childcare and domestic responsibilities in ways that strikingly resemble the hierarchical gendered conventions of heterosexual relationships. The perspective of accumulating affective intensities in gender assemblages makes it possible to approach these issues from a nuanced perspective that goes beyond fixed ideas about LGBTQ+ women's relationships. My analysis shows how the complex and shifting gender assemblages, which are a co-constitution of many elements (e.g. sexual desire, psychic entanglements, cultural norms and ideas about gender, (shared) interests, events and material spaces), have an ability to bring certain gendered bodies closer to one another, affecting the closeness and 'smooth sailing' of everyday life for certain LGBTQ+ female relationships. On the other hand, binary ideas of gender and gender segregation in many different fields of society affect the assembling of gendered bodies in different spaces, in such ways that can also have a distancing effect between partners in mixed-sex relationships. Gender assemblages have multiple effects, as some LGBTQ+ women experienced the closeness of female relationships as a 'strain'. Closeness can also become straining in the course of a relationship, although experienced as energising in the beginning.

Often when a child was brought into a gender assemblage it could both enhance the closeness and proximity between the partners or create distance between them, as an effect of various elements in the gender assemblage. For instance, the arrival of a child could mean that heteronormative ideas of gender are plugged into LGBTQ+ women's gender assemblages and affect the ways of taking care of children and dividing housework. Yet, although it entailed heteronormative elements, childcare and housework were often divided in more complex ways. The analysis also shows how equalities and inequalities emerge in temporally shifting ways in LGBTQ+ women's gender assemblages and how this is entangled with closeness and distance in their relationships. They emerged as an effect of multiple elements in gender assemblages, which could include and extend to differing generations of women, to the biological mother carrying the baby for nine months, to the repressive cultural ideas that she should also carry the main responsibility for the child's care when it was born, to spatial and geographical living arrangements after the separation and to disputes about how to appear in public as an LGBTQ+ family. Importantly, the various elements and power dynamics come to matter differently in the course of the relationship, depending on relational processes that shift over time. By approaching gender as assemblages, I have revealed the multiplying effects of different elements in those assemblages and highlighted their ongoing processes.

In order to illuminate the multiplicitous nature of gender, I have analysed gender as a productive assemblage (Bennet, 2010). While my analysis shows that gender assemblages are complex and multiple, I do not treat them as random (see also Lahti and Kolehmainen, 2020). Often the elements and dynamic processes are assembled in certain ways, such as in gendered power dynamics, or gender segregation that can diminish the vitality of bodies when being part of an assemblage. Multiplicity means that gender is in a constant state of change and becoming. Yet this does not always mean becoming in a radical sense (Linstead and Pullen, 2006). When plugged into a gender assemblage, unjust gendered ways have a power to diminish affective capacities of partners, although they would not attach only to certain gendered bodies or be always organised in similar ways during the course of a relationship. However, my analysis also highlights the vitalising aspects of certain LGBTQ+ women's assemblages that have the capacity to bring the partners closer together and energise their bodies as they are becoming with these vibrating and intimate gender assemblages.

Notes

1 Please see interviewees' definitions of their gender on page 181.
2 The acronym LGBTQ+ women refers to lesbian, gay, bisexual, trans and queer women, where + is an acknowledgement of non-cisgender and non-heterosexual experiences that are not easily captured by the aforementioned identity categories in my data. The letters 'I' referring to intersex people and 'A' referring to asexual people are left out, when referring to my data, because none of the interviewees identified with these terms.

References

Aarnio, K., Kylmä, J., Solantaus, T., and Rotkirch, A. (2018), *Sateenkaariperheiden vanhemmat: Kokemuksia lasten hyvinvoinnista, perhesuhteista ja tuen saannista. Väestöntutkimuslaitoksen julkaisusarja* D 63/2018 (Helsinki, Finland: Väestöliitto).

Ahmed, S. (2000), *Strange Encounters: Embodied Others in Post-Coloniality* (London: Routledge).

Balsam, K. F., Rostosky, S. S., and Riggle, E. D. B. (2017), 'Breaking Up Is Hard to Do: Women's Experience of Dissolving Their Same-Sex Relationship', *Journal of Lesbian Studies*, 21:1, 30–46.

Balsam, K. F., Rothblum, E. D., Beauchaine, T. P., and Solomon, S. E. (2008), 'Three-Year Follow-Up of Same-Sex Couples Who Had Civil Unions in Vermont, Same-Sex Couples Not in Civil Unions, and Heterosexual Married Siblings', *Developmental Psychology*, 44, 102–16.

Bennett, J. (2010), *Vibrant Matter: A Political Ecology of Things* (Durham, NC: Duke University Press).

Blackman, L. (2012), *Immaterial Bodies: Affect, Embodiment, Mediation* (London: SAGE Publications).

Bolin, M. and Olofsdotter, G. (2018), *Our Culture Can Be Described as 'Management by Excel': Challenging Inequality in the Forestry Industry*, conference presentation at 9th Nordic Working Life Conference, 13–15 June 2018 (University of Oslo, Norway).

Brewster, M. E. (2016), 'Lesbian Women and Household Labor Division: A Systematic Review of Scholarly Research from 2000 to 2015', *Journal of Lesbian Studies*, 21:1, 47–69.

Buchanan, I. (2015), 'Assemblage Theory and Its Discontents', *Deleuze Studies*, 9:3, 382–92.

Causby, V., Lockhart, L., White, B., and Greene, K. (1995), 'Fusion and Conflict Resolution in Lesbian Relationships', *Journal of Gay and Lesbian Social Services*, 3:1, 67–82.

Coffey, J. (2020), 'Assembling Wellbeing: Bodies, Affects and the "Conditions of Possibility" for Wellbeing', *Journal of Youth Studies* (online, 2020). doi: https://doi.org/10.1080/13676261.2020.1844171

Coleman, R., and Ringrose, J. (2013), 'Introduction: Deleuze and Research Methodologies', in *Deleuze and Research Methodologies*, R. Coleman and J. Ringrose (eds) (Edinburgh: Edinburgh University Press), 1–22.

De Landa, M. (2006), *A New Philosophy of Society: Assemblage Theory and Social Complexity* (London: Continuum).

Deleuze, G., and Guattari, F. (2004), *A Thousand Plateaus: Capitalism and Schizophrenia* (London: Continuum).

Duncombe, J., and Marsden, D. (1993), 'Love and Intimacy: The Gender Division of Emotion and "Emotion Work": A Neglected Aspect of Sociological Discussion of Heterosexual Relationships', *Sociology*, 27:2, 221–41.

Ellis, S. J. (2015), 'Lesbian Psychology', in *The Palgrave Handbook of the Psychology of Sexuality and Gender*, C. Richards and M. J. Barker (eds) (London: Palgrave Macmillan), 109–28.

Fox, N. J., and Alldred, P. (2015), 'New Materialist Social Inquiry: Designs, Methods and the Research-assemblage', *International Journal of Social Research Methodology*, 18:4, 399–414.

Fox, N. J., and Alldred, P. (2021), 'Bodies, Non-Human Matter and the Micropolitical Production of Sociomaterial Dis/advantage', *Journal of Sociology* (online first, 2021). doi: https://doi.org/10.1177/14407833211002641

Frost, D. M., and Eliason, M. J. (2014), 'Challenging the Assumption of Fusion in Female Same-Sex Relationships', *Psychology of Women Quarterly*, 38:1, 65–74. doi: https://doi.org/10.1177/0361684313475877

Frost, D. M., and LeBlanc, A. J. (2019), 'Stress in the Lives of Same-Sex Couples: Implications for Relationship Dissolution and Divorce', in *LGBTQ Divorce and Relationship Dissolution: Psychological and Legal Perspectives and Implications for Practice*, A. B. Goldberg and A. P. Romeo (eds) (New York, NY: Oxford University Press), 70–86.

Goldberg, A. E., and Garcia, R. (2015), 'Predictors of Relationship Dissolution in Lesbian, Gay, and Heterosexual Adoptive Parents', *Journal of Family Psychology*, 29:3, 394–404.

Gotta, G., Green, R.-J., Rothblum, E., *et al.* (2011), 'Heterosexual, Lesbian, and Gay Male Relationships: A Comparison of Couples in 1975 and 2000', *Family Process*, 50:3, 353–76.

Gottman, J. M., Levenson, R. W., Gross, J., *et al.* (2003a), 'Correlates of Gay and Lesbian Couples' Relationship Satisfaction and Relationship Dissolution', *Journal of Homosexuality*, 45, 23–43.

Gottman, J. M., Levenson, R. W., Swanson, C., *et al.* (2003b), 'Observing Gay, Lesbian and Heterosexual Couples' Relationships', *Journal of Homosexuality*, 45, 65–91.

Greene, K., Causby, V., and Miller, D. H. (1999), 'The Nature and Function of Fusion in the Dynamics of Lesbian Relationships', *Affilia*, 14:1, 78–97.

Ilmonen, K., Danbolt, M., and Lund Engebretsen, E. (2017), 'Narrating the Nordic Queer: Comparative Perspectives on Queer Studies in Denmark, Finland, and Norway', *Lambda Nordica*, 22:1, 95–113.

Jurva, R., and Lahti, A. (2019), 'Challenging Unequal Gendered Conventions in Heterosexual Relationship Contexts through Affective Dissonance', *NORA – Nordic Journal of Feminist and Gender Research*, 27:4, 218–30. https://doi.org /10.1080/08038740.2019.1682662

Kauhanen, A., and Riukula, K. (2019), 'Työmarkkinoiden eriytyminen ja tasa-arvo Suomessa', in *Näkökulmia Sukupuolten Tasa-arvoon: Analyyseja Tasa-arvobarometrista 2017*, J. Närvi, S. Aapola-Kari and M. Teräsaho (eds) (Helsinki, Finland: Terveyden ja hyvinvoinnin laitos), 80–100.

Kelly, M., and Hauck, E. (2015), 'Doing Housework, Redoing Gender: Queer Couples Negotiate the Household Division of Labor', *Journal of GLBT Family Studies*, 11:5, 438–64.

Kinnunen, T., and Kolehmainen, M. (2019), 'Touch and Affect: Analysing the Archive of Touch Biographies', *Body & Society*, 25:1, 29–56.

Kolehmainen, M. (2020), 'Re-Imagining Gender and Sexuality: Feminist New Materialisms, Affect Theory and the Feminist Futures', presentation at Gender Studies Conference 2020, 15 November 2020 (Tampere University, Finland).

Kolehmainen, M., and Juvonen, T. (2018), 'Introduction: Thinking With and Through Affective Inequalities', in *Affective Inequalities in Intimate Relationships*, T. Juvonen and M. Kolehmainen (eds) (London: Routledge), 2–15.

Kuosmanen, P. (2007), 'Johdanto: Sateenkaariperheet, julkiset tilat ja queer-politiikka suomessa', *SQS Journal*, 2:1, i–xxi.

Kurdek, L. A. (2008), 'Change in Relationship Quality for Partners from Lesbian, Gay Male, and Heterosexual Couples', *Journal of Family Psychology*, 22:5, 701–11. doi: https://doi.org/10.1037/0893-3200.22.5.701

Lahti, A. (2015), 'Similar and Equal Relationships? Negotiating Bisexuality in an Enduring Relationship', *Feminism & Psychology*, 25:4, 431–48.

Lahti, A. (2018), 'Listening to Old Tapes: Affective Intensities and Gendered Power in Bisexual Women's and Ex-Partners' Relationship Assemblages', in *Affective Inequalities in Intimate Relationships*, T. Juvonen and M. Kolehmainen (eds) (London: Routledge), 49–62.

Lahti, A. (2020), 'The Becoming of Family Relationships and Friendship Circles After a Bisexual Break-Up', in *Bisexuality in Europe*, R. Baumgartner and E. Maliepaard (eds) (London: Routledge), 85–99.

Lahti, A., and Kolehmainen, M. (2020), 'LGBTIQ+ Break-Up Assemblages: At the End of the Rainbow', *Journal of Sociology*, 56:4, 608–28.

Laird, J. (2000), 'Gender in Lesbian Relationships: Cultural, Feminist, and Constructionist Reflections', *Journal of Marital and Family Therapy*, 26:4, 455–67.

Latimer, J., López Gómez, D. (2019), 'Intimate Entanglements: Affects, More-Than-Human Intimacies and the Politics of Relations in Science and Technology', *The Sociological Review*, 67:2, 247–63.

Linstead, S., and Pullen, A. (2006), 'Gender as Multiplicity: Desire, Displacement, Difference and Dispersion', *Human Relations*, 59:9, 1287–310.

Malins, P. (2004), 'Machinic Assemblages: Deleuze, Guattari and an Ethico-Aesthetics of Drug Use', *Janus Head*, 7:1, 84–104.

Mazzei, L. A. (2013), 'Desire Undone: Productions of Privilege, Power and Voice', in *Deleuze and Research Methodologies*, R. Coleman and J. Ringrose (eds) (Edinburgh: Edinburgh University Press), 96–110.

Rich, A. (1976), *Of Woman Born: Motherhood As Experience and Institution* (New York, NY: Norton).

Ringrose, E., and Renold, J. (2014), '"F**k Rape!" Exploring Affective Intensities in a Feminist Research Assemblage', *Qualitative Inquiry*, 20:6, 772–80.

Schuller, K. (2020), *The Future of Gender: Rethinking the Sex/Gender Distinction*, keynote speech at Gender Studies Conference 2020, 13 November 2020 (Tampere University, Finland).

Sevón, E. (2009), *Maternal Responsibility and Changing Relationality at the Beginning of Motherhood* (Doctoral dissertation, University of Jyväskylä, Finland: Jyväskylä Studies in Education, Psychology and Social Research), 365.

Seyfert, R. (2012), 'Beyond Personal Feelings and Collective Emotions: Toward a Theory of Social Affect', *Theory, Culture & Society*, 29:6, 27–46. doi: https://doi.org/10.1177/0263276412438591

Smart, C. (2007), *Personal Life: New Directions in Sociological Thinking* (Cambridge: Polity Press).

Stewart, K. (2007), *Ordinary Affects*. (Durham, NC: Duke University Press).

Strazdins, L., and Broom, D. H. (2004), 'Acts of Love (and Work): Gender Imbalance in Emotional Work and Women's Psychological Distress', *Journal of Family Issues*, 25:3, 356–78.

Umberson, D., Thomeer, M. B., and Lodge, A. C. (2015), 'Intimacy and Emotion Work in Lesbian, Gay, and Heterosexual Relationships', *Journal of Marriage and Family*, 77:2, 542–56.

Warner, M. (2000), *The Trouble With Normal: Sex, Politics, and the Ethics of Queer Life* (Cambridge, MA: Harvard University Press).

Weston, K. (1995), 'Forever Is a Long Time: Romancing the Real in Gay Kinship Ideologies', in *Naturalizing Power: Essays in Feminist Cultural Analysis*, S. J. Yanagisako and C. L. Delaney (eds) (New York, NY: Routledge), 87–110.

Zengin, A. (2016), 'Violent Intimacies: Tactile State Power, Sex/Gender Transgression, and the Politics of Touch in Contemporary Turkey', *Journal of Middle East Women's Studies*, 12:2, 225–45. Available at Project MUSE: muse.jhu.edu/article /625055 (Accessed: 16 March 2021).

Index

Note: Photographs and poems can be found under author's name.

Lightning Source UK Ltd.
Milton Keynes UK
UKHW041254250722
406342UK00004B/46